Touching the Mind

Applied Yoga Psychology

Asad Ullah Adnan

ISBN: 978-93-343-0721-4

Cover design by: Asad Ullah Adnan

Contents

Title Page
Copyright
Acknowledgements 3
Preface 6
Introduction. 12
Chapter 1 22
Chapter 2 31
Chapter 3 36
Chapter 4 54
Chapter 5 57
Chapter 6 67
Chapter 6 69
Chapter 7 75
Chapter 8 80
Chapter 9 83
Chapter 10 88
Chapter 11 95
Chapter 11 100
Chapter 12 105
Chapter 13 109

Chapter 14	123
Chapter 15	130
Chapter 16	139
Chapter 17	143
Chapter 18	154
Chapter 19	163
Chapter 20	167
Chapter 21	174
Chapter 22	181
The Agony of Seeking.	189
The Divinity in Goodness.	191
The Mechanisms of Influence: The Aspects That Brainwash Any Unaware Person.	193
How to Not Take Offense at All	206
How to Achieve a Euphoric State Without Drugs.	210
Everything You Need to Know About Increasing Cognitive Function.	216
The Practice of Brahmacharya	222
Chapter 23	226
Chapter 24	234
Chapter 25	253
Chapter 26	260
Chapter 27	268
Chapter 28	276
Chapter 29	283
Returning to Yourself	286
Appendix A – Classical Kriya Yoga Cross-Reference	296
Appendix B – Practical Sequencing for Teachers	299
Appendix C – The Integrated Approach	304

Touching the Mind

Asad Ullah Adnan

Touching the Mind: Practical Yoga Psychology

First Edition – December 2025

Author: Asad Ullah Adnan

Title: Touching the Mind: Applied Yoga Psychology

ISBN: 978-93-343-0721-4

Printed in India

All characters, examples, and narratives used illustratively within this book are either products of the author's reflections or presented in a generalized manner. Any resemblance to actual individuals is coincidental unless cited explicitly.

For permissions, inquiries, or author contact:

Email: asadullahadnan@gmail.com

Acknowledgements

I want to begin by acknowledging the Tathāgata, Gautama Buddha (may peace be upon him), whose teachings continue to illuminate the path of awakening for countless seekers.

I also extend my deepest respect to Prophet Muhammad (may peace be upon him), whose wisdom and compassion have guided the hearts of millions across centuries.

I want to acknowledge all the teachers and writers whose books and teachings have enlightened my mind — the great Indian philosophers, Rishis, and ancient seers whose wisdom forms the foundation of our spiritual traditions. I offer my respects to Sage Patanjali, whose Yoga Sutras remain an unparalleled guide to inner transformation, and to the Ayurvedic masters whose science of life continues to heal humanity.

Among modern teachers and philosophers, I express gratitude to J. Krishnamurti, Osho Rajneesh, Rabindranath Tagore, Swami Sivananda, and Swami Sarvapriyananda, whose works on Yoga, Vedanta, Tantra, and meditation have shaped my understanding. I would also like to mention the Western thinkers — Socrates, Plato, Immanuel Kant, Ludwig Wittgenstein, and Spinoza — who have profoundly influenced my mind in my endeavor to seek the truth. If I begin naming everyone, this brief note will not suffice; the references are provided at the end.

I deeply appreciate the unwavering support of my father and mother throughout the journey of creating this book. Their presence, faith, and blessings have been my foundation.

I also wish to honor Ibn Arabi (may peace be upon him), Imam Ghazali (may peace be upon him), and Maulana Rumi (may peace be upon him) — I will forever remain indebted for their contributions to the rich heritage of Islamic knowledge.

Many names escape my mind but I bow down to all of them with utmost respect.

I will never forget the mosques, shrines, and ashrams where I stayed during these transformative times. India is a land of diversity, and I consider myself fortunate to have lived and breathed its divine air.

Without all of you, this work would not have come into existence.

For every light that shines upon an object,

there is a source.

Light upon light is the nature of reality.

To touch the mind

is to enter this eternal presence.

To touch the mind

is to see through the illusion of the world.

To be free,

one becomes light upon light.

Truth lies in understanding the mind

and its subtle nature.

And to truly touch the mind,

one must first be free from it.

Preface

Anything you read in this book is conceptual until realised or experienced first hand,I have tried as much as I could to resist further Intellectualisations or explanations,I have emphasised only a few points that can direct the reader's mind to a certain practical way of thinking.

Thinking in a certain way often is a byproduct of the practical way of life you live,a lot of our philosophies are sometimes rationalisations for our actions,which are sometimes not even in our control. We defend, protect and try to uphold our beliefs through intelligently crafted words and influential linguistics to both ourselves and to others around us.

Practical actions and lived words resonate and make a difference in the world, thoughts no matter how romantic they may sound, can somehow be an obstruction in precious matters of life But that is not to say I don't like poetry or essay writing,infact this book came from poetic essays ,which you will find plenty here. I like rhythm and so does your mind,things woven in rhythm are remembered easily.

You will learn a lot of concepts from different traditions in this book but all are stages that you can reach simply by being mindful of your own self.the more you grow in awareness the more this wisdom will actually make sense to you This is not teaching ,it is simply a reflection of what the mind is.

The pages that follow are not merely ideas but living threads of thought, stitched together from questions that never left me. Psychology is not abstract; it breathes through the body, it sings in the mind, it struggles in the emotions. I have never written to prove a system, but to open doors—doors that you may step through into your own experience.

We live in a time of overexposure to information but starvation of meaning. I wanted this book to slow down the noise, to speak to the soul that still asks: what does it mean to be alive? This condensation is not a summary but a distillation, like reducing a vast forest to its fragrance. The trees are still here, though closer together. The silences remain, though more deliberate.

This work asks not for agreement, but for attention. It asks you to hold still long enough for words to do their secret work. If you walk away with more questions than you began with,slightly more aware and smarter than before, then the book has succeeded.

Entering the World Where we can Touch the Mind

To enter the world where we can touch the mind is to abandon the illusion that reality is dead matter awaiting our use. The ancients knew what we forget: that stones carry memory, rivers possess voice, and the wind speaks in riddles if we dare to listen. We live surrounded by presences, not objects.

But modern life has trained us otherwise. We see the tree only as timber, the body only as a machine, the self only as a consumer. Yet somewhere deep, the heart resists. It whispers that perhaps the world is enchanted, that perhaps meaning still hides in the pulse of things.

To begin this journey is not to adopt a belief, but to recover a sensitivity. It is to see your body as part of the earth's body, your breath as part of the wind's rhythm, your thought as part of the larger weave of life. The world is alive because you are alive within it, and because both are inseparably bound in mystery.

The Meaning of Life ?

The question "What is the meaning of life?" has followed humanity for as long as consciousness itself. It feels strange, unsettling, and often remains unanswered throughout our lives. And if I claim that I have an answer, you will probably not believe me. Something in you insists that the question is either unanswerable, or that the answer changes from person to person, shaped by their experiences and beliefs.

But what if I tell you that something is wrong with the question itself?

Would you believe that the confusion begins long before the search for meaning even starts?

Why Do We Seek Meaning?

Meaning, in our everyday use, implies something objective—something to be grasped and understood. When you say, "I don't understand what this means," it simply indicates that the words or the idea are not yet familiar to you. But the moment someone explains it clearly, something inside you clicks. Neural connections form, your mind adapts, and suddenly the same sentence makes perfect sense.

So meaning is born from explanation, and explanation relies on the mind's ability to connect, interpret, and resonate.

Meaning Depends on the Mind That Seeks It

When you reject an explanation and say, "This makes no sense," it is because the explanation clashes with the knowledge you already have. Your conditioning, your background, your experiences—all of these shape what seems meaningful or meaningless to you.

Meaning, therefore, is not fixed. It shifts as we grow. As our understanding deepens, our answer to the question "What is the meaning of life?" also changes.

And here lies the first error:

We Are Trying to Build Something Rigid on Something Changeable

If meaning depends on the ever-changing mind—its knowledge, its memory, its conditioning—then any answer we produce will also constantly change. A meaning based on knowledge can never be stable, because knowledge itself evolves every moment.

The Case for an Unchanging Ground

But what happens if we base meaning not on knowledge, but on something unchanging?

Wisdom is unchanging.

Truth is unchanging.

The essence of life—beyond concepts and explanations—is unchanging.

If we seek something eternal rather than something merely informative, the mind becomes naturally quiet, and the so-called "meaning of life" stops being an object to acquire. Instead, meaning begins to appear as a living presence, an expression of life itself.

In that state, meaning is not understood—it is felt.

It is not constructed—it is experienced.

It is not an answer—it is a state of being.

Meaning reveals itself not through explanation, but through the natural, unconditioned awareness that arises when the mind stops chasing and simply becomes aligned with life as it is.

In that sense, the meaning of life is not a fixed sentence or idea.

It is a living, eternal movement—something you touch only when you stop seeking and start experiencing.

Definitions and Foundations

Words are dangerous. They tempt us to think we have captured reality when in truth we have only sketched its shadow. Yet we cannot do without them. To speak of truth, mind, freedom, or the sacred, we must define—but never imprison—them.

Definitions in this book are foundations, not fences. Truth here is not a fixed proposition but the resonance of reality

when encountered honestly. The mind is not a static organ but a stream, changing with every act of attention. Freedom is not license but clarity. Ethics is not law but alignment with what is deeper than preference.

These foundations allow us to build, not walls but pathways. They let us walk through difficult questions with steadiness. For without grounding, philosophy and psychology simply floats away; without openness, it hardens into dogma. The foundation is both firm and porous, strong enough to walk on, loose enough to let life breathe through.

Notes :

Introduction.

Perspective and the Mind

“Perspective depends on the mind and can be shaped through experience.”

When we see a room, we are not all seeing the same thing —we are seeing different things. This is because the room exists in relation to us, and we form a connection with it. The more we live in it, the more we experience it, and the more we know it. As our experience with the room deepens, we feel increasingly connected to it. Our emotions become attached to the room, and it eventually becomes our room. A new person entering this same room will not experience it first-hand in the same way; they will, in some sense, encounter our room through our relationship with it.

Life mirrors this process. We form relationships with everything around us, and the more we live and experience, the more attached we become. This raises an important question: why is it necessary to examine perspective and relationships—not as external objects, but as products of our own minds?

We must carefully examine relationships, to see what they are and why we become attached to or detached from them. The relationship we have with ourselves is perhaps the most important of all, because above everything else, we are most deeply attached to ourselves. This attachment is uniquely ours—nobody else can know "our room" better than we do.

However, being in your own room does not mean you grasp reality. Over time, you form a concept of the room shaped by your experiences in it. Emotions, events, and associations color your perception, so what you see is not the raw room but your mental construct of it. In actuality, the room is nothing but empty space bounded by four walls. Your perspective has given it meaning. Reality itself is emptiness; perspective is the reflection you project upon this emptiness.

Perspective is always tied to the mind. If you and your friend look at the same object, each of you perceives something different in your minds—two separate concepts of the same physical thing. The object itself remains constant, but its interpretations are many. In Jainism, this principle is known as anekantavada: the belief that everything has multiple dimensions and countless reflections projected onto the screen of consciousness. Each reflection may differ, each perspective may even contradict the others, but ultimately, the thing itself is empty of inherent meaning. Life, without our interpretations, is inert and almost lifeless.

Perspectives about the external world often differ, shaped by experience and conditioning. But the perspective of perspectives—the awareness of how the mind generates these views—is more universal. Many philosophers and psychologists have worked to interpret the mind and its patterns, studying behavior, instincts, and thought processes. Through this investigation, we now know enough about the mind to build artificial models of it.

Artificial intelligence, modeled on neural processes, is a great achievement. Yet what has been replicated so far is only a fraction of human intelligence—mainly the capacity for learning patterns. To make AI more intelligent, it must be continually trained with accurate behavioral data.

Even so, perspectives can be faulty. If parts of the mind fail to work in harmony, disconnection arises, causing mental imbalance and suffering. Poor coordination between different functions of the mind may result from unhealthy habits, emotional turmoil, or biological factors.

The mind operates in complex ways, starting and stopping different functions throughout the day depending on situations and experiences. We cannot fully control which aspects of the mind will become active unless we engage in certain practices of self-awareness.

Changing perspective is possible, but the external world alone may not radically shift it. By adulthood, we are deeply entrenched in our habits, impressions, and personality traits, which reflect long-standing thought patterns. This book, therefore, concerns itself with the perspective of perspective: learning how to touch and transform the aspects of the mind that are within our control.

The first half explores different workings of the mind, while the second presents practices designed to activate specific functions of it. The investigation itself is valuable. It provides tools for approaching patterns of the mind and reshaping them.

One can skip directly to the second part if one chooses to practise different methods of controlling the mind.This wisdom comes form a long lineage of "Yogis", seers who observed their whale subjective being.It is purely scientific in nature and does not require any faith or belief, it is a systematic process of developing consciousness over the body and the aspects of the mind to reach a state of superconsciousness, known by many names "Samadhi", "Fana Fi Allah" and many other terminologies which can fill up this entire book and create controversies.There are many approaches to reach an elevated level of consciousness, and different personalities will be attracted to different methods and practices and thought systems, but it is helpful to keep in mind that the goal is the same.

This investigative method—learned from many great philosophers—is something anyone can practice without relying solely on books. By persistently questioning the dimensions of our own minds, we can observe, analyze, and better understand their functions and interconnections.

Tracing causes back to their roots is one of the most powerful intellectual skills we can develop. Whether for understanding our own mental processes or navigating relationships, this ability allows us to see the true motivations and intentions behind actions. In doing so, we learn to read people more clearly while grasping the deeper reality of the perspective of perspectives.

On Controlling the Mind

The mind is the greatest gift and the greatest burden. It is the flame that has lit up human history — the mind built temples, carved poetry into stone, measured the stars, dreamed of eternity. And yet, the same mind tortures us with worries that never come true, regrets that cannot be undone, cravings that leave us emptier than before. A single memory, replayed endlessly, can paralyze a life. A single imagined future can drain years of peace. We speak of freedom, but most of us live as prisoners in the invisible cage of our own thoughts.

Every tradition that has touched the depths of human life knew this. The Buddha said the mind untamed is like a wild monkey, leaping from branch to branch, never resting, never satisfied. The yogis of India compared it to a restless lake, agitated by every wind of desire and fear — only when it grows still can it reflect the truth of reality. The Stoics, so sober and practical, warned that man is enslaved not by events but by the judgments he makes of them. And in every culture you find the same recognition: unless you learn to guide the mind, you will be dragged by it.

And yet how many of us, in the quiet of night, lie in bed and find that our own thoughts are louder than the city outside? You try to rest, but the mind begins its endless parade: things left undone, things that might happen tomorrow, things that happened years ago that still ache as if they were fresh. You scroll your phone to silence it, but the silence does not come. We all know this struggle — perhaps it is the most human struggle of all in this day and age.

When we speak of "controlling" the mind, we often imagine a battle. We imagine silencing it by force, crushing it into obedience. But anyone who has tried knows the futility: the more you fight a thought, the stronger it becomes. Tell yourself not to think of sorrow, and sorrow blooms tenfold. Tell yourself to stop worrying, and the worry grows louder. Control, in the sense of domination, fails. What is required is subtler: understanding, redirecting, befriending. The mind is like fire. Left untended, it burns down the house. But when cared for, when guided, it becomes the warmth of the hearth, the forge of creation.

The first step is attention. Our culture has stolen our attention and sold it back to us in fragments. We live surrounded by screens, each one shouting for our gaze. Our attention is pulled in a thousand directions, until we can barely sit still with a single thought, a single image, a single person. But attention is the currency of the soul. Whatever you give it to, grows. Attend only to distractions, and your mind becomes shallow. Attend to beauty, truth, silence, and your mind deepens. To reclaim your attention is to reclaim your life.

But attention alone is not enough. We must also learn detachment. The mind produces thoughts the way lungs produce breath. You cannot stop it. A memory, an image, an anxiety — they arise on their own. The suffering begins when we identify with them. A fear appears, and we clutch it as prophecy. A memory arises, and we relive it as if it were happening again. But the mystics remind us: you are not the thought. You are the witness of the thought. The thought is a cloud; you are the sky. When you begin to see this, the tyranny loosens. A thought can pass without dragging you into its storm.

Still, understanding and detachment must be grounded in discipline. The mind, like a wild horse, must be trained with patience. Not beaten, not crushed, but guided daily. Ten minutes of meditation, done every day, begins to change the landscape. The repetition of prayer or mantra gives the mind a rhythm, a form to rest in. Journaling, sitting in silence, walking without headphones — these are not small practices, but acts of sovereignty. Without discipline, the mind scatters endlessly. With discipline, it learns to serve. And once it serves, it reveals its brilliance.

And then there is love. At first glance, love seems far from the question of mental mastery. But love is the greatest silencer of noise. Think of the way all distraction falls away when you hold a newborn child. Think of the way the chatter ceases when you sit across from someone you love deeply, truly listening. Think of the way devotion — to a person, to a cause, to God — dissolves self-centered thought. Love focuses the mind as nothing else can. In its presence, worry seems small, obsession loses power, the mind bends willingly toward what matters most.

To weave these together — attention, detachment, discipline, and love — is to begin to place the mind in harmony with the soul.

Each balances the other. Attention without detachment can become obsession. Detachment without attention can become indifference. Discipline without love can harden into rigidity. Love without discipline can scatter into chaos. Together they create a balance, a rhythm, a way of being where the mind is neither enemy nor tyrant but companion.

And yet, perhaps the deepest truth is that the mind was never the enemy. It is not something to conquer, but something to see clearly. When you see it for what it is — a flow of images, words, impressions, constantly arising and dissolving — you realize that it is not the whole of you. Beneath the mind is consciousness itself, vast and silent. Thoughts pass through it like waves upon an ocean, but the ocean is not disturbed. You are not the thought; you are the awareness in which the thought appears. To know this not just intellectually but experientially is liberation. The chatter continues, but it no longer rules you. The storms come, but the sky remains vast and still.

This realization is not abstract. It changes how you live. A harsh word spoken by another no longer festers endlessly, because you see it as a passing wave, not a wound in your essence. A fear about the future loses its claws, because you recognize it as imagination, not destiny. A memory of failure dissolves, because you see it belongs to the past, not the present moment of awareness. This is not cold detachment. It is freedom — a freedom that allows you to meet life more fully, not less.

But we must be patient with ourselves. No one tames the mind overnight. Even the saints and sages wrestled with it for years. The desert fathers of Christianity, living in solitude, confessed to endless battles with thoughts. The Zen monks speak of decades of sitting before the mind grows still. It is not about perfection but about practice, not about silencing thought completely but about loosening its grip. Each moment of awareness is a step. Each act of choosing presence over distraction is victory.

And let us not forget the human side of it. We are not machines striving to optimize brain function. We are beings who suffer, who laugh, who love, who long. To control the mind is not to become robotic, but to become more human — to reclaim the capacity for wonder, for joy, for presence. The goal is not a blank mind, but a mind that serves life instead of obstructing it. A mind that can reflect beauty without distortion, hold pain without being consumed, listen without interruption. A mind that allows the soul to speak.

Perhaps this is why every great teacher speaks of silence. Silence is not the absence of thought, but the presence of being. When you sit quietly, even for a few minutes, you begin to feel the mind settling, like dust in a sunbeam. At first the noise grows louder, but if you remain, something shifts. The thoughts become less urgent. Space opens. In that space, you begin to sense something deeper — the stillness that was always there. That stillness is you. The mind is a guest.

And so, the work is not about crushing the mind, but about remembering who you are beyond it. The thoughts will come, but you need not be swept away. The memories will arise, but you need not drown in them. The future will tempt you, but you need not abandon the present. You are the witness, the awareness, the vastness in which all of it appears. To live from that space is to live freely.

"The mind is fire. Left untended, it burns you. Guided with care, it becomes light."

And you, who have spent years enslaved to its chatter, can awaken in an instant to the truth: you were never the prisoner. You were the master all along.

Awareness Evolves

Awareness is the most mysterious thing about us, and yet we take it for granted. We wake each morning and immediately fall into its spell, without ever questioning it. We say, "I am awake," but what does that mean? We are awake enough to check messages, to plan, to worry, to chase, to speak. But are we awake enough to see who it is that is doing all this? Most of us never ask. We live half-dreaming, half-seeing, assuming we already know what awareness is, when in truth it is the most astonishing mystery of all.

And like everything alive, awareness itself evolves. It does not stand still. It expands, contracts, deepens. The awareness of a child is not the awareness of a lover. The awareness of a soldier in battle is not the awareness of a monk in silence. It shifts with our lives, with our struggles, with our loves and losses. Awareness is not a light switch but a flame — flickering, sometimes dim, sometimes blazing, sometimes hidden entirely under smoke.

As children, we are raw, unfiltered. The world is alive: toys have voices, trees have faces, shadows terrify or enchant us. Wonder is natural. But as we grow, awareness narrows. We learn names, labels, categories. We are told who we are: male or female, citizen of this country, follower of that religion. Awareness puts on clothes, layers of costume. And slowly we begin to mistake the costume for ourselves. We stop seeing the world directly and see only through labels.

Most people stay here. Awareness half asleep, trapped in identity, endlessly circling around memory and habit. But sometimes, life shocks us awake. Death, love, loss, beauty — they tear holes in the veil. Suddenly the ordinary room feels infinite. Suddenly you see the other not as an object in your story but as a soul shining before you. Suddenly time feels different, stretched or dissolved. These are glimpses of awareness evolving, leaping into another dimension.

The mystics knew this. They taught that these glimpses are not accidents but invitations. Awareness is always infinite; it is we who live small. To awaken is not to invent something new, but to remove what blinds us.

And yet, the path is not easy, because awareness challenges everything we cling to. It asks us to question not only society but ourselves. It asks us to surrender illusions. And human beings cling to illusions like a drowning man to a piece of driftwood.

Perhaps this is why the great teachers used stories. Because sometimes, to wake awareness, you cannot argue — you must surprise.

There is a story of Mulla Nasrudin. One evening, his neighbors found him on his hands and knees under the streetlamp, searching the ground.

"What are you looking for, Nasrudin?" they asked.

"My key," he replied.

So they all joined in, searching with him under the light. After a long while, someone asked, "Are you sure you dropped it here?"

"No," said Nasrudin calmly, "I lost it inside the house."

"Then why are you looking out here?"

"Because here," he said, pointing to the lamplight, "the light is better."

Everyone laughed, but the laughter has teeth. For this is what we do with awareness. We search for meaning, for truth, for peace — but we search only where it is convenient, where the light is easy. We avoid the dark house within us, where the real key lies. We distract ourselves with surface knowledge, with clever theories, with endless entertainment, because it is easier to look where the light already shines. But the key is within. Until we dare to step into that darker, more intimate space, we will never find it.

Awareness evolves when we stop looking outside and turn inward, even if it feels uncomfortable, even if it feels uncertain. The light of the lamp is not enough; the fire must be lit inside.

This is the essence of every practice — meditation, prayer, art, silence. They are ways of stepping into the house of ourselves, fumbling, searching, slowly learning to light our own lamp. With each act of courage, awareness expands. You notice not just what is easy to see but what was hidden in shadow. You realize that the world was not flat but layered, luminous, alive.

And yet, awareness does not only expand in moments of stillness. It evolves in the messy, ordinary encounters of life. When you pause before reacting in anger, awareness deepens. When you realize that the story you are telling yourself is only a story, awareness awakens. When you choose compassion instead of judgment, awareness grows roots in your heart. Evolution does not only happen in monasteries or caves. It happens at the dinner table, in traffic, at work, in the smallest choices of attention.

Still, many resist. Because awareness dissolves illusions, and illusions are comforting. It shows us we are not who we thought we were. It reveals the fragility of our identities, the impermanence of what we love, the emptiness of our fears. It strips us bare. Most prefer to remain clothed in distraction. But those who dare to stand naked in awareness discover something astonishing: beneath the illusions, there is freedom. Beneath the fragility, there is strength. Beneath the impermanence, there is eternity.

Awareness evolves not only for us individually, but for humanity as a whole. A society rooted only in survival wages endless wars. A society rooted in individuality produces wealth and invention but also loneliness and greed. A society rooted in compassion begins to heal. A society rooted in wisdom learns balance. And a society awake to awareness itself becomes sacred, living not just for survival but for beauty, truth, and love.

Each of us is part of this unfolding. Each of us is a flame in the great fire of consciousness. And each of us has the chance, each day, to grow that flame or to dim it.

So do not search under the streetlamp forever. Dare to look within, where the light has not yet reached. The key you seek — to meaning, to peace, to wholeness — is already there, waiting in the dark. And when you find it, you will realize that awareness was never really evolving at all. Awareness itself is infinite. What evolves is our courage to recognize it, to embody it, to live it.

And then the search ends where it began — here, now, in this moment, which contains eternity.

Chapter 1

A Search for Peace Beyond Morality

There's a strange paradox in our lives: ethics, arguably the most important force shaping our destiny, is something we rarely stop to truly understand.

We've taken countless courses—finance, math, physics, philosophy, art—all of which fed our curiosity. But when it comes to morality,we have a "family" system. That's it. No real exploration of virtue, right and wrong, or the meaning of a moral life.

Now, in the midst of chaos, as we seek peace and salvation from the disorder that our life has become, we finally understand the value of morality. The kind of morality we once mocked, scorned, and ignored. We used to see moral people as naive fools—too innocent for the world. But today, we must know: the biggest fool is the one who leads an immoral life.

A moral life is not just about righteousness. It is peace. It is tranquility. It is divinity. And, when you strip everything else away, isn't that what we're all really chasing? Our deepest desire is not power or pleasure. It is peace.Nietzsche spoke of the "will to power." Schopenhauer, of the "will to live." But perhaps the deepest force in us is the will to be peaceful.

Every night, you fall into sleep—a great, quiet ocean of forgetting. In that space, your desires vanish, your problems dissolve. It's a place where nothing exists but stillness. And every morning, you hope for one thing: a good night's sleep. That's the silent proof of what we truly crave.

And so, day after day, you dive into life again—searching, often unknowingly, for that inner stillness.

But sometimes, life becomes so chaotic, so distorted by desire, that we forget our original aim. The mind gets clouded. Judgment collapses. And reality itself begins to warp. When we lead immoral lives—driven by unchecked desires—we lose our grip on goodness. That inner compass grows silent. And all that remains is an endless cycle of craving. One urge after another. Pulling us deeper into blindness.

Spinoza's ethics offers a different path. It is neither traditionally feminine—submissive and meek—nor hyper-masculine, glorifying conquest or control. Instead, it is a balanced integration of both energies. A unity of strength and serenity. This same balance exists in Tantra and many Indian philosophical systems. Here, good and evil aren't enemies. They are part of the same process. Male and female energies are not in opposition, but in harmony.The man was shunned by his on society for he spoke a new language , he gave the eternal religion, the religion which has always existed and will never die a voice.

This is why an ethics based on acceptance—rather than rigid rules—can build a society that is not torn by inner conflict. A society where problems are faced, not denied. Where people stop pretending to be someone they're not, just to appease others or win the approval of a god.

You've heard the question: "Why do bad things happen to good people?" It carries a kind of bitterness—as though goodness should automatically be rewarded. But maybe that question is rooted in misunderstanding. Often, it comes from people who feel wronged for reasons they can't understand. There's a sense of entitlement there, an expectation that the universe should trade peace for virtue.

But ethics doesn't work like that. Morality isn't transactional. It's transformational.

There's a daily battle inside us. Between the urge to lash out and the strength to smile instead. Between the shadow and the self. This isn't a debate about rules—it's about expression. What we choose to express, and what we choose to repress, defines who we are.

Every expression begins in the quiet depths of our subjective experience. We know that no one can see into it—unless we let them. And yet, from that space, we choose: what part of ourselves do we reveal to the world? What part do we hide?

Over time, these choices shape us. A harsh rejection, a painful failure—these impressions leave marks. They recalibrate our behavior. They become part of our story.

Some impressions go even deeper—beyond birth, perhaps. No two brothers are alike. Our karma, our emotional memory, runs far beneath the surface.

Spinoza believed in a deterministic world—one where metaphysics, ethics, psychology, and politics are all interwoven. His thoughts echoed into the minds of Rousseau and other naturalistic thinkers. But even before Spinoza, there were sages—original naturalists—raised under open skies, guided by stars, using only awareness and consciousness as their instruments of truth.

In that world, there is no good or evil in the simplistic sense. Both paths—whether of light or darkness—lead to a just universe. A universe where karma is as real as gravity.

So perhaps the goal is not to be good for the sake of reward, or to avoid evil for fear of punishment—but to live awake. To express the truth of who we are. To seek peace—not as a prize, but as our natural state.

And in that pursuit, maybe we will finally meet the divine—not in heaven, not in doctrine, but in the stillness within.

There is value in retraining our lower instincts. We tend to evolve in character and become wiser or more intelligent the more we refuse to let our lower instincts take hold of us. The more you resist the urge to fall for cheap dopamine hits and erratic sensations, the more you will grow as a mature person. And it is not a matter of reward—it is a matter of growth in intelligence. Being good is simply wise and intelligent. It helps us remain undistracted in life, and it allows us to climb further up the ladder of intelligence. The good things you do bring happiness to you, while the bad things you do bring sadness, paranoia, and anxiety. All of our psychological problems are rooted in bad actions—things we thought we could somehow escape without being caught—but we failed to realize that we ourselves were falling into the trap.

A person who prides himself on monetary achievement tends to become lonely, to discriminate in life, and to pursue only what money can buy. But freedom sometimes comes in simple things, like offering a helping hand to a stranger or supporting old parents. Your whole body-mind complex lights up when you do good. Certain neurochemicals are released only when you are kind to someone, when you are generous, and when you decide to forgive. In those moments, you become glorious, you become noble, and you rise in wisdom.We suffer for our sins. I do not say this to belittle anybody, but to point out the law of this land: we suffer for our sins. The sins we commit might escape everyone's notice—nobody may ever know—but we know, and they are embedded in our personality. The more we repeat them, the more our personality changes. The more you sin, the more you lose self-control. You become foolish and make reckless mistakes. You tend to be cruel, your anger slips out of your control, and it only takes a second to make the biggest mistake of your life. Only a second to trip you up, and in that blindness you fall deep into the states of hell. Hell is here, and heaven is here too. We can decide where we want to tread. If we simply ask ourselves whether our actions are good or bad after each step, much can be learned.If we are mindful of the impact of our actions—both on the outer world and within ourselves—we can drastically change our lives. We can gain the natural wisdom of morality, we can see the natural laws that Spinoza advocated, and we can then decide whether we want to live a good life of intelligence, or a bad life of endless pleasure-seeking. This is "yama" the first limb of Yoga.

As a young person, anxiety is natural because you haven't reached a point where you see that your actions are all validated. This invalidation of action by others is what causes anxiety in us, especially those who feel socially crippled.Social validation needs to be a healthy consumption for the young mind. If you do not feel validated, you will always be trying to learn how to act, when simply you should be yourself no matter what, and let the world accept it.

People might call you crazy, people might say something is off with you, or try to correct your actions, but often this traumatizes,even as a child, especially as a child.

You remember the rejections and the failures more than the successes,because your mind was shocked at that event.

Gabor Maté, a psychologist who mainly worked on children's psychology, says that whenever there is a response of unacceptance by society, the child receives mild trauma. When asked what to do as parents to "discipline a child," he says that the only way is to tell them they are fully accepted. This radical approach is hard to adopt. We simply cannot resist the urge to teach a child the ways of the world, always treating them as if we know better than they do, as if we are somehow superior and know how to behave.

A child acts instinctively; he or she doesn't care what response they get. They act well instinctively too—there is a good instinct that counterbalances the natural bad instincts.

This might be a little fearful for some parents, where they think, "It's really not good to not discipline a child."Well, you see, discipline is also a natural instinct, says Gabor Maté.

The story we tell ourselves about our lives is not free from fiction. In fact, much of it is self-told. The events that happened were interpreted by the mind in some way, and you accepted them that way. Unless and until you have gained the capacity to know events as they truly are, you are moving from one end of fictional storytelling to another end of interpreting facts.

Is all of life then a lie? Told to ourselves? It kind of is, I'm afraid—unless somebody points out the mistake.

When someone points out an error in our interpretation of an event, we realize that a fundamental aspect of our psyche is hurt. Our core concepts of truth and falsehood are challenged. And if this process continues—through education, through experiences of hurt, through the constant struggle between what is right and wrong, truth and falsehood—we gradually move away from the natural instincts we once had as children.

If we look at our instincts and see they are in conflict, we become anxious. We don't know how to respond. There is a battle between the mind, the heart, and the gut. What do we do? Who do we choose?

More open-hearted people will choose their hearts no matter what, but they may fail to use their minds when necessary. Some rely solely on their minds and fail to express emotions when needed. A balance is struck when you become natural again—when you recognize the difference between instinctual actions and mental actions. Then, you will be aware enough to see your responses and channel them accordingly.

The solution for many people who are anxious and lonely is simply this: learn to trust your instincts and pause your mind for a while. Become a child again, play, and express.

Expression – Being Seen

Being seen is an instinct we all have. We want to show ourselves, present ourselves beautifully, and let people know that we exist, for God's sake! We want to express ourselves, share our stories and feelings, and be seen and accepted as we are.we choose communities who accept us, we choose families who accept our instinct, if your don't have such a family you will leave or feel uneasy.You expression matters ,your way of expression matters and the acceptance of your expression also matters.even those who say,I don't care about what other people think are often lying to themselves and to others, because like Aristotle says, Man is a political animal,we just cant get rid of society even if we wish we could.

Why Does Parental Trauma Even Exist?

Because parents are always on a mission to "mold" the child.

Even governments are no exception to this tendency. They are always thinking of hiring young recruits as political executives so that they can "mold" them easily into their administrative processes.

Unknowingly, the child is traumatized and enclosed because their natural instincts weren't accepted. Their inclination towards certain choices wasn't acknowledged. They were told they were failures —again and again. They failed to recognize that there was an inner instinct guiding them, but it was repressed. It disappeared, and now they are crippled, suffering from anxiety, and afraid to talk to people.

Life is especially hard for young people these days. They are being thrown into an unnatural world —a world where intellect is valued much more than instincts and the natural yearning of a person.

There is a misconception, in my opinion, about self-development. We assume that self- development is about learning things that others have discovered and putting them into practice. I have often found that this approach does not work.

The idea that you need to mold yourself into perfection is false, in my opinion. I believe that one must approach everything in life as a discovery— discover your inner talents, your inclinations, your passions, and move forward rather than trying to behave like someone you idolize. Simply idolize yourself and try to become that version.

Even the ideas of success are very abstract and differ from person to person—parent to child, brother to brother, friend to friend. So why stick to abstract ideas when you can simply create your own and work on them instead?

You are better off happy than successful. You are better off blissfully enjoying what you want to do rather than doing what others tell you to do.

Self-discipline arises naturally when you recognize its value. Until then, you need not fret about it—but one day, it will arrive naturally.

All self-help books are written by middle-aged people who struggled with the same things you have struggled with. And one day, you will see that you are capable of writing a self-help book— maybe even better than the popular ones that sell a lot.

You inherently know what you want to become. You know what to do and how to behave instinctively. You know how to express yourself. You know all these things because you are human—you are born with such knowledge, just as a cat is born with the knowledge to stretch and do yoga poses.

There is also value in learning from wise people, but unless you recognize that what you are learning from them is experiential wisdom—a law that always works regardless of the person performing the act—you won't truly learn from them.

Until then, if you feel anxious, know that it is alright, and everything will be okay if you simply learn to trust your instincts and speak the truth that comes to your mind.

Practical Takeaway:

Observe your "bad" friend's behavior long enough. When it comes to making a big decision in life, would you really trust him or her?

Question to Self:

How many times have you felt the paranoia of your own lies, of your own words?

Chapter 2

Introduction to chakras and swara yoga

What do you experience?

Your body is both an objective and a subjective thing. It can be looked at from an outer perspective by dissecting it and analyzing it, which is the general view, or it can be looked at subjectively, with all of its functions regarded purely from within. The latter is accessible to everyone; you need not be a specialist doctor to observe the various activities and their effects on your body. You need not even be skilled in anything or "know" anything. You can simply observe, and believe that observation is the key to knowledge in any area. What firsthand experience can teach you is far greater than reading or listening to another person's experience because your whole being goes through the experience and changes as a result.

The various functions of the body can be classified purely subjectively. Where do you feel your stomach? How can you control the movement of the inner organs? Can you control the inner organs? What if I decide one day to simply observe all the happenings in my body—the nerves, the information these nerves send, and how they reflect on my mind? What kind of thoughts do I generate when I eat a certain food, or when I sit in the morning sun? If we observe, if only we observe, we can come to remarkable conclusions given by the yogis in many spiritual texts like the Siva Samhita, the Gheranda Samhita, or various other ancient Ayurvedic texts.

Medicine in ancient and medieval India was completely different from what it is now. We assume that the most effective medicine these days is allopathy or modern medicine. Various institutions prefer allopathic doctors and aim to educate themselves on allopathy, which started roughly 200 years ago. Remember, in the early 1900s, "doctors" were actually transmitting viral diseases from patient to patient because of their lack of knowledge about sanitation.

We also prefer allopathy because we see the effects it has directly. A painkiller ingested can have immediate effects because it interacts directly with your bloodstream, manipulating it in a drastic way. If you observe the mind while the whole process happens, you will see how it affects even your thoughts. You may feel a bit focused for a while and then lack enthusiasm later. Maybe you experience a "fog" afterward. We brush these symptoms off with disregard. "They are merely harmless side effects," we may say. But on further investigation, you will find effects that are irreversible.

A person whose mind has changed doesn't realize that he has changed because his whole perspective is now completely different. An outsider may tell him that something has changed, but he wouldn't realize it. Similarly, there are a lot of things in our environment related to these "modern" scientific revolutionary technologies that are affecting us, but we seem too ignorant of their effects because we are essentially hypnotizing ourselves.

The chakras are nerve clusters in your body that you can interact with if you put awareness toward these centers. Each center responds to the environment in a certain way, and these centers are very much connected to the thoughts you generate.

If we focus our awareness on these centers, knowledge of how to work with them is very helpful not only for balancing one's life but also for balancing the lower chakras in order to attain a higher consciousness of the upper chakras, which can lead to mystical or transcendental experiences.

Our lives are filled with wisdom that we cannot easily translate into words. We try to transmit it to our loved ones, and we try to articulate it, but it's hard to explain all of the realizations one has throughout life. Different centers activate at different stages of our life. You never really think about earning for your survival until you grow older and realize that your parents will not always provide for you. Your body, through these chakras, signals you and urges you to think of such things.

Prana is the life force and energy that you can direct toward these chakras. Imagine pushing energy towards your tightened fists. How do you do that? How do you direct energy there? It is similar but slightly different. You can direct prana through these chakras and balance them to achieve a wholesome, balanced life where you are capable of thinking clearly about all aspects of life in a healthy way.

The subjective experience of directing prana toward these chakras can be thought of as an inner exercise, where instead of clenching your fists or feet, you inwardly direct the life force to the center. We cannot really point out the exact center of the chakras, but through continuous practice of directing the life force, you gain an intuitive feeling of where they are. The lower ones are harder to put awareness into, but it is not impossible.

Prana and mind are therefore intricately connected with each other, and prana and breath are intricately connected as well. Hence, the Buddha prescribed only Vipassana, or careful observation of either bodily sensations or the breath, in order to let wisdom flow naturally.

All of this can be accessed by any person who is "conscious."

Prana controls the mind. A man with less energy cannot really think thoroughly or direct his mental energy toward something. This point leads us toward two types of energy that arise in our daily life—one is mental energy, and the other is physical, or life force energy.

Yogis try to balance these energies, which are related to the nostrils. If you observe that your left nostril is predominantly open, it means that your system is moving more toward mental energies. If your right nostril is dominant, your energy is outwardly flowing. You can divide your daily activities according to your breath and the optimal efficiency of these two important nerves called the Ida (connected to the left nostril) and the Pingala (connected to the right nostril).

With awareness, you can also observe which chakra is dominating by noting not only the kind of thoughts you have but also your unconsciously habituated bodily positions. You can simply glance or take note of which chakra has more prana in it.

Prana naturally flows throughout your body. There is conscious willing movement of prana and unconscious movement. This unconscious movement happens in your sleep too. Hence, the content of your dreams and feelings are closely interrelated to the prana flow in your body while you are asleep. Releasing prana from your body before sleep can aid in getting sound sleep.

Prana Vidya is part of the wisdom traditions in India. Vidya has a literal transliteration as "wisdom," but it is much more than simply wisdom. To define Vidya, one must first glimpse how maturity ripens within a person. Have you ever known a friend who was far too mature for their age? Most of us have had a friend or even a sibling who is mature enough to solve familial conflicts. That is special—almost a superpower in plain sight. If we understand how maturity arises, we gain insight into how the ancient seers of India attained these “Vidyas.”

Maturity develops when we glimpse the nature of reality and align our words to make sense of it. True maturity is glimpsing something of the eternal truths. Eternal truths are those that are applicable to any human being, regardless of tradition, organization, color, or race. These truths are timeless and philosophical, valid across centuries, and would be recognized in the minds of people even a thousand years from now.

If we strive in our lives to glimpse eternal truths and deconstruct them, we can reveal to ourselves the basic functioning of the mind. The mind, as we experience it, is the constant chatter in our heads—conscious thought processes, desires, urges, blame, excuses, family drama, the entire psychodrama that plays out within. This drama is governed by certain laws, just as astronomy and the physical and chemical sciences are.

The laws of the mind can be referred to as eternal, because as long as we have minds, we can observe these laws in action. Many are familiar with the saying "the macrocosm is reflected in the microcosm." This is an eternal truth, applicable to everyone. Quantum physics even confirms this eternal law, which may be called an axiom. All laws are basic observations that humans have made about the workings of the universe, with consistent accuracy. A law must be dependent on the observer's report, and it must be universally applicable.

Thus, eternal truths are "observed" fragments of reality linked to the human mind. We can know the intricacies of how our mind and the relation of this mind with the universe by simply observing the mind.Those who dedicate themselves to observing the mind and its patterns over long periods develop the wisdom known as "Vidya".The Neural networks that are used to power a lot of Artificial intelligent systems and machine learning algorithms are also a similar kind of "Vidya",externalised or computerized.

There are many Vidyas that ancient rishis, seers, and meditation practitioners have uncovered, each reflecting an important aspect of the mind. One of them is Prana Vidya—the wisdom of life energy, the wisdom of life itself.

Practical Takeaway:

Gently observe your nostrils and the flow of your breath, noticing the subtle patterns and their connection to the energies stirring within you.Which nostril is blocked and which one is flowing more?Pay attention if any frustration or discomfort arises when you engage in activities that do not align with you. Reflect on whether you can enhance the effectiveness of these actions simply by harmonizing with the natural rhythm of the Swara pattern.

Question for Self-Inquiry:

What insights or Vidya have you uncovered through your practice?

Consider listing some eternal truths—such as gravity, the simple yet profound fact that an apple falls from the tree to the ground—that serve as anchors of wisdom in your journey.

Chapter 3

Unknown, Known, and the Unknowable

The mind seeks what can be known, always striving to create a sense of security around the unknown—most notably, the uncertainty of tomorrow. Societal progress as a scientifically minded community depends on confronting and uncovering this unknown. Through remarkable advances, information hidden in the unknown has been transformed, manipulating and expanding the boundaries of the known world. Diseases once unimaginable have now been identified, predicted, and cured, thanks to scientific and biological progress. Research and analytical thinking cultivated through universities and colleges have turned many unknowns into known realities.

The unknowable, however, exists beyond both the known and the unknown. It represents what cannot ever be fully known or expressed—only experienced. For example, while love can be explained as a product of chemicals in the body, its subjective experience remains unknowable. The workings of thought processes and the experience of enlightenment also belong to this domain; these can only be directly experienced, never fully articulated. Enlightenment itself cannot truly be claimed as having "happened" to someone, since that would transform it into something knowable. Consciousness cannot be shared entirely with another; the unknowable remains the realm of meditators and spiritual seekers who continually turn inward, striving to dive deeper into themselves in search of what cannot be named.

When the unknowable is glimpsed, the world and

everything in it become seen as direct manifestations of that mysterious source. All emerges from a space of awareness beyond the mind—a mirror reflecting the known and the unknown with equal clarity. The unknown becomes accessible through the analytical and investigative abilities of intelligence, but truly seeing oneself as the "Self," "Atman," or "Soul" is the simplest doorway to this profound space. This is the beginning of self-inquiry: asking questions such as, "What and who am I?" Such questions, posed sincerely, can open the gate to the unknowable. Meeting the unknowable with clear seeing leads to natural happiness and the deepest, most effortless state of consciousness.

The Evolution of Knowledge and Consciousness

Knowledge is one of humanity's oldest hungers. Before fire, before language, before temples or machines, there was this single burning question in the human heart: *What is this?* A rustle in the grass, a flicker of light in the sky, a cry of birth, a silence of death — each awakened wonder, each demanded an answer. And so knowledge was born, not from certainty but from mystery.

But knowledge has never been static. It evolves, just as rivers carve new paths, just as trees reach higher toward the sun. At first, it was instinct: a bodily knowing, wordless. The hunter knew the wind, the gatherer knew the plant. The child knew the mother's heartbeat as surely as breath. This was the first layer — intimate, embodied, woven into survival.

Then came the myth. To explain thunder, men spoke of gods. To explain love, they sang of spirits. To explain death, they wove stories of journeys beyond. Myth was not "false knowledge" but symbolic knowledge — a way of containing mysteries too vast for literal thought. These myths were not lies; they were bridges, artful translations of infinity into human speech.

Later came philosophy — the leap from myth to reason. "What is justice?" asked Plato. "What is being?" asked Aristotle. Reason carved new channels for knowledge, demanding clarity, coherence, universality. It sought to replace the poetry of gods with the rigor of logic. Yet even philosophy, at its highest, remained half-art, half-science, reaching with words toward what words could never hold.

Then came science — a revolution in seeing. The telescope and microscope turned our gaze outward and inward, revealing galaxies and cells. Knowledge became measurable, testable, repeatable. The myths of gods gave way to laws of physics, the cycles of the stars, the unfolding of evolution. Science claimed the throne, declaring itself the only true knowledge. But in its pride, it forgot that knowledge is not a thing but a journey — a living, evolving movement of consciousness itself.

And so we stand now, in an age where knowledge has multiplied beyond comprehension, yet wisdom often lags behind. We can split atoms and splice genes, map the brain and simulate worlds, but we still struggle with the same ancient questions: Who are we? Why do we suffer? How should we live? Knowledge grows in power, but consciousness grows slowly, often painfully.

To see this clearly is to understand that the evolution of knowledge is inseparable from the evolution of consciousness. Knowledge without consciousness is dangerous. Consciousness without knowledge is blind. Together, they are the two wings of the bird that has carried humanity across millennia.

Consciousness is not a static thing. Like knowledge, it grows, deepens, evolves. The consciousness of a child is not that of an elder. The consciousness of a tribe is not that of a global civilization. To speak of "the evolution of consciousness" is to recognize that humanity, as a whole, is still waking from its long sleep.

At first, consciousness was fused with nature. The earliest humans did not stand apart from the forest or river; they *were* the forest, the river. Identity was porous, fluid. There was no sharp distinction between self and world. Animism, the belief that everything is alive, was the natural worldview — not superstition but direct perception. Consciousness was relational, embedded in the web of life.

Then came separation. With agriculture, cities, empires, humans began to stand apart from nature, to dominate it, to measure it. Consciousness became more self-centered, more individual. The ego was born. For the first time, man said "I" with power. This "I" created wonders — pyramids, philosophies, sciences — but also horrors — slavery, war, oppression. The rise of the ego was both triumph and tragedy.

And still consciousness evolves. Mystics and sages throughout history have spoken of higher stages — awareness beyond ego, unity beyond division. They tell us that consciousness can awaken from its dream of separation, returning to the sense of oneness but now enriched by self-awareness. The child's openness becomes the sage's clarity. The circle closes, but at a higher turn of the spiral.

Knowledge, too, reflects this spiral. Myth corresponds to the fused stage, philosophy to the emerging ego, science to the rational individual. But what comes next? What knowledge corresponds to the consciousness of unity? Perhaps it is not a new science or philosophy, but a synthesis — a way of knowing that is both rational and poetic, empirical and mystical, outer and inner. A knowledge that does not divide but integrates.

This is what we are groping toward in our time. For as technology accelerates knowledge, we are forced to confront our own consciousness. Artificial intelligence can calculate faster than us, but it cannot tell us who we are. Genetic engineering can alter bodies, but it cannot answer why we long for eternity. Space exploration can carry us to Mars, but it cannot teach us how to live on Earth. Knowledge without consciousness becomes monstrous. Consciousness without knowledge becomes impotent. Their union is the next stage of evolution.

There is an old story of Nasrudin.

One day, he was seen pouring spoonfuls of yogurt into a lake.

“What are you doing, Mulla?” asked the villagers, astonished.

“I am making yogurt,” he replied calmly.

“But Mulla, you can’t turn a whole lake into yogurt with just a few spoonfuls!”

Nasrudin smiled. “True. But imagine if it *did* take.”

We laugh, but the story points to something essential: great changes begin with impossibility. Consciousness evolves not because the conditions are certain but because someone dares to pour a little yogurt into the vastness of the unknown. A few prophets, poets, thinkers, mystics — their spoonfuls have transformed civilizations.

The same is true of knowledge. At first, the telescope seemed like Nasrudin’s yogurt — absurd, impossible. The idea of invisible microbes? Madness. The thought of human flight? Folly. And yet, spoonful by spoonful, knowledge ferments, consciousness shifts, the impossible becomes the new ground of possibility.

Knowledge is the expansion of map. Consciousness is the expansion of territory. One without the other is useless. A detailed map with no land to walk is fantasy. A vast territory with no map is confusing. Together, they dance, one shaping the other. And humanity’s story is nothing but this dance, playing out over millennia.

But here is the danger: we mistake accumulation for

evolution. More facts, more data, more information — but does this make us wiser? The internet is the greatest library ever created, yet it also breeds distraction, addiction, and confusion. We swim in knowledge but drown in meaninglessness. Consciousness does not evolve by quantity of data but by depth of presence. It evolves not by hoarding more, but by *seeing differently*.

Thus the challenge of our time is not merely to expand knowledge but to deepen consciousness. For without this depth, our progress becomes self-destruction. Nuclear weapons, climate change, AI — each is knowledge unbalanced by consciousness. We must grow in both, or we will perish in the imbalance.

When we trace the story of knowledge through history, we notice that it does not advance in a straight line but in cycles of construction, collapse, and renewal. A new framework emerges, dominates for a time, then eventually reaches its limits and is replaced.

The mythic stage was not simply error or ignorance. It provided a coherent worldview that bound people together, explained existence, and offered meaning. It collapsed not because it was entirely false, but because consciousness itself outgrew it. The same can be said of philosophy: it offered clarity where myth could not, but it could not account for empirical discovery. Science then rose, providing a reliable method of testing claims. Yet even science shows signs of strain in our time — overwhelmed by its own specialization, distorted by economic incentives, and unable to provide meaning in a fragmented world.

Each stage of knowledge corresponds to the level of consciousness that produces it. Myth expresses a fused, collective consciousness. Philosophy expresses the rational ego discovering itself. Science expresses the individuated mind harnessing reason and experiment. What might come next? Perhaps a form of knowledge that integrates these — a synthesis of empirical rigor, philosophical reflection, and mythic depth. A mode of knowing that honors both outer measurement and inner experience, both fact and meaning.

Some thinkers call this "integral knowledge" or "metamodern consciousness." It would not discard science, but situate it within a larger framework of values and lived experience. It would not discard myth, but understand it as symbolic truth rather than literal description. It would not discard philosophy, but recognize that rational analysis is one tool among many. The evolution of knowledge may therefore be toward integration, not replacement.

Consciousness does not evolve only in individuals; it evolves in societies. The individual's awakening contributes to the collective, and the collective atmosphere shapes the individual.

In tribal societies, consciousness was embedded in community and nature. There was little sense of separate individuality. Modernity, in contrast, elevated the individual — with all the freedoms and alienations this brought. Postmodernity, which we live in now, deconstructs narratives and identities, often leaving people in disorientation. What is needed next is not a return to older stages but a movement forward — toward a consciousness that is both individual and collective, both free and connected.

This collective evolution mirrors the individual's journey. A child begins in fusion with the world (tribal stage), discovers autonomy in adolescence (modern stage), questions narratives in early adulthood (postmodern stage), and ideally matures into integration later in life (integral stage). Societies move through parallel arcs, though more slowly and unevenly.

This suggests that the crises we face today — political fragmentation, ecological collapse, technological disruption — are symptoms of consciousness outgrowing its current frame.

We cannot solve them with the same mindset that produced them. We require an evolution not only of knowledge but of the way we experience ourselves and the world.

If knowledge outpaces consciousness, disaster follows. The ability to split the atom without the wisdom to restrain violence produced nuclear weapons. The ability to manipulate the environment without the consciousness of ecological interdependence has produced climate change. The ability to design digital platforms without awareness of human psychology has produced mass distraction and polarization.

The inverse is also true. Consciousness without knowledge can become superstition or naïve idealism. A desire for unity without empirical understanding can devolve into dogma or fantasy. The harmony of knowledge and consciousness is not optional; it is necessary for survival.

This is why many contemporary thinkers argue that the next great challenge is not technological but psychological. We have built tools we cannot yet wield wisely. Artificial intelligence may extend human knowledge beyond our capacity to even understand it. Without a parallel deepening of consciousness — humility, ethical reflection, a sense of interconnection — this power will be destructive. The bottleneck is not intelligence but wisdom.

What might an evolved synthesis of knowledge and consciousness look like?

First, it would integrate subjective and objective modes of knowing. Science studies the external world, but subjective experience is equally real. Practices such as meditation, contemplative inquiry, and phenomenology are not enemies of science but partners in a fuller understanding of reality.

Second, it would unite analysis and meaning. Facts alone do not tell us how to live. Philosophy, art, and spirituality provide frameworks of value that science cannot supply. A mature synthesis would see them as complementary.

Third, it would balance individuality and collectivity. The modern emphasis on the individual brought freedom, but also loneliness and fragmentation. An evolved consciousness must recover a sense of belonging — not in the tribal sense of conformity, but in a higher sense of interdependence.

Finally, it would cultivate humility. Every stage of knowledge has believed itself final, only to be transcended. Science today, for all its achievements, will one day be seen as a stage, not the end. An evolved consciousness knows this, and remains open.

Perhaps it is worth returning to Nasrudin one last time.

He was once seen riding his donkey backwards.

"Nasrudin," someone asked, "why are you facing the wrong way?"

"I am not," he replied. "It is the donkey that is facing the wrong way."

This is the predicament of humanity. We believe we are progressing, riding forward on the donkey of knowledge. Yet if consciousness does not evolve, we may be riding backwards — mistaking speed for direction. True progress is not only about how fast we move, but about whether we are facing the right way.

Knowledge gives us the donkey. Consciousness tells us which way to face. Only together can we move wisely.

We live at a hinge point in history. Knowledge has never been greater; consciousness has never been under greater strain. The task is to bring them into balance — to cultivate not only sharper tools but deeper wisdom.

This will not be achieved by one discipline, one nation, or one leader. It requires a global evolution, a shift in the way humanity sees itself. It requires education that cultivates not only information but awareness. It requires technology designed with ethics, governance guided by humility, culture infused with meaning. It requires each of us, in our ordinary lives, to evolve our own consciousness, however small the step.

For the evolution of knowledge and consciousness is not abstract. It is lived in the way we treat one another, the way we face uncertainty, the way we live with ourselves. Each moment of clarity, each act of compassion, each refusal to be swept away by distraction is part of this evolution. The great story of humanity is not written only in laboratories and books, but in the choices of every mind, every day.

Future Scenarios: what we do next, and why it comes back to the inner work

If the previous pages laid out the pattern — myth, philosophy, science, fragmentation, then the call to integration — the question now becomes practical: what could the near future look like if we try to align knowledge and consciousness rather than let one outrun the other? There are several plausible trajectories, and each one depends less on technology than on the maturity of the human systems that operate it.

First scenario: acceleration without interiority. This is the default. We keep building faster computers, more persuasive platforms, more efficient production systems, while neglecting moral education and depth of character. The result is a hyper-capable civilization that amplifies short-term incentives, exploits systems, and accelerates collapse dynamics — ecological, social, psychological. The risk here is systemic: more power in fewer hands, faster feedback loops, less capacity for collective reflection. Knowledge grows geometrically; wisdom lags linearly. The catastrophe is not inevitable, but the probability increases with every neglected prefrontal cortex: tools without restraint mean unintended consequences multiply.

Second scenario: technological maturity married to ethical governance. Here we deliberately design institutions that slow certain impulses, create friction where necessary, and enforce long-term accountability. We invest in education that teaches not only expertise but meta-cognition and moral imagination. We build governance that places ecological stability, human flourishing, and intergenerational justice at its center. In this future, AI, biotechnology, and energy innovations are harnessed, but they are offset by cultural incentives to care for common goods. Knowledge proceeds, but it's guided by frameworks that cultivate restraint and foresight. It's not utopia — no system avoids trade-offs — but it's survivable and human-scaled.

Third scenario: planetary maturity — the evolution of a civic culture that treats the biosphere as an identity marker as powerful as nationality or religion. This involves a cultural reorientation: people see themselves as members of a living planet. Policies follow. Economies are redesigned for regeneration instead of extraction. Technology serves restoration. Such a shift requires both structural redesign (new legal and economic forms) and a mass-scale interior maturation — people who practice attention, who can defer immediate gratification for shared, long-term goods. It's conceivable, and certain communities already point in that direction; scaling it is the practical challenge.

Fourth scenario: transhumanist bifurcation. We choose to decouple consciousness from biology through uploads, cognitive enhancements, or networked minds. This would produce radical new forms of intelligence that may not share the values of unenhanced humanity. If such advances occur without broad, ethically mature deliberation and shared governance, they could produce extreme inequality and even existential risk. The technical problems are enormous; the moral problems are larger. Knowledge would have outrun the kind of consciousness necessary to steward it.

None of these paths is a technical inevitability; they are social possibilities. The common variable that shifts the probabilities is not a piece of software or a discovery in a lab. It is how we cultivate inner capacities, how we change education, economics, and governance so that knowledge has a guiding intelligence — not merely intelligence-as-capacity, but intelligence tempered by care.

So what are the practical levers?

— Education reform toward depth: curricula that combine rigorous empirical training with exercises in attention, ethical judgment, conflict resolution, and systems thinking. Teach students how to hold paradox, how to understand causal chains over decades, how to recognize bias in their own thinking. These are skills; they can be taught and measured.

— Institutional redesign: laws and incentives that make long-term thinking rational. Try this simple design principle: if a decision will have multi-decadal externalities, require multi-level review and broader representation. Institutions that reward quarter-to-quarter gains need to be counterbalanced by institutions that reward durability, resilience, and ecological health.

— Technology with humility built-in: auditability, transparency, and purpose-limitation as standard design norms. If a system manipulates attention, it should be tested for social fragility before wide release. If an algorithm can shift civic norms, it should be subject to civic oversight, not only corporate profit.

— Cultural habits of presence: rituals, arts, silence, and regular practices that train attention. These are not a retreat from modern life; they are preventative medicine. People who practice presence are less likely to be polarized, less likely to be seduced by simplistic narratives, and more capable of long-term planning.

— Global governance and solidarity experiments: not utopian world-state designs, but practical experiments — commons-based resource stewardship, planetary monitoring with transparency, multinational pacts focused on remediation and restoration. We do not need one single global culture, but we do need reliable protocols that cross borders when biospheric thresholds are at stake.

None of this happens by decree. It happens by accumulation of small, consistent choices. The future that values wisdom is created by millions of practiced moments when people privilege reflection over reaction, when institutions accept slower but safer options, when designers accept moral constraints as part of competence.

A final caution: even at our best, any civilization is transient. The question is not immortality for the human project but whether we act in ways that extend the possibility for more meaningful life for many generations. That ethical horizon — our duty to future persons, possible sentient beings, and the living systems that support them — is both practical and spiritual. It depends on the external systems we build and the internal systems we cultivate.

Which brings us — inevitably, properly — to the place this essay must end: the most reliable lever for any future scenario is inner clarity. The broadest changes in education, governance, and technology are asymmetric when matched with a culture that inclines toward presence, humility, curiosity, and compassion. There is no substitute for inner work; the technical fixes are scaffolding. Knowledge without interiority amplifies harm. Interiority without knowledge is insufficient. Together they are the necessary conditions for a viable future.

It is useful to close this long arc with a small human

image — because policy and philosophy eventually meet the kitchen table, the hospital ward, and the bedside of the grieving. Years ago, in a village I once passed through, an old woman tended a communal well. Children played, arguments flared, strangers traveled through. She never wrote a paper on governance, never designed software, but when disputes arose, people sat in that square and she would ask a simple question: "What do you need?" Her glance was not legalistic; it was not ideological. It was a call to attention. People often found the answer after hearing her question. Systems are built by people who notice. If we shift the habit of notice from novelty to depth, the architecture of our institutions will follow.

That attention — the habit of noticing what is actually happening rather than the stories we tell about what is happening — is precisely what the next chapter turns to. Because all the structures we sketch as necessary depend on one simple but radical capacity: the ability to observe our inner process honestly. The rest follows.

The Answers Are All Within

Many of the questions we run after outwardly — meaning, justice, truth, peace — are in truth questions about our interior procedure for knowing. We think: if I find the right book, the right teacher, the right data, the right leader, the right policy, then the problem will be solved. Often what we gain in those outward searches are fragments, helpful but incomplete. The fuller answer is located in a different register: how we receive, process, and integrate information. Before trying to fix external systems, it is efficient and durable to first learn to read the machinery within.

Why is misunderstanding so persistent? Not because people are stupid or malicious in the majority of cases, but because the mechanics of understanding are rarely taught. We assume that once information enters a mind, understanding follows naturally. In practice it does not. Misunderstanding often arises because people mistake perception for comprehension, confound opinion for synthesis, and treat memorization for mastery. The great global conflicts of our era are not only political disputes; they are disputes rooted in diverging, unexamined epistemologies — different assumptions about what knowing actually is.

This matters because the remedies are practical. If we can teach people a meta-level of how to approach knowledge, many disagreements thin out; two parties may still disagree about values, but they can at least recognize where their mental processes differ. That recognition makes conversation possible.

A pointed corrective comes when we reconsider Descartes. His "I think therefore I am" was revolutionary — he sought a secure foundation for knowledge in a time of uncertainty. Many Indian and existential traditions invert that observation: "I am, therefore I think." They start from presence rather than thought as the primary datum. This matters: presence provides a stable field in which thinking happens. When you search for truth from a place of reactivity, your mind is already biased. When you search from a place of calm attention, the same evidence reveals itself differently.

Five steps toward real understanding

Once you understand soemthing truly you are freed from it and if it is misunderstood it clings like a

Perceive. The first move is clean perception. Like assessing the outside of a fruit, you look without immediate judgment. Perception must distinguish between surface appeal and substance. Advertising and charisma are designed to look like understanding; training perception means learning to delay the rush to conclusion.

Peel. Don't stop at the surface. Peel the fruit. Suspend premature evaluation and pay attention to the structure beneath the glossy exterior. This is not mere skepticism for its own sake; it's disciplined curiosity. For example: read a text twice, then trace its internal logic before reacting. Ask: what are the assumptions here? What terms are being used without definition?

Experience. Enter the domain you study. Experiment, practice, or simulate the claim. Reading about meditation is different from sitting on the cushion. Reading about markets is not the same as participating in one. Experience tests the internal coherence of knowledge.

Digest. Integrate new material with what you already know. This is the slow work. Weeks or months after exposure, insights coalesce — or they fail to. Digesting is the ability to synthesize, to make a new configuration of understanding that fits the rest of your map. It often involves critique: you hold the new idea against existing frames and either accommodate it or revise your map.

Express. Finally, test your understanding by teaching, writing, or action. Excretion — the metaphor is crude but apt — removes what doesn't assimilate. Expression reveals gaps and consolidates insights. If you cannot explain an idea simply, you probably have not digested it. Intentional articulation also yields practical consequences: the way you act will show whether integration is real.

These five steps are not a rigid hierarchy but an iterative cycle. Perception leads to peeling; peeling leads to provisional experience; experience calls for digestion; digestion invites expression; expression invites new perception. The important point is that understanding is procedural. It is an activity, not a state you arrive at by acquiring a single fact.

Practical examples

— A manager confronted with a new policy must not

immediately implement or reject it. Perceive the policy objectively; peel back the incentives and assumptions; if practical, pilot it (experience); collect data and internalize findings (digest); then share results and adjust (express). This slow loop reduces costly mistakes.

— A reader encountering a spiritual text: perceive the voice and context; peel through metaphors to the intended meaning; practice the suggested exercises; allow insights to be integrated into daily life; then write or speak about what genuinely changed. That cycle distinguishes piety from transformation.

Why does this matter for collective life?

When institutions teach only content and not process, they produce citizens who can recite facts but not deliberately. Public life suffers when debate becomes performance rather than inquiry. The five-step method is mundane, but it builds a culture of epistemic humility: a recognition that understanding takes time, that one's initial reaction is provisional, and that disagreement often reflects differences in stage rather than malice.

If our earlier chapters argued that the survival of complex civilization depends on aligning knowledge with consciousness, this chapter insists that the most tractable place to begin is inside each mind. Systems change slowly; habits change faster. Cultivating the capacity to perceive, peel, experience, digest, and express is the most pragmatic civic technology we can practice daily. It makes debates less destructive, decisions more robust, and communities more resilient.

So start small. Before you forward an article, try the five steps on it. Before you adopt a policy, run a micro-pilot. Before you argue in public, ask yourself: which stage of the cycle am I operating from? Over time, such discipline accumulates, and the density of shared wisdom grows. The external institutions we redesign will then rest on a more competent substrate: minds trained to know more than they assume they know.

From here, the book moves inward — into practical essays about how to practice presence, how to read the body and mind, and how inner work concretely reshapes external behavior. The answers are indeed within; learning how to retrieve them is the skill of our age.

Practical Takeaways:

Learning how the mind works has never been a priority in most education. Understanding how information is retained, concepts analyzed, and problems solved is essential.

The mind operates as a daydreaming mechanism; desires originate in the heart and are expressed in dreams. Mindfulness and emotional awareness are crucial for improved focus. Ramana Maharshi, a renowned South Indian mystic, stated that thoughts arise from the heart rather than the brain, and observation of this can lead to greater focus.

Focus does not work like an uninterrupted beam; it must be continually brought back to the object of attention. Cultivating this habit of awareness enhances all areas of life.

Chapter 4

The Brain as an Associative Machine

The brain forms associations, which enable deeper understanding by connecting information to broader perspectives. Reinforce these links by writing about subjects or discussing them with peers for extended periods. Associative learning often occurs unconsciously, sometimes even during sleep—so prioritize association over rote memorization for stronger retention and adaptability.

The more memories you create with a piece of information, a book, or a course, the more you will connect physically and emotionally, generating a retentive force that helps you form stronger associations. Learning need not be monotonous; it must be multidimensional and experiential. Otherwise, unfortunately, you may not truly learn and may instead merely impress upon yourself the illusion that you have learned.Organizing your mental space is like organizing your room. If the room is tidy, you know exactly where everything is, and you can retrieve items easily, without needing luck or stumbling upon them by chance.Mind PalaceNever underestimate the power of mental imagery. Forming vivid "mind pictures" makes recalling concepts easier. Yes, the famous fictional detective Sherlock Holmes used this technique, creating "mind palaces" where he stored relevant information. This method works tremendously well because our minds are deeply connected to the spaces we dwell in.Think of your home—a sanctuary where you can relax and intuitively know the location of things. Similarly, create a mind palace: perhaps a beach house, a multi-storied skyscraper, or a garden with fountains. Design compartments: beautifully decorated rooms, grand halls, or even hidden alcoves. Store specific information in each space. Imagine yourself walking into a particular room, embedding a piece of knowledge on its walls, and revisiting it whenever needed.

Before an exam, for instance, you might "open" this palace in your mind and retrieve the stored material. Use imagination as it was meant to be used, for memory becomes your strength when you learn how to harness it. Everything you are is the accumulation of experiences, books read, thoughts contemplated, and memories formed. You are the embodiment of all that you have lived.Memory enhances both associative power and problem-solving speed. Strong memory allows you to recall tools and insights with ease. Over-reliance on notes or apps can hinder your capacity to address real-world issues. Instead, practice with simple tasks—like memorizing your grocery list. Make the act playful and imaginative. Soon you will notice another benefit: the ability to discard unwanted mental imagery. Awkward moments, negative impressions, and distracting thoughts can fade when you actively replace them with new, vibrant memories.Problem-Solving and TestingProblem-solving is a lifelong discipline that strengthens your ability to apply techniques in real life and recognize underlying issues. Testing, too, is indispensable—not for measuring scores alone, but for revealing gaps in understanding and teaching through error correction. Welcome opportunities for testing—whether through self-quizzes or digital tools—since every mistake transforms into a memorable step toward mastery.

Practical Takeaway

Build a mind palace.Play with memory; it is your hidden superpower.

Questions to Self

Do you remember trivial things from two years ago—details that now hold no practical use?
If so, why do such memories linger more vividly than the important ones you wish to keep?

Chapter 5

Touching the Mind.

"A Meditation on the Senses and Instincts."
Reading this can help a lot in "expanding" your consciousness, as you read the following words, considering opening yourself up to certain possibilities that you may connect to your "True Nature". We will go through all of the aspects of this experience starting from the senses, to the deeper Unconscious Instincts.

Conception.

The senses are the doors to perceiving this reality. All of our Thought constructs are based on the senses.A fact that is ignored and needs attention.Whatever has happened in this life has been through the senses.

Thought constructs have also developed, evolutionarily, according to the senses.

For example, we have words like "focus" or "attention," which imply a kind of action that we do with our eyes. When we listen to a word like "focus," we first put that sense there. We move our eyes towards the objects of focus, we look at it from different angles and turn around to receive information.

The words have developed through the senses too,like

"control",for
example,we figured that we could control things with our hands first and most basically,then this relationship with "control" eventually, evolved.

Our day-to-day life is also a continuous interaction with this world through the senses.

But the extraordinary thing that human beings have developed over time is the ability to Conceptualize and Abstract.

We looked at and touched the sharpness of a knife, we felt that it is sharp and can be used for cutting various things, like a tool.

Our minds are developed enough to make this sharpness abstract and make it something measurable so that we can compare the sharpness of two things.

The intensity of darkness and light can also be measured and somehow sensed. Smell and its pleasantness or unpleasantness can be conceptualized.

In conceptualizing, we may have gone too far.

If we look closely and pay attention to our daily thought patterns and desires, we see that it is a conceptualization of a certain sensory experience.

Whether it be a conversation with a loved one or a professional meeting, we often suffer due to conceptualizing the sensory experience, looking at it from different angles, thinking about things before they happen, and so on.

It is sometimes essential that we do that, and it actually helps a lot to pre-analyze and abstract certain events to try to enhance the sensory experience, the thrill of it all.

This is the basis of our minds; the root of its workings is desire and abstraction.

Without desire of the senses, without abstractions, without even the senses, what are we?

Douglas Harding wrote a book called On Having No Head. His whole philosophy revolved around this concept, which stems from a practice in Zen Buddhism. This practice was simply to notice that we don't have a head, purely subjectively speaking, actually, without abstracting the head. If we notice that everything takes place in the place of the head,

Even if we look at our reflection, we are still looking at a reflection; we are not really looking at our head, which is above our shoulders.

This method evokes a certain connectedness to the essential "root" of ourselves.You may notice a natural openness or clarity that is already existing.

Here is a thought experiment:

Have you ever wondered

what life would be like

without mirrors, without the

thought that we look a certain

way?

Don't you think our

abstractions would be reduced

a little? Do you think we

would live a more contented

life?

Without a head?

My answer would be that we certainly wouldn't survive in a society that has abstracted the "head." We certainly wouldn't even look presentable. But we would definitely be more comfortable and carefree.

The abstraction of the head is also a very interesting thing I like to talk about. Because we have all kinds of things we struggle with.

For example, if I define my personality with the head that looks at me in the mirror, I would be completely off. There wouldn't be a single thing that matches. I would have to repent so much, sometimes even play down things, say things that are appropriate for the "head," do things that are appropriate for the head – basically act like the face is mine.

Feelings and the Heart.

Feelings are usually sensed in the chest area, more accurately in the middle of the chest. In this area, we encounter the most connection to the heart. The heart is always pumping and working. Sometimes it slows down, and sometimes it beats faster. This is felt, but it's also translated by the mind as a certain feeling. Once this is conceptualized, the mind brings up memories or imagines based on previous memories.

These memories may even be completely fabricated or false. Some might even be coming from memories that are far back in our childhood, or from what Carl Jung called the collective unconscious. These are tendencies and impulses of the instincts.

The fabrications can also take an extreme direction and start projecting outwards, towards the person. Here, of course, if there was a certain memory that created a certain imprint on your heart, then this is justifiable. But if it keeps repeating, then it needs attention. That's what your heart is trying to tell you; it's continuously trying to point out that a feeling needs attention.

Another thought experiment:

What if the senses – the eyes and the ears – slowly started to stop receiving signals? This process is called Pratyahara in Yoga philosophy, withdrawal of the senses.

Imagine looking without the eyes. Imagine hearing without ears, and imagine touching without your body. What will you be feeling then? Aliveness? Awareness?

The thing is, you will simply be connected to your

purest self and be close to what you are naturally, without the abstraction. And this is the essence or a taste of what a meditator feels in deep meditation. He simply withdraws his senses and rests in this purely natural space.So, the senses which receive information pass through the interface of mind and heart, and we experience it.

Touching the Mind

I like the idea of touching the mind, because just how we touch the senses, we are also touching all kinds of things in our mental space, like a thought. You are either hearing a thought or you are looking at a thought. There are certain thoughts that are "ours" and we claim them. Sigmund Freud called them the thoughts of the ego, that is, "I," "me," and "mine." We certainly claim the thoughts that are happy and joyful; we never say, "”This”

happiness is in my heart," but we often don’t claim other thoughts like anger or anxiety. We say, "This anxiety is stressing me out." Or “I cant get rid of “this” anger”.

We speak of certain thoughts as if they are not “ours”,even they are clearly coming up in “our”
minds, we refuse them, just like how we refuse certain physical sense objects.

We also sometimes "grab" thoughts and ideas, as if they were objects, and we "let go" of certain ideas or feelings, as if they are objects, and so on.

They are all parts of us,they are Instinctual.Different instinct centres in our bodies and
accumulated minds produce different “instinctual” thoughts.

The training of these Instinctual thoughts is mainly done through education or "thinking" a
a certain type of way.

For example if You are a mathematician very much proficient in Logic, you will be instinctually logical or Philosophical, or Psychological.And be slightly biased towards such Constructs.

So, this conceptualization and its dynamics are obviously very similar in all of us, and if the

"roots" are understood it is

easily trainable or re-trainable.

Interesting Thing:

Children rarely conceptualize; they are very instinctual. They don't care if you are annoyed by their crying or shouting. They feel an instinct and act naturally upon it.

Suppose there are a bunch of toys in front of two children of completely opposite temperament. One kid chooses a doll, and the other kid chooses a toy police car. What attracted them towards these objects? The senses received the information, went into the mind, and for the child who liked the doll, his heartbeat rose a little, and he felt an attraction towards this doll instinctively and grabbed it.They are not yet trained in "following or not following a certain instinct.

They are natural,but also unique in a way that they respond.

So, instincts are usually driven from the unconscious. That doesn't really mean that they aren't controllable. It means that as adults, when we are capable of touching and feeling instincts more deeply, we can slightly attune them in a different direction.The kid choose “naturally what his/her instinct calls out to him,he doesn't suffer for the instinctual reaction.This predisposition towards certain things is kind of a built-in software in each of us.Some of us just wanted to be writers,and we just couldn't really avoid it,because it is simply just natural to you.

Whereas others don't care about writing,because it is not natural to them.Getting in touch with what is most natural to us , is essential to removing all kinds of worries and anxieties.

Education of Instincts

Suppose you wanted to change an instinct that you touched upon, an instinct like a reactionary habit of maybe biting your lip, in my case, how would I go about this process? I would first need to acknowledge that this needs to be changed. Then, whenever the instinct is being touched, I can slightly remind myself by counteracting it with another instinct. The more instinctively the negation of the previously instinctive act happens, the more progress I am making. There is a catch here: a rejection is being made, we are rejecting a certain instinct, and this comes at a cost. We tend to hate that instinct. That’s how we usually judge others by their instincts too. But in actuality, we are not judging them; we are judging our own instincts that we have rejected.A pile up of such judgements leads to all kinds of hatred.Freud called this Repression.

The problem then comes when we find ourselves in the middle of our lives and recognize that we have almost rejected all the instincts that we had as children, through conceptualization, through all kinds of abstraction and education.

There is a solution to this. Simply put in simple terms, the answer would be to reduce the abstraction of the outer senses and move to the more natural sense of the body.

The instinct will be heard once you restrain yourself from the ongoing mind chatter. A naturalness will come to your instincts and your actions. The abstractions that are produced will also be much more intuitively right. You will start to read not only yourself more easily but even those surrounding you. You will recognize the instincts that they are unconsciously following.

Withdrawal from the senses doesn't really mean making them function less, not at all. In fact, with the practice of instinctual awareness, your senses too will also become much more heightened. Suddenly, you start tasting things in a better way, seeing things in a better manner with reduced judgments and add-ups. Even while talking to a loved one, you will talk much more instinctively, which is always good and natural. It doesn't really feel bad or immoral; you don't really have to conceptualize all that.

Above everything, this helped me connect to the unconscious mind in a deeper manner. I was able to recognize certain tendencies that come naturally and balance the other tendencies in a much more healthy manner.

A last Thought experiment:

Is your phone sensorily connected to you?

Yes actually it has become for most of us,I feel hurt when my phone falls down.Why is that?,because we have expanded our sensory body and whatever is in our sensory body is somehow “ours”.This is not bad in any way,consider what happens if you expand yourself to the whole Universe, wouldn’t you then be connected to the whole Universe and say things like “my universe” instead of ,”the Universe out there”?

Practical Takeaway:

Live a day without a head or maybe the rest of your life.

Question to self:

Can you stop thinking of controlling the things that are not in your control?
Why don't you do it already?

Chapter 6

Individuality and Identity

Everyone has heard at some point in life the advice: "be yourself."

What does this mean, and why is it so challenging to find purpose and meaning? This essential question deserves attention, especially in youth—who am I, and what do I truly want to become? What comes naturally, and what kind of identity genuinely aligns with the future self?

Many live life unconsciously, unaware of their actions and associations and how these shape them. It is common to move through life absorbing whatever society imposes, continuing the desires of parents during childhood, later taking on the ambitions of friends and society. People often drift from one desire to another without ever pausing to watch the mind and its movements or become mindful of the games played by themselves or, even worse, by society upon them.

Identity is largely inherited from parents and the surrounding society. People are labeled for the mind's convenience—labels make the unknown familiar. In practice, however, no one can ever truly know another person's being, yet people convince themselves otherwise. Instinctively, questions like "What do you do?" or "Where are you from?" arise in order to place strangers in predefined categories.

Society has spread many such stories, telling individuals that they belong to certain countries or lineages, and these identities are often unconsciously accepted. It is easy to behave according to labels, such as a company employee or a member of a particular race or gender, or as a boy or girl before these roles are personally discovered. True identity forms only when a person deeply resonates with a philosophy, discovers work that brings real enjoyment, or feels genuinely aligned with a religious path. Individuality arises once these externally imposed identities are examined and cast aside, revealing purpose, calling, and meaning from within.

Many cling to imposed identities without daring to pursue individuality. It takes courage to explore the deeper self and create uniquely meaningful work. Following the herd leads to disappointment because such a life is built on accumulating borrowed desires and constructed identities.

To seek the truth, uncover hidden potential, question deeply, and self-reflect. Rather than only asking parents or society, turn inward and investigate this body and mind until the true calling becomes clear and individuality is embodied. Though this path may feel lonely—requiring distance from the herd—it is ultimately rewarding. Genuine individuality brings uniqueness, and those who embrace it rise to lead and inspire.

Consider the lives of the great people often admired: their journeys were marked by time spent alone, self-discovery, and relentless pursuit of their passions. Only after mastering what they loved did society celebrate them as ideals. Most desires are borrowed. Like a child who begs for a toy in a store, adults now want jobs, relationships, and status. The discovery of true individuality lies not in external pursuits, but by looking within and realizing one's own unique capabilities.

Practical takeaway:

Look at the practical talents that you have,like rose flowers uniqueness is in its mystical fragrance,

Question to Self:

What is unique in you.what fragrance do you emit to the world around you?

Chapter 6

Rituals as Spiritual Devices and Synthesis of Knowledge.

"Lost wisdom is not necessarily untrue."

Knowledge has experienced its share of ups and downs. It has been rejected, refuted, synthesized into new forms, and continuously transformed over time.

Past traditions and their wisdom have often been lost, rendering them seemingly irrelevant in
today's world, where they hold little to no material value.

To some, these traditions are nonsensical; to others, they remain significant only in the context of a single "true" field of knowledge or tradition that they believe offers the definitive path.

While it's true that knowledge must evolve and adapt over time—being created through the dual processes of synthesis and criticism—our focus here is on these two modes of knowledge creation.

Today, knowledge is being generated rapidly through synthesis, yet the critical aspect of knowledge evolution seems to lag. Before delving into this, let us first explore the concept of spiritual devices.

A Glimpse into the Past

Life in ancient times was both simple and complex. Without modern technology, communication across the world was nearly impossible, and there was minimal exchange of information and goods.

The world was a place of hunting, scavenging, discovery, conquest, and endless curiosity. People sought knowledge by traveling to scholarly centers and engaging with extraordinary individuals, often through word-of-mouth introductions.

Accessing wisdom often required years of arduous journeys through deserts, forests, and mountains.

Back then, curiosity was ever-present: "What lies across the sea?" "What would happen if I explored that unknown land?" Knowledge creation was a slow process, often hindered by the lack of efficient communication.

For instance, an experimenter working in isolation might not live long enough to see conclusive results. This slow pace meant that life was strange, mysterious, and full of challenges.

The advent of technology marked a turning point. Communication became more accessible, reducing the need for physical travel in search of knowledge. Printing enabled the dissemination of ideas, fostering cultural exchange and unifying human understanding.

However, invasions—once an "innocent" act of curiosity (and also a pastime for power-hungry warlords)—served as both destructive and synthetic forces, blending knowledge and traditions to create new paradigms.

The Explosion of Knowledge

Over time, the linear progression of knowledge gave way to exponential growth, driven by improved communication and technological advancements.

This explosion of information has brought us to our current state, where erudition is more valued than ever. Regardless of race or culture, the ability to acquire and create knowledge is the most valuable asset in today's world.

Knowledge now encompasses not only traditional disciplines but also coding, data, and software—new forms of intellectual capital.

Data has become the fuel of our era, and everything related to it holds immense importance. But what does this

mean for knowledge and its evolution?
Evolution of Intelligence and Problem-Solving.
The rapid pace of knowledge creation has significant psychological and physiological implications.
Technology produces devices to solve problems, yet the presence of a problem is a constant in human life.

"Problems are Inevitable.
- David Deutsch."

As long as the mind exists, it will perceive problems and seek solutions. Technological devices solve specific issues, and those who invent them are often deemed successful.
However, solving one problem does not eliminate all challenges—it simply plays a part in the broader human effort.

In the past, before the scientific revolution, knowledge was localized. People devised solutions to their immediate experiences, often in philosophical or religious contexts.
When rejecting old knowledge, we must be clear about what we are discarding.
In this era of rapid knowledge creation, there is a risk of losing valuable wisdom.

Spiritual Devices and Their Role

Technology has become an integral part of our reality, influencing how we perceive the world. Similarly, spiritual devices—concepts or practices developed by sages—offer tools for understanding deeper realities. These devices operate on intricate levels, shaping our perceptions when engaged with regularly.They reveal aspects of existence that might remain hidden without them.

Looking deeper the greatest gift that western thought has given us,and by western thought I mean the scientific revolution that began with europe and spread rapidly across the whole globe,through its procedure of thought that based itself on very intricate and critical levels of logic,is that it create d a space for technological growth in term of converting the seen and experimental,like the radio waves into transmittal waves used for communications,this technology or device slightly manipulates the laws of the radio waves and transforms them into a materially observable thing that can be perceived by the sense.

Spiritual Devices for example a ritual like the device called the Namaz,which was “given”,to Prophet Muhammad,has an ability to act as a psychological device which overtime has an effect of inducing a serenity on the mind, like a mantra that is done though the whole body.
“The coolness of my eyes is in prayer.- Prophet Muhammad.”

These devices can be seen everywhere in all esoteric traditions of the world.These devices actually do give comparable and evidential experience, often not as easily materialised, which hence is rejected by the scientific community.

But considering the human system as a subjective experience through an objective medium, these devices which are all over the world, are mere means to experience certain things in the world.

The mind is also a device.Its workings can either be understood through self-awareness or through wisdom.

In India, these devices are used all over the place,and have an effect on the consciousness of the person performing using the device,often leading to similar effects,if performed consistently with diligent effort.

They are called Tantras,or techniques,and according to the book Vignana-bhairava(Knowledge of Divine Consciousness) a treatise and a collection of all these techniques,leads to a unifying experience,which opens the consciousness to the highest state of realisation called the ,Shiva nature.
However, spiritual devices are often overlooked for three main reasons:

The overwhelming pace of knowledge creation makes it

difficult to focus,rapid generation means
the refuted things are "false".

In an era of unified knowledge, attractive ideas are embraced while less appealing ones are dismissed, obscuring alternative realities for misleading desires.

Non-judgmentalism (which is now due to this diversity is seen as a virtue these days), can hinder the critical thinking necessary for deeper understanding,

which is actually necessary to protect oneself from self created delusions,even in spiritual traditions.J.Krishnamurti, an Indian Philosopher way ahead of his time,often stressed on this point , because dogmatism and belief leads to a perception of "duality" and this duality is even more strengthened because of the benefits of the Devices, like these Tantras or

Namaz or the benefits of other various devices from tradition like Christianity,Judaism and so on.

you are bound, consciously or unconsciously, through fear , to the dogma or the tradition in which you have been brought up.
— J.Krishnamurti

It just so happens that we tend to get lost in other traditions, we fear our own,Only to end up realising that it was not bad at all.

Yet at the same time the conservatives who often uphold their beliefs and traditions,do it unknowingly for the greater good,that is to preserve wisdom.

The Importance of Criticism

Criticism is essential for the evolution of knowledge. Without it, humanity risks stagnation, clinging to outdated ideas and authority figures unable to address current challenges. Observing and addressing global problems, even those outside one's immediate profession, is crucial. We are all interconnected, and solving issues beyond our personal scope contributes to collective progress.

Knowledge has advanced through synthesis, conjecture, and criticism—not dogmatism or blind belief.

In our information-rich society, the implications of accessible knowledge are profound. Life becomes far more exciting when we realize not only the breadth of problems but also the availability of research and solutions.

Spiritual devices can address psychological and spiritual challenges. Though prone to dogmatic misuse, their benefits often outweigh their risks. Our ancestors' beliefs, deeply rooted in our consciousness, shape our inclinations and perceptions. By acknowledging our interconnectedness and addressing shared problems, we honor the collective effort of humanity.

Knowledge grows on the pillars of synthesis, integration, conjecture, refutability, and criticism. Weakening these foundations leads to stagnation and ignorance. Strengthening them, however, allows society to evolve and thrive.

Chapter 7

Your Body as Nature: Ayurvedic Insights

"Listen to the Body."

Understanding and connecting with the body's functions is crucial. Extensive research and wisdom from multiple healing traditions suggest that esoteric knowledge can assist in identifying imbalances and guiding adjustments to align with different lifestyles. This awareness helps in detecting potential diseases, mental states, and emotional patterns beforehand, allowing proactive care of overall well-being.

The information here is presented in a simple, relatable manner—not from a strictly professional standpoint—but in a way that anyone can understand and apply. The guide is divided into two parts: the first concerns the body, and the second addresses the mind—and, for those interested, the soul.

> This wisdom is deeply spiritual, viewing the body through the lens of disciplines like Ayurveda, Unani, Traditional Chinese Medicine, and Yoga. These systems, known collectively as AUSH in India, emphasize preventive care. While not all conditions can be "cured" instantly, these traditions offer profound insights into understanding the body and mind, invaluable for maintaining health.

The Body and Its Aspects Concerning Health

The body is primarily sensed through the nervous

system. If the nerves are damaged or unhealthy, interaction with specific parts of the body becomes impaired. The functioning of nerves can also be observed subjectively through heightened awareness. In Yogic practices, these nerves are referred to as nadis. It is believed that there are 300,000 nadis carrying information and energy throughout the body. Proper functioning of these nerves is essential for health.

Exercise is often associated with gym workouts or walking, but such activities rarely train the nervous system directly. In some cases, they may even strain it. Observing nerve function helps in recognizing whether they are in good health. Signs of a robust nervous system include strong coordination, a precise biological clock, and restful sleep.

Sleep is one of the most significant indicators of a healthy nervous system. Deep meditation is another. Practices such as Yoga, Namaz, Tai Chi, and related exercises strengthen the nervous system. Waking up naturally with the sun, going to bed on time, and ensuring quality sleep between 12:00 midnight and 3:00 a.m. are crucial for nervous health.

A vital practice for the nervous system involves neck exercises, especially in the morning when the body is stiff. Slowly rotating and stretching the neck improves blood flow in this critical junction where nerves connect brain and body. Practiced daily with awareness, this yields significant long-term benefits.

The Digestive System

The digestive system plays a central role, connecting to many bodily functions and significantly influencing emotions and mental states. A well-functioning digestive system ensures stability in emotions and overall balance. Emotions are closely tied to digestion, and a proper diet deeply affects energy levels, efficiency, and health.

Eating for health is an essential life skill. Meals ought to be chosen not for indulgence but to nourish and support the body. Simple, balanced dishes which nourish without overburdening the system, exemplify this principle. Mindfulness around food—being aware of what is consumed and how it moves from taste to digestion—is critical. Eating passively, such as while watching television, diminishes this awareness.

The Lungs

The lungs are intimately connected to the nervous system. Air quality, breathing patterns, and temperature impact the body's energy, heart, and nerves. Conscious breath control regulates emotions and decision-making.

The lungs link directly to the brain, heart, and circulatory system. In Yogic traditions, the nostrils are associated with the Ida and Pingala nadis, which connect to the Sushumna nadi along the spine. This alignment is vital, as the spine plays a crucial role in nervous and brain health.

Breathing practices such as alternate nostril breathing rejuvenate nerves over time. A clean environment with pure air supports both mental and physical health, making it particularly important for those managing low energy or emotional imbalances.

The Heart and Blood System

The heart sustains the body by pumping oxygenated blood throughout. Inner temperament, goals, and even thought patterns are influenced by the heart's condition and experiences. The heart retains trauma, joy, and emotions, circulating these impressions through blood and body.

Mindful eating, particularly when done with gratitude, is held in spiritual traditions to affect both energy and emotional balance. Physical aspects such as food quality and eating habits have a direct influence on both body and mind.

Heart-centered practices like chanting or meditating on the heart space can consciously awaken inner energy. However, balance is key—placing excessive strain on the heart risks long-term complications.

Ayurvedic Time Cycles

Ayurveda explains that daily cycles are governed by elemental dominance (Pitta, Kapha, Vata). Between 10:00 a.m. to 2:00 p.m., during the Pitta period, the digestive fire is strongest, emotions heighten, and energy peaks. This is the optimal time for productivity or physical activity.

At night, between 10:00 p.m. to 2:00 a.m., the body naturally detoxifies and restores itself. Adequate sleep during this phase is vital.

Activities are best aligned with the solar cycle: rising with the sun, working in the afternoon, and resting in the evening. Creative and contemplative work flourishes during times of Vata dominance, especially in the early morning golden hours, also called Tahajjud in Islamic tradition and Brahma Muhurta in Sanskrit. Spiritual practitioners across traditions consider the pre-dawn hours (4 a.m.–6 a.m.) sacred, a time when divine presence is closest.

The Third Eye

The third eye, or pineal gland, regulates sleep, focus, and memory. While often mystically interpreted, its key biological role is releasing melatonin, vital for sleep-wake cycles. It also contributes to flow states and elevated awareness.

Simple eye exercises, such as moving the eyes in different directions, foster cranial nerve health and better thought patterns. Yogic techniques like Shambhavi Mudra, Child Pose, and prostration postures in Namaz enhance blood flow, relax the mind, and sustain third-eye vitality.

This guide touches only a fraction of the Ayurvedic perspective on the body. The journey requires patience, not perfection. The next part will explore body behavior as a bridge between body and mind, showing how posture and emotional expression affect overall harmony.

Practical takeaway:
Try waking up at brahma muhurta (2 hours before sun-rise) and feel the natural stillness in the air.
Judge whether your body goes through the ayurvedic cycle as mentioned in the chapter.
Question to self:
Do you feel the synchronicity with the sun and the moon cycle?

Chapter 8

Body Behaviour: The Bridge Between Mind and World

Behaviour is the crucial interface between deeper instincts, the mind, and the outer world. Outer personality is largely reflected through behaviour. The mind is shaped by behaviour, and others form perceptions of a person through it as well. Behaviour also includes the proper coordination of body and mind—when expression matches intention and restraint aligns with wisdom, there is harmony. Yet, this system is not flawless. Emotions often override intended actions, or the mind blocks behaviour entirely. This behavioural field has long been a mystery to psychologists, some of whom specialize solely as "behavioural therapists." However, their studies are sometimes dismissed as secondary, since behaviour does not always reflect the true intentions of the mind.

For instance, behavioural psychology can explain patterns in sales and marketing strategies within a supermarket, but it cannot reveal the deeper truths of the mind, which are of a more profound nature. In this sense, behaviour lies in the space between intention and action.

This bridge, however, is valuable, because it offers insights into understanding the self. Much of behaviour arises from automatic responses, outside conscious awareness. Still, behaviour can be trained through experience. This requires not formulas or repetition, but deeply involved, lived experiences. Only then does behaviour shift meaningfully for the future.

Take the example of entering a mall and encountering a salesman who skillfully uses persuasion techniques. If there has been no prior experience with such tactics, behaviour will likely align with the majority: responding automatically. Robert Cialdini, the well-known behavioural psychologist, called such responses "click and whirr," revealing how blind many of our reactions can be. A sign announcing a sale instantly triggers desire. Observing a crowd purchasing a product leads to unconscious validation: "So many people are buying it—this must be good." Similarly, habits like smoking have often been justified by individuals imitating admired figures, despite personal awareness of their harmfulness. Behaviour, in this sense, is easily shaped by external triggers.

Yet, behaviour can be trained gradually through practice. Behaviour in relationships with family and friends shapes one's egoic or inner personality. Many have felt the urge to stop overthinking about past words or actions in social situations, yet such reflection plays a vital role. Overthinking is not necessarily an enemy—it is the natural process that refines future behaviour. Instead of stopping it, one can use it as a tool for growth in social responsibility, communication, and expression.

This shows that behaviour is not entirely under control. However, with patience and practice—especially through bodily awareness—it can be refined. Awareness is the first step to understanding anything. In this way, behaviour becomes the social expression of inner personality. When it seems to contradict self-perception, it often creates anxiety or issues of self-esteem. The root lies in misalignment between body and personality.

A person may imagine themselves as a king, yet unless they behave like one, the imagination remains unrealized. One may read of kings and their ways, yet still act in unkingly fashion. Actions must align with awareness. Every movement, whether of the eyes, face, or hands, reflects personality. Observing oneself—through awareness, even by looking into a mirror—can reveal whether expressions and movements match inner intention. This is not perfectionism, but self-alignment.

There is no requirement to imitate another's style of awareness. Movements and expressions, practiced with awareness, will naturally become uniquely one's own. This is where alignment with the higher self begins to unfold.

Practical Takeaway:

Sit in a simple calming posture and observe how the mind changes its pattern simply because your body behaviour is calm.
Pose a certain posture and reflect how the mind changes.

Questions to self:

How many times have you said things you didn't really mean and how did you rectify or reason with your behaviour?

Chapter 9

The Mind According to Ancient Indians: Its Functions and Causes

The body holds the mind. It is a vessel that not only contains and sustains it but also transforms and molds it. Every aspect of the mind is related to some part of the body. Therefore, health is of utmost importance—not just for longevity, but to allow the mind to flourish. Only a healthy and natural mind can produce thoughts and ideas that align with nature's rhythm and purpose.

Nature is self-sustaining. It is only man who strives to destroy it, because he has somehow lost touch with the wisdom once inherent in a natural human being—a person connected to the soul.

> Discussing the body is relatively easy; its laws are more tangible. Eat proteins to build muscle mass. Exercise regularly to reduce cholesterol. Eat seasonal foods and avoid others in certain months. But the mind defies such logic. It is illusory and intangible—almost like a hypnotic trance. To understand the mind, one must first awaken from this trance. When you see the elements by which you are hypnotized, you gain the potential to change. But that effort must come from within you.

There are, however, certain observable laws of the mind. Let us explore them.

The Flow of Mental Functioning

Desire → Emotion → Thought/Action → Consequences → Results → Reactions → More Desires → More Emotions → More Thoughts...

This cycle continues endlessly. Some call it the law of karma. Others call it cause and effect. Regardless of the terminology, you can observe this pattern within yourself.

Aristotle once said that virtue leads to peace of mind. But why should virtue, of all things, bring peace to a random cluster of molecules called a human being? Is every human born with a conscience—or at least a degree of it? This leads us to the psychology of children.

Children are unique beings. Each child has a mind with varying gifts and talents. As we grow into society, these raw gifts become shaped and often suppressed. Until the teenage years, we are open vessels, discovering our inner blessings. There is much to learn from children—and more from realizing that we were once like them.

What changed? Certain qualities diminished while others strengthened. Your memory grew, your muscles developed, and your reasoning matured. Emotions once centered around parents now encompass friends and others. You've discovered parts of yourself and even learned how to learn.

At every stage of growth, new emotions emerge: the desire to control, the urge to be important, patriotism, or even brotherhood. Qualities like honesty, loyalty, integrity, and helpfulness arise naturally. Ethics and morality begin to make sense.

As a child, you were simply "being." Yet even then, some inclinations appeared. Perhaps you were drawn to music or writing. These were your innate gifts—your jewels in seed form. Nurturing them is your duty.

We may say these seeds are inherited from the Universal Mind. According to the law of karma, we are enjoying the fruits of past actions. These seeds become our individuality as we grow into adults. Everyone has the choice to understand their talents, strengths, and weaknesses—and to move with intelligence.

Hermetic Principles and Ancient Perspectives

The *Kybalion* is often quoted by modern artists and philosophers. Its hermetic principles describe mental laws observed by the ancients. The ancient human was deeply connected to being. He had not lost his sense of wonder, observation, or ritual.

Instead of microscopes or machines, ancient men experimented with worship, with reverence for nature. Nature was their God. There were no axioms, no rigid dogmas. They regarded themselves as souls and used their own consciousness as the primary source of knowledge. Experience was the laboratory.

They saw the divine in trees, stars, and rivers. Worship wasn't based on fear, but connection.

Hermes devised several mental principles, the foremost being: *All is mind.*

The sun gave them energy, the moon gave them peace, the waters cooled them, and the wind dried their sweat. These people were naturalists. They believed in the five elements—earth, water, fire, air, and ether—and found balance within them.

Over time, however, rituals turned to dogma, and sacrifices replaced reverence. Philosophers emerged to question it all—and so we continue.

Ayurveda and the Balance of Elements

Ayurveda still views the world through a primal yet powerful lens: man is born of the elements. When the mind and body are balanced, wellness follows. When imbalances occur, so do illness and dysfunction.Virtue is an aspect of health. Choosing happiness over indulgence in alcohol or fleeting pleasures like sex is a step toward balance. Such activities, though instantly gratifying, often lead to depression or hysteria. Pleasure, then, can be harmful to health.

The Ayurvedic view is that pleasure disrupts elemental balance. True happiness is found within awareness, not in objects. Once this is realized, we can seek to realign our elements through practice, self-discipline, and external aids.If you wake up irritated, ask why. Don't just blame others. Look within. Irritation could stem from indigestion, overstimulation, or unaddressed emotions. Awareness reveals that the mind projects outward what begins within.

Consciousness and the Functions of the Mind

To understand the mind, one must first understand consciousness. Consciousness is like light. It doesn't relay information instantly; it reveals things slowly. Sometimes it may take years just to become aware of certain nerve signals.Why enhance consciousness? Simply put: to live fully.

Great inventors and artists all had one trait in common: the ability to understand their own minds. Their consciousness was refined. This clarity allowed them to operate at high levels of creativity and intelligence.Enhancing consciousness involves focusing the mind until perception becomes clear. This clear perception allows us to see things as they are—not through the mind's filter.

The light of consciousness is a subtle, subjective experience. Sometimes it brightens, sometimes it vanishes. But when it returns, it feels like a gift—not something conjured by will alone.In that state, the world feels alive. Events seem to unfold synchronously. This is the "flow state," sought by artists and thinkers alike. Flow is a high-vibrational experience. It can be induced through deep concentration and surrender.

Once we attain flow, we can begin to study the mind more deeply. Thoughts and responses can be classified. Just like in programming, we create functions. Actions like riding a bicycle or driving a car become automatic.The ultimate goal? Transcend default functions. Enter deeper awareness.

Ritual and Mastery

Rituals, when practiced mindfully, can induce flow. Yogis and religious practitioners use repetition to deepen awareness. Though often misunderstood, these practices can cultivate strong concentration.The problem arises when the practice is mistaken for the cause of awareness. Consciousness comes from within, not from the external act.

Your mind's functions drive your personality. As psychologist Robert Cialdini notes, automatic "click-and-whirr" responses can be manipulated—even in sales. Awareness of these responses is essential.To grow and evolve, we must uncover these unconscious functions and bring them into the light of awareness. In doing so, we enhance consciousness and become the best version of ourselves.

Practical Takeaway:

Observe the thoughts patterns.
Try to analyse them if it seems easy to catch those thoughts patterns which seem too repetitive and mundane.
Question to self:

What does the mind comprise of?

Chapter 10

Everything is Alive

Do some of us ever examine what our life feels like from a purely subjective perspective? Do we recognize that what we call ourselves was never really born to say the truth? Yet there was something that began to happen when we realized that we were somebody like other people. This idea probably originated when we saw ourselves in the mirror. When we first recognized and looked at our faces and bodies, and were told that we should dress properly and comb our hair before boarding the bus to school. But before that, where did we dwell? What was our nature?

The thought that the self that exists now as I type these words also existed when I was first born is something that presents a surprising shock. When did this being called "me" really start?

These questions may seem absurd and, as they did to me, lead a person nowhere because they do not have definitive answers. They are confusing questions that generate a tremendous source of energy and curiosity. Curiosity, when nurtured, can lead a person who takes these questions very seriously to the depths of the oceans of knowledge that humanity has collected over ages and built upon. However, rarely does one get true answers to these questions. Whatever one may find will be complete paradoxes. Every approach to knowledge seems fallible. It seems that the nature of knowledge keeps changing, as does everything else in the world.

The idea of a separate self generally emerges after the age of 2-3 years old when a child recognizes that it has a will, a certain attraction to toys, or certain tendencies. But I doubt that the people who question such matters ever had such tendencies even when they were children. I presume they were quiet and didn't even play with other kids. But setting presumptions aside, when the idea of the separate self starts, memory also seems to arise. Although it's hard to truly understand the subjective experience because it can never be put under a microscope, the best one can do is go back as far as possible in their memory. Wherever they go, they find a separate self and nothing besides that. However, if we closely examine our direct experience, we might notice a stark difference between the direct experience of the self and the small self that we recall a moment later. There is this direct experience and there is the interpretation of that experience constantly happening.

This interpreter, which we might imagine as a character in our head, is what we often take for ourselves. This is where important things are happening: thinking and dreaming. But if we detach a little and look behind our eyes, we see a kind of transcending, simple existence that is directly experiencing the moment as it passes. It seems to me that there are two modes we can "live" in (there might be more that someone with a higher consciousness could access). These two modes provide different types of information. One mode gives us information about direct experience, and the other provides information about interpretation. This interpretation and its different aspects are what constitute the separate character, which varies through attributes such as intelligence, mental health, language, and numerous theoretical factors.

But we are here now, without indulging in interpretations. Where are we really?

The closest explanation of this "isness" and its qualities can be found in various esoteric texts. However, I have realized that reading about these qualities is not particularly useful. If we change and "modulate" ourselves to be in this state, our interpreting self will eventually interpret the same things found in these texts. Rightly so, our interpreting selves will interpret this experience—or should I call it being?—in different languages, with different backgrounds and different stories, based on different knowledge, which are all fallible and subject to change according to Karl Popper and David Deutsch. Yet we can all agree that we somehow just exist.

Through this experience of being the experiencer, if I say that all is one entity and that you are not a separate self but part of the whole universe, it suddenly makes sense, at least for a moment before the interpreting self starts its business.At least for a moment, it seems as if we might be connected to a whole "thing" in which we somehow live and act, and our actions have consequences, and so on. We find that to live or be, we really do nothing; we just find ourselves here. Simply finding ourselves in this world, all the interpretations follow this according to our culture, education, experience, and so on. So simply being is what is called in Buddhism "tathata," suchness. The Buddha stressed simply being and observing. If you simply be for a while, you will start to see a certain peace coming into your heart. Even a change in vision, as if things are brighter and feelings are heightened

So, all in all, what I am trying to convey is that knowledge is refutable; all kinds of knowledge are refutable and based on the interpreter and their experiences. Yet there is the knowledge of the NOW, which is always here observing even the interpreter. This knowledge of the NOW doesn't require doing as we usually think. It is somehow just there, and we find ourselves engulfed as part of this universe. This is all interpretation of that suchness.

> The concept of space varies according to the traditions one is born into. While many traditions may outwardly appear different, they share remarkable inward similarities. Although the sacred center might differ in location, nearly every tradition has a place where Creation is believed to have begun.

The sacred space that a religious mind holds is one of sanctity and tranquility, a place of holiness where they can immerse themselves in the sacred. What is the religious mind, and is everyone able to perceive this holiness? The concept of holiness is intriguing, as it arises from a profound religious experience. To a layperson who believes all space is homogeneous, there is no significant difference between one place and another, apart from their utility. A holy place, however, is where one transcends the confines of the mind and body, experiencing a unique peace.

Why is this? And is it possible to consecrate a place to make it holy? Many cultures believe it is possible, with various rituals such as placing a cornerstone, creating a sacred fire, or chanting mantras at specific intervals.

Is this holiness a universal phenomenon? A person detached from cultural biases and theories can perceive holiness everywhere. However, it is rare for someone to intuitively sense such spaces. A person deeply immersed in consciousness may recognize subtle shifts in energy. While there is no material evidence of how one perceives this, it remains a possibility.

To the layperson, space is homogeneous; to a person viewing the world through a materialistic lens, space is the same everywhere. But to a religious or spiritual person, space fluctuates, evoking different feelings and associations. For an enlightened person, the holiness of a sacredsite from one tradition is no different from a sacred site in another. They may have their own rituals for sanctifying a place, bringing it to life through these personal practices.

Similarly, a spiritual person believes that people are not homogeneous; each individual is unique, shaped by their spiritual growth.

The Emanation of a Saint

A saint emits an essence that can be perceived by those sensitive to it—a scent or a light that emanates from their being. While this may sound far-fetched, many people who seek the hidden truths behind the material world have experienced this mysterious quality in saints. It soothes the soul and brings instant calm.

The Rational Side

The scientific revolution, beginning in the late 17th century, introduced a system of thought to investigate the material world with evidence and logical methodology. This led to rational thinking, where people began to reject superstitions and authoritative beliefs ingrained in human thought. For the first time in thousands of years, humanity began examining the objectivity of subjective experience.

Rational concepts also spurred desires, including an increased emphasis on physical desires. The logical conclusion that humans are biological animals has, for some, placed physical desires like sex at the center of existence. However, this belief that we are merely biological beings has caused confusion and harm, as it reduces humanity to bodily needs alone.

I believe this perspective has led to a detrimental shift. While such goals may be logical and rational, they are also life-denying. The more one studies biology and science, the more thoughts align with materialism, leading to desires for wealth, alcohol, or sex as ultimate pursuits.

Is there a purpose in life that transcends mundane existence? Is there something beyond merely living for these goals and dying? Logical conclusions alone do not provide a satisfactory answer.

Is Scientific Knowledge Wrong?

Scientific knowledge is an unripe wisdom, revealing only half of the truth—the material causes of experience. It has yet to address the deeper issues of human existence. Yet, before the development of science, there were many who claimed to understand the nature of the world and achieve liberation.

Science will eventually reach remarkable conclusions that will bring rationality and integrate the system of thought initiated by the Enlightenment with the already existing great traditions. This will, in turn, eradicate the contradictions in the outward forms of religious experiences and foster a unity and deeper understanding of the inner workings of the soul.

A point where the rational aligns with the sacred will create a different kind of person—someone more accepting and profound in both religion and science.

Chapter 11

What will people think?

This thought obstructs you from liberation. The feeling that you need to be appreciated by everyone around you can be your downfall in creative or even professional growth. People don't think anything significant about you—we simply assume they do. But why?

Have you ever thought deeply about what someone else is doing, what they've gone through, or even their misdeeds? And how has this affected you? How has it changed your behavior or your perspective? If you fail miserably in your professional life, more than despairing over losing what you wanted, you may feel crushed by the thought that others will look at you through distorted lenses. You may start hearing imagined voices speaking behind your back.

What is this? Why do we feel this way? And do we ever do something purely for ourselves, without seeking acknowledgment from others? Is there an act—just one—that we do solely for ourselves?

One can become great at experiencing things by adopting identities. But clearing yourself of all identities is like emptying a bowl. It's liberating, so liberating that you may never want to adopt an identity again. The process of liberating oneself from identities and making oneself grow into

Individuality is part of the elaborate games that you are playing in this World.

We develop a "social measurement device" in our minds at the age of about 6 or 7. This device constantly reminds us that we are in society, evaluating ourselves based on this measurement, trying to satiate our parent and making th people around us happy. It's difficult to turn this off unless we empty ourselves of all identities and see life simply as it is in the present moment.

Identities of all kinds—professional, familial, moral, recreational—are all roles we adopt. You have learned the advantages of certain identities and the disadvantages of others. You strive to become more like one identity and less like another. An identity inference diagram shows how we adopt "truths" when we accept an identity and defend those truths when our identity is threatened.

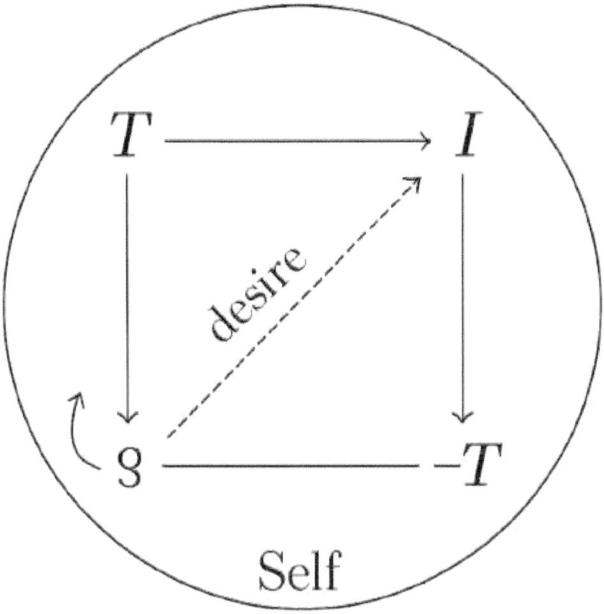

Identity Inference Diagram

The O is the original self and the I is the identity and the negating Identity and in adopting these identities we accept the truths pertaining to each identity. Even if they contradict basic common sense.

Identities mask our true nature; they steer us away from the truth, making life appear as a constructed reality. Some people excel in certain identities, and others don't. Those who fail can sometimes fall into despair. But do not despair because your identity is threatened; defend your individuality with all your might. Embrace what is truly yours and dance with the false identities.

Sometimes I am a king, and sometimes I am a beggar, and I am alright with both because I know I am neither. It's a play, a game—what Indian mystics call Leela. In this Leela, learn which role suits you best. Part of self-development is recognizing your talents and understanding what you're truly fit for.

Once upon a time, in a jungle, there was a deer who roamed freely, embracing the forest and grazing where it wished. The deer's father had taught him to avoid certain places where danger lurked, and the deer had accepted this.

After his parents passed, one day, the deer sat by a lake, lost in thought. Suddenly, he smelled something mystical, something heavenly that invoked a sense of sacredness within him. He rose, searching for the scent but found it everywhere he went. Eventually, he wondered if the scent had come from the forbidden place his father had warned him about. Curiosity grew until he finally ventured there.

As he neared the forbidden place, he encountered a lion's den. His eyes widened, and his ears perked as a lion spotted him. The deer ran with all his might, but the lion chased him relentlessly until the deer fell into a ditch. As the lion prepared to strike, the deer surrendered, and in his last moments, his eyes fell upon his own belly—the scent emanated from him. It was musk.

We all emanate a unique scent. Unlike musk, ours is a metaphorical scent we sense when we are lost or in despair. This search to uncover the truest part of ourselves—the individuality within us—is the journey of self-discovery. Through trials and hardships, as our bodies and faces change, we adopt and drop identities. One day, we come to a point where we recognize the unique scent we each carry. Follow that scent, and don't worry about what others might think, because they are all in deep waters too.

Chapter 11

Prana Vidya.

"Your life is in your hands."

Prana is invisible. It cannot be seen through the physical eyes, and yet it is always present. It flows within us, sustains us, and gives us vitality. In yogic and Ayurvedic traditions, prana is understood as the universal life force that animates not only human beings but all existence. Though invisible, its expressions can be felt, observed, and even directed through conscious awareness. The study and practice of this inner force is known as Prana Vidya—the wisdom of prana.

The Nature of Prana

Physically, the life energy is closely linked to the circulatory system, as blood acts as a carrier of pranic force throughout the body. If we develop sensitivity, we can become aware of this flow—not in the sense of mechanical blood circulation alone, but as a subtle pulsation of life energy. It manifests as pressure in the veins or as a vibration in the energy centers, commonly known as chakras. What we are sensing is not just the physical stream of blood but the subtle current of vitality moving along with it.Prana is not limited to the body. Yogic philosophy maintains that prana pervades the environment. A mature practitioner can direct prana into a room to change its atmosphere, energize an object such as a stone, or even transmit it to another person for healing. The life force is fluid and responsive, moving in alignment with consciousness.

The Connection of Prana and Mind

The ancient sages observed that the mind and prana are deeply interconnected. They found that when the mind is disturbed, the pranic flow becomes irregular, and when prana is calm, the mind follows. For this reason, they emphasized prana as a bridge to mental balance.Consider a person suffering from high blood pressure. If we tell him simply, "Do not be angry," he will not succeed. In fact, attempting to suppress anger directly through control of the mind may even harm him, creating more stress. On the other hand, if his blood pressure is brought down, his anger will subside naturally. The tension in his body will release, and his mental state will shift instantly.Prana Vidya extends this practical wisdom to a much deeper level. Just as lowering blood pressure can calm the mind, learning to regulate the subtle current of prana brings clarity, awareness, and equanimity. This is why the yogic path does not rely solely on suppressing thoughts but teaches a more refined approach—observe and shape the flow of life force, and the mind will reflect harmony.

Although connected to blood circulation, prana is much more than a physical function. Blood is merely the carrier, while prana is the animating essence behind it. The ability to perceive prana requires sensitivity and inner awareness. The first signs may be subtle: a gentle vibration under the skin, warmth radiating from energy centers, or a tingling sensation in certain postures. With sustained practice, these sensations grow clearer, and the practitioner becomes capable of directing prana consciously.Young people naturally radiate higher amounts of prana. Their vitality is not only obvious in their strength and enthusiasm but can also be subtly felt by those around them. Unfortunately, much of this prana is unconsciously wasted. Lack of awareness, harmful habits, and shallow pursuits often cause young people to deplete the very force that gives them vigor. Instead, if this energy were consciously cultivated and directed, youth could be a time of building inner reserves of force and using them for creativity, healing, and service to others.

The Temple and Prana Pratishtha

In Indian spiritual culture, the importance of prana is reflected in the sacred practice known as Prana Pratishtha. This is the process by which life force is infused into an idol in a Hindu temple. Without this process, the idol is simply a carved stone or metal structure. But when prana is installed through proper rites, the idol becomes alive in the spiritual sense and worthy of worship.To the uninitiated, this ritual may seem superstitious or merely ceremonial. However, it carries deep scientific and spiritual logic. Through specific mantras, meditations, and energy transmissions, prana is invoked from the cosmos and stabilized in the idol, making the deity's presence accessible to the devotee. In this way, prana is not limited to the body; it can be intentionally directed into objects, spaces, and even collective environments such as temples.

Cultivating Awareness of Prana

Once a person begins to perceive prana within themselves, their life changes. They gain insight into which environments, conversations, or people support their vitality and which ones drain it. They become aware of activities that waste their life force, such as excessive indulgence in pleasures, anger, or overwork. With this knowledge, one naturally gravitates toward practices and environments that nourish prana.Such awareness also transforms daily living. Eating becomes more than consumption; it becomes a practice of drawing prana from food. Breathing becomes more than oxygen exchange; it becomes communion with universal life force. Relationships become more than transactions; they become exchanges of vitality.

Prana and Yogic Disciplines

Prana Vidya is closely linked with both Yoga and Ayurveda. A Vaidya, or practitioner of Ayurveda, cannot be complete unless they understand prana, for it is the very foundation of healing. Likewise, yoga in its true form is not merely physical exercise. Every asana (posture) subtly alters the flow of prana in the body. Yoga without pranic awareness is incomplete.For example, certain postures push energy upward toward higher centers of consciousness, while others ground prana in the lower centers, stabilizing emotions and vital functions. Without the awareness of what an asana is doing to prana, yoga becomes mere gymnastics. With awareness, however, yoga becomes a transformative science.

The Bandhas: Locks of Prana

Among the practical methods to regulate prana are the bandhas, or locks. Bandhas involve specific muscular contractions that control the movement of energy in the body. There are three main bandhas:Mula Bandha (root lock): Located at the perineum, it seals prana at the base of the body and redirects it upward.Uddiyana Bandha (abdominal lock): Practiced by contracting and lifting the diaphragm and abdomen, it draws prana upward from the navel region.Jalandhara Bandha (throat lock): Achieved by lowering the chin to the chest, it redirects prana at the throat level and prevents its dissipation.Bandhas are not mere physical locks but energetic controls. By applying them, the practitioner creates internal pressure that guides prana into desired channels. Over time, this grants mastery over the nervous system, glandular functions, and even mental states. Of course, this does not happen overnight. Like all yogic practices, it requires patience, discipline, and humility.Prana within an individual is not isolated. The flow of life force is influenced by cosmic rhythms—the movements of the sun, moon, and planets. This is why Jyotish Vidya (Vedic astrology) is often studied alongside Prana Vidya. For example, certain lunar phases increase pranic receptivity, while others may reduce vitality. Planetary alignments can influence the way prana flows, making one more prone to fatigue, enthusiasm, or agitation.For instance, during a full moon or eclipses, many people report heightened sensitivity or fluctuations in mood and energy. Yogic texts even prescribe specific practices and fasting days aligned with these cosmic events, maximizing pranic benefit and spiritual growth.The yogic seers understood this interconnectedness and aligned their practices with cosmic cycles. Breathing exercises such as pranayama were synchronized with lunar rhythms. Fasts were undertaken at specific times when prana was more easily conserved and redirected inward. This synchronization is not superstition but an acknowledgment of how the microcosm within us mirrors the macrocosm around us.The Path of Prana AwarenessThe journey of Prana Vidya begins with simple recognition—becoming aware that you are not merely a body, nor merely a stream of thoughts, but a pulsating life force on the fabric of consciousness. Once this truth sinks in, every breath, every gesture, and every experience becomes a touchpoint for prana awareness.In practice, this involves cultivating sensitivity through meditation, breath control, and inner listening. Techniques such as pranayama refine the pranic flow, while visualization practices help direct prana to energy centers or specific parts of the body.

Over time, one learns not only to conserve prana but also to project it outward—into healing, creativity, and spiritual development.The highest goal of Prana Vidya is not simply personal health or vitality. These are natural outcomes, but the deeper aim is awakening. When prana flows freely and harmoniously through the channels of the body, the mind becomes luminous, and consciousness expands. One begins to sense the unity of all life, realizing that the same prana vibrating within oneself is also vibrating in others, in nature, and in the entire cosmos.

Chapter 12

Make and Break Habits by Will.

"Understand the Mind."

The most important aspect of understanding how habits are formed is precisely that— understanding the mechanism behind their formation. Once you grasp how habits are created, most of the work is done. You simply need to apply this understanding to the workings of your habitual mind.

Understanding the nature of the mind is crucial for anyone who wants to change their life, break a bad habit, or achieve something remarkable by acquiring positive habits. As we grow, we tend to become automatons—many aspects of life become habitualized, such as our work, social interactions, and daily routines.

Breaking habits can teach you a lot about life. Acquiring habits is also valuable, but I believe that understanding how to break habits reveals essential insights into the workings of your mind.

These insights, if utilized correctly, can help you grow in all areas of life: building relationships, achieving financial growth, pursuing spiritual practice, and improving health. At their core, these areas are shaped by habits.

In our youth, many of us experiment with bad habits and may even find ourselves in trouble. Often, people who struggle later in life fail to break these habits. The issue with such "bad" habits is that they are not inherently bad if approached with curiosity. If you have acquired bad habits but successfully outgrown them, recognizing their lack of real-world advantage, you become stronger—perhaps even stronger than those who never acquired such habits. Rising from the depths of unconscious behaviors and taking control of your life can make you a better leader and enable you to help others who are still struggling.

The First Step: Cultivating Awareness

Awareness is the key to emotional intelligence and personal growth. A person may be highly intelligent in terms of IQ, but without emotional awareness, sustaining success becomes challenging. Cultivating awareness can be achieved through various methods, but the best method is to strive for constant self-awareness. The more aware you are of yourself and your actions, the better you can calibrate them. Eventually, you'll recognize the excuses you make to indulge in bad habits and catch the urge as it arises.

People may suggest practices like meditation, breathing exercises, or journaling, and these methods work. However, unless you develop awareness in the midst of conflicts and triggers— when the bad habit feels like an option—it won't fully go away. Cultivating awareness doesn't have to be daunting. It can even begin while indulging in the bad habit. For example, have you ever noticed the changes in your mind and body while consuming alcohol, smoking, or gossiping? If you're aware of the effects on your body and mind, you will naturally start to restrain yourself over time.

The Second Step: Supplement the Habit

Dopamine is generated in your body when you perceive a reward at the end of an action. The trick is to fool your mind into associating dopamine release with a "good" habit. If you can redirect this mechanism, your body will produce similar results for the new habit.

Understanding this is critical. By consistently tricking your mind into engaging in long-term beneficial habits, you can condition it to prioritize these over short-term rewards. If you quit a bad habit like smoking but replace it with shopping, you haven't made a real change; you've merely swapped one short-term reward for another. Instead, think long-term.

The Role of Self-Control

In a famous experiment on delayed gratification, psychologists tested children with the option to receive one marshmallow after 10 minutes or two marshmallows after 20 minutes. The children who opted for immediate gratification were found to struggle more in life decades later, even if they were otherwise intelligent.

This experiment highlights the importance of self-control. The best way to build self-control is to discipline your body and resist overindulgence. Over time, this discipline strengthens your ability to make better decisions and avoid destructive habits.

The Role of Philosophy.

Philosophy can profoundly impacted your life,evn though it mind sound utterly unbenefecial in the race for material possesions. Philosophy broadens your understanding of the sciences, religions, logic, and various fields of research. This passion can keep you curious and constantly striving for improvement. When you immerse yourself in a meaningful pursuit, bad habits lose their grip.

Philosophy, for me, is an endless adventure, and such pursuits can shield you from the temptations that often plague young people.

Following a Passion

Discovering your passion is one of the greatest things that can happen to you. When you realize your purpose, obstacles naturally fall away. All barriers to achieving your goals diminish. The simplest way to overcome bad habits is to identify what drives you and pursue it relentlessly.

Breaking and forming habits is not just about discipline; it's about understanding the mind, cultivating awareness, and redirecting your focus toward meaningful pursuits. By doing so, you can unlock your potential and achieve extraordinary things.

Chapter 13

Mystical Psychology: Unlocking the Inner Self

The world has mastered the art of cutting open the body, of weighing, measuring, and diagnosing it, but the mystery of the soul remains untouched. Modern psychology walks with sharp tools and clever terms, but it forgets the essence. It forgets that man is not merely a cluster of neurons, not simply the chance spark of chemicals flickering in a skull. He is something vaster — an uncharted depth where thought, memory, and silence meet. The ancients knew this. They never divided man into flesh and mind alone. They spoke of the soul not as a metaphor but as the most intimate truth of existence.

Ayurvedic sages mapped the inner terrain with the same precision that surgeons cut into flesh. They spoke of sattva, rajas, tamas — clarity, restlessness, inertia — not as abstractions but as living tides in the human sea. The Sufis spoke of the ruh, the breath of God hidden in man, waiting to be remembered. The Chinese masters tied each emotion to an organ, each mood to the turning of the seasons, as if grief, anger, and joy were not disorders but rhythms of the cosmos echoing through the body. To them the psyche was not a problem but a mirror of the universe.

Our age, armed with pills and formulas, tries to quiet the storms of the mind by muting them. But the soul does not surrender so easily. When it is ignored, it rebels. That rebellion is called depression, anxiety, the dull ache of emptiness that no entertainment or substance can soothe. What we call mental illness is often the hunger of the soul — a hunger for meaning, for silence, for beauty, for contact with the eternal. And so the one who feels restless at two in the morning, endlessly scrolling through a glowing screen, is not sick in the way we think. He is starving. He is thirsty for the water that no drug can pour.

To walk the path of mystical psychology is to refuse the lie that suffering is an error. Suffering is not a flaw in the system; it is the knock of the soul upon the door of consciousness. Every pang of sadness, every tremor of fear, is a messenger whispering: *Something in you longs to be known.* And if you turn away from the messenger, the knocking grows louder. Until at last, you have no choice but to listen.

The self is not one, but many-layered. On the surface we wear the mask — polite, smiling, acceptable. This mask is necessary; society demands it. Yet when the mask fuses with the face, when you forget that it is only a mask, life begins to feel hollow. Beneath it surge the emotions, waves that lift us and drown us in turns. Beneath the emotions swirl thoughts, patterns, the endless chatter that spins our identity. Beneath the thoughts is a stiller chamber — the witness, the one who sees without judgment. And deeper still is the soul, silent, luminous, untouchable. It does not come and go with moods. It does not break when the world breaks. It is the eternal ground of being, unnoticed yet always present.

To unlock the inner self is to walk through these chambers one by one. Not to deny them, but to embrace them until they open into the next. When you touch the soul, you do not reject the body or the emotions; you see them as instruments, sacred and alive. You understand at last that the body is the harp, the mind is the hand, and the soul is the silent musician behind the music.

Suffering, then, is no enemy. It is the fire that refines the gold. The ancients called it tapas, the heat of transformation. Without this fire, the ego remains hard, unyielding, proud.

With it, the ego cracks, and light enters through the wound. That is why those who suffer deeply often become wise. Their wounds have become windows.

What opens this window wider is not theory but practice. Silence is the first medicine. In silence, the chatter grows unbearable at first, but slowly it loses its claws, and then, beneath the noise, you begin to hear the song of stillness. The breath, too, is a key — for breath is the bridge between the visible and invisible. To watch the breath is to watch the soul's thread weaving the body to eternity. To write is another key — to pour words upon paper not to impress but to listen, to let the soul reveal itself in ink. And art, too, in all its forms — the brush stroke, the melody, the dance — is a secret language of the inner self speaking.

The point of mystical psychology is not merely to cure an ailment, not to reduce man to normalcy, but to lead him into wholeness. A man who has glimpsed his soul is no longer terrified of failure, because failure no longer defines him. He does not need to escape suffering, because suffering has become his teacher. He does not need endless validation, because he has found a deeper ground of being. He becomes alive in a way that words cannot capture.

Perhaps this is why every true tradition, whether it prayed to Christ, chanted to Shiva, or bowed in the direction of Mecca, sought not merely to explain but to transform. They knew the mind was a labyrinth and that only by passing through its shadows could the self arrive at light. They knew that man is not born merely to survive but to awaken.

So let us awaken. Let us stop treating our pain as a disease to be numbed, and begin to treat it as a teacher to be listened to. Let us stop imagining ourselves as bundles of thought and flesh, and remember that we are also soul. Let us learn again the art of silence, of breathing, of creating, of praying. For these are not hobbies or superstitions. They are the ancient sciences of the self.

And when you begin to practice them, when you allow suffering to soften you instead of harden you, when you sit with yourself not as an enemy but as a friend, you may find that the door opens. You may discover a presence within that has always been there — steady, radiant, infinite. You may realize that you are not merely alive. You are life itself, experiencing its own mystery.

Archetypal Psychology and Its Relation to Our Worldview or Philosophy

Human nature is inherently archetypal; we live through stories and events. By examining the stories we were told as children we can see how this archetypal story mind was developed in us.

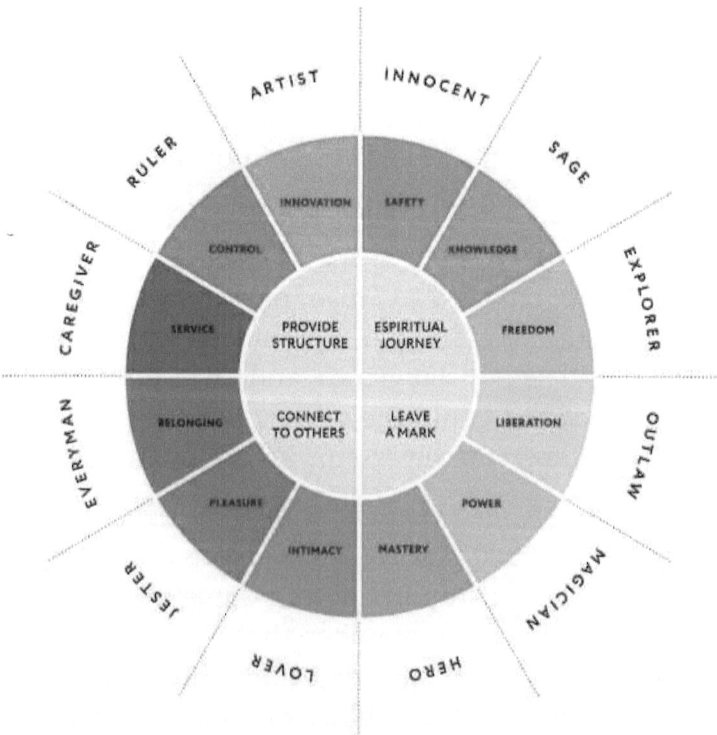

The 12 Archetypes that Arise from the Collective Unconsious.

Human nature is inherently archetypal; we live through stories and events. By examining the stories we were told as children or those that captivate us, we can gain insight into our nature.
Humanity is in a constant struggle between repressive and expressive forces within us. The repression of one archetype leads to the expression of another and the expression of one archetype results in the repression of another. This constant interplay of duality reveals itself in our lives.

Understanding that the world around us and every aspect of it is in continuous movement between these dual natures helps us grasp the hidden wisdom behind our problems. This explains why there are always rises and falls, calm before the storm, and why love can precede hatred.

Yes, Satan might be real, but it is simply a force that leads you toward a life of pleasure and ennui. A life that seeks pleasure constantly follows this unrestrained mode of expression, which unfortunately leads to the destruction of intelligence and holiness.And yes, angels might be real too. They may guide us toward repression, goodness, and piety, but this also comes at the cost of naivety.We all know that life is often a struggle, an internal battle. Those who succeed in life intuitively learn how to fight this battle, to manage themselves within it, and to stay carefully aware at every step of what they are following.The mind, as we all know, is difficult to manage. If it were easy, we would all be successful and happy. There seem to be a thousand influences acting upon it, and if this resonates with your own struggle to take control, then it is crucial to understand the archetypes—mentioned in the Bible, in the Quran, and in ancient stories—all of which reveal aspects of our psyche. Brothers are often jealous of one another; they are competitive by nature, striving for a parent's approval.

Mothers, by instinct, tend to indulge their children, while fathers often play the role of structure and rule. These roles shape our inner and outer lives, and each of us embodies a small set of archetypes at most. You can be a devoted lover to someone, but you cannot play the same role in your office—you may need to become a strategist or even a wizard. You can be a great poet, but lack the rigor of logic and rationality required for searching after truth through research.

The task, therefore, is to balance the archetypes. We must first recognize that we are, in a sense, slightly schizophrenic—but in a productive way. The more adept we become in managing social relations, the more we realize how many selves live within us. Consider inviting a teenage friend with whom you once shared conversations about youthful exploration to a formal family dinner. How awkward would that be? Which role would you play? This awkwardness emerges from uncertainty, because the mind loves roles—it even thinks through them.

The way you perceive yourself, therefore, is

of the highest importance. Pay attention to your daydreams—those fleeting visions you have while walking down the street or before going to sleep. These wanderings of the mind are not trivial; they are the very place where decisive moments arise.

Many of life's most important decisions are formed in these dreams—dreams in the shower, in silence, in the background of your ordinary hours.

Our character can be seen as a program with specific calibrations, adjusted according to our experiences and awareness. The experiences of these archetypes often depend on our relationship with the external world. Interacting with and experiencing this world reveals different archetypes in various situations. For example, we may be cunning with our siblings but extremely loving to our friends, or great lovers to our partners but harsh with our coworkers.

Both men and women must eventually realize that they are playing roles and fluctuating between these roles. This is not schizophrenia but a normal occurrence in human psychology, deeply rooted in archetypes. The sages of India refer to this nature as "Leela," meaning play, which holds profound wisdom. Understanding this concept leads to insights similar to those Carl Jung discovered with his psychoanalysis, approaching psychology from this perspective and deriving groundbreaking ideas.

By reflecting on the stories we tell ourselves about our experiences and events, we can see where we suppress or elevate certain voices in our lives. For instance, a father who works hard may become a tyrant at home, while a daughter who was obedient might suddenly choose to leave her parents. What drives such irrational behavior, even in the so-called obedient ones? It is the archetypes craving expression. We have been conditioned to suppress certain aspects by those who were themselves suppressed.

Through introspection, one can observe the unfolding of these personalities. Why might you be a king among friends and a servant to your partner? Eventually, one must confront these archetypes shaped by external influences and decide to create their own life, calibrate themselves, and perfect their individuality. Your worldview depends on this process.

Every philosophy we encounter and hold changes over time, especially those we held during adolescence. As we mature and recognize the need to be an "adult," we may question whether we can transcend philosophies or understand the origins of our worldview. In Tantraloka, Abhinavagupta discusses transcending religions and philosophies, similar to what Shri Krishna talks about in the Bhagavad Gita regarding transcending the mind's attachment to rituals and practices.

Understanding the nature of the mind and the concept of Leela is key to transcending philosophies. This paradoxical transcendence means that one person's way may differ from another's, which makes each path valid and justifiable.

Historically, human nature has remained constant despite changes in outer appearances and civilizations. Tyrants and dictators have existed throughout history, and they will continue to do so, regardless of the form of government. This highlights the importance of understanding not just the archetypal nature of humanity but also the nature of future humanity. The advent of technology has shifted the value of knowledge, with technological expertise becoming more influential. However, the core nature of humanity remains unchanged.

The balance of duality occurs in subtle and drastic ways, with wars being the drastic and prophets the subtle forms. Prophets, being archetypes, often gain recognition posthumously for their subtle yet impactful contributions. Analyzing religions or philosophies through this lens reveals their
archetypal balance. It is unwise to generalize those who do not adhere to specific philosophies, but it is insightful to observe those who adhere firmly to one.

Transcending philosophy involves understanding our nature to align with philosophies that express our instinctive or archetypal tendencies. Although recognizing this is not extraordinarily difficult, we often fall prey to these tendencies. By observing archetypes and addressing their inner shadow aspects, we can identify areas needing improvement and remove blockages on our path to achieving our goals.

The nature of someone who has transcended philosophies might seem indifferent, seeing every person as a manifestation of the divine. This observation and questioning are central to Jnana Yoga, as discussed by Swami Vivekananda. Among various paths to understanding existence, the path of questioning appeals to intellectuals seeking truth.

Many religions suppress questioning tendencies to maintain control and doctrine. This suppression is often unconscious, a continuation of the conditioning of predecessors. However, examining the lives of the founders of these religions reveals the archetypal balance they embodied.

Albert Machotte and Daniel Kahneman highlight that humans have predetermined tendencies from infancy. Kahneman's concept of System 1 (fast, impulsive thinking) and System 2 (slow, deliberate thinking) shows how our immediate impressions often seem true but may be impulsive. Those who identify with System 2 tend to make more reasoned decisions, whether in abstract concepts or spiritual endeavors. Distancing ourselves from our impulsive tendencies allows us to recognize different aspects of ourselves and address underlying issues.

Understanding these dynamics helps us comprehend the changes in the world and ourselves. Observing and analyzing these archetypes lead to greater self-awareness and the resolution of personal challenges.

King, Magician, Warrior, Lover.

"Balancing the Soul."

Life is art. You are the creation of all creators, an embodiment of all that God could think of. Every side of his attributes lies within you, because you wouldn't be able to assign these attributes to God if you didn't recognize them in yourself in the first place. Life is art, and being connected to your nature will make this statement even more profound. When you look at life as art, you start to wonder about its intricacies, its qualities. You begin to see the beauty, the fullness, and the emptiness. The trees become vibrant for the first time, and the colors shine on the woman's face.

There are 99 names of God in Islam. These are different attributes we have assigned to the One, the creator of all creators: the Magnificent, the Compassionate, and the Lover of all lovers. These attributes, surprisingly, are our inner nature. We experience them and hence give them to The One, the Unlimited Boundless Being of all beings. And somehow, if we look closely at those around us, we see that people too embody these attributes. Some of these attributes are vibrant and blooming in them, and some are dim and dull. But to a certain extent, some of them are truly alive.

If we divide these attributes into four subcategories, we see that the King, the Magician, the Lover, and the Warrior all embody these attributes.

When we daydream, when we imagine ourselves in the future, we dream of being these. We dream of being a king living in a palace and ruling with might. We dream of being a wise magician giving orations and solving problems. We dream of being a lover, passionately loving or being in inner connectedness with life. And we dream of being a warrior, waging courageous wars and adventuring across the world.

Of course, the appearances of these may look different in our heads. Each of us tries to be kings in our domains, and each of us tries to be magicians and technicians in our own domains. But to some extent, we all dream about this. Some dream more and some less, but we all do. And what we want is to accomplish all of these. We want to be masters of all these archetypes, and if one is achieved, we move to the next and the next, and so on.

These dreams come from the Collective Unconscious, the memory storage of all human beings who existed at all times. We access it unconsciously, only when it comes into our awareness do we then recognize it. Now, how can this really change our perspective?

How can it help? It can help us integrate and understand them. It can help first to understand that we will only be satisfied or move towards contentment when the attributes and the nature of these archetypes are balanced in us. When the lover is accessed in a balanced way and is not turned into an addictively passionate over-indulger, when the king balances the lover, and when the magician advises the king and the warrior is in command of the king – when all of these archetypes are balanced and run in smooth fluency, with each having their power, their time, their indulgence, and their impulses in balance, we will see that life actually starts to become balanced. An inner calm is invoked, and a boy turns into a man.

Some of us do this unknowingly. We figure out some terminology and figure out a way to actually integrate ourselves through some other terminology, not necessarily the terminology that I am mentioning here. The wisdom of different cultures has different language and different flavors to point out the same thing. But balance can really be struck if we are patient enough and able to recognize this. An enormous amount of energy is generated, and sources of energies are in our access at our will.

How to access them?

The methods are:

* **Interactions**: Previously, I had talked about how different personalities or how different sides of our personalities are revealed to us when we have interactions with each other. Some side of you can appear when you simply have interactions with different people. The more you interact, the more you see that different sides seem to be revealing themselves to you. You might even be surprised. So, it's important to tune into our warrior spirit and engage in conversations, move ourselves to interact, and yet remain uninfluenced by the interaction.

* **Active Imaginations**: In this method, you are consciously imagining and looking at, or writing down, your imaginations, daydreams, passions, and desires. The best time will be in the morning when you wake up and write down your dreams too, because your dreams can tell you a lot about the collective unconscious.

* **Invoking Them**: In this method, you actually call upon the forces by acting like the king you have in mind, by acting and feeling the presence of the

magician in you and acting like the magician.

I personally divide the day into 4 activity zones where I access each archetype for a certain time and act them out, doing the activities they would do. The magician writes, for example. The lover paints and sings. The king consults his advisors and works. And the warrior exercises and plans his next moves strategically.

You can also figure out certain activities you are already doing and do them by invoking the energies and calling upon them.

Balance is the key to good integration. Hence, it will help you perfect yourself and lead a happy, contented life. Life is art. It is the creation of all creators. When we access the Source of all these archetypes, when we are in communion with the Source of our existence, we see that everything is vibrant, shining, and mesmerizing. Work becomes dance. Appearances start to look like paintings, and the sounds appear musical. Energy flows and is accessible. With effort, it turns to play.

Chapter 14

The Dance of Polarity

Observing this universe reveals one undeniable truth: everything is linked to its opposite polarity. These opposites, at first glance, appear completely different—sometimes even utterly unlike one another—yet nothing about them is the same. Still, they persist side by side, inseparable in their existence. This interdependence is nothing short of fascinating.

Opposite polarities generate a profound attraction for one another, a force so immense that when they clash, the energy unleashed could rival that of a nuclear bomb capable of annihilating entire countries. But beyond this dramatic example, what exactly is polarity? How does it weave into the fabric of our daily lives? And what wisdom did ancient civilizations pass down regarding this primal force?

This chapter immerses itself in the exploration of polarity: first within the individual, then within social relationships, and ultimately within the very structures of our bodies.

Curiosity is the invisible thread that draws men and women toward one another. The moment a woman becomes aware of her distinction from men, an intense curiosity about the masculine energy flickers within. Likewise, when a man recognizes his inherent tendencies toward dominance and assertiveness, a compelling fascination with the delicate and passive feminine arises. Society often reduces this profound energetic alchemy to frivolous flirtations or the use of perfumes, yet these superficial expressions only scratch the surface of a deep inner transformation that unfolds when maturity dawns, revealing that boys and girls embody fundamentally distinct energies.

Sexual discovery for men introduces awareness of the power a woman holds over him, and for women, the immense pleasure a man can provide. However, considering polarity solely at this surface level is shortsighted. Polarity permeates all dimensions of the body and being.

According to ancient Hindu and Chinese philosophies, the human body is multilayered. Beyond the visible physical form—the aspect of ourselves that interacts with the material world—lies the Sukshma Sharir, or subtle body. This subtle body perceives energies invisible to the naked eye, housing both masculine and feminine forces. The sensations of masculinity and femininity differ dramatically here—these polarities manifest not just externally but deeply within every layer of our being.

A brief overview of these layers clarifies this intricate architecture:

- **Annamaya Kosha:** The physical sheath, intimately connected to nourishment, digestion, and the generation of vital energy.
- **Pranamaya Kosha:** The body's vital energy system, the channel through which consciousness harnesses and utilizes energy.
- **Manomaya Kosha:** The heart-mind layer, where thoughts and emotions arise and intermingle.
- **Vijnanamaya Kosha:** The sheath of consciousness, home to the soul itself.
- **Anandamaya Kosha:** The bliss sheath, the source from which all existence radiates.

Though some traditions speak of even higher bodies—the ethereal or astral—perceived only by enlightened beings, this framework is sufficient for understanding the practical experience of polarity.

The energies drifting within these subtle bodies—masculine and feminine—engage in an inner dance of alchemy. When balanced, their energy is magnified; a sense of calm settles around the presence of the opposite polarity, not due to mere physicality, but to energetic resonance. This resonance fosters a magnetic attraction. Absent this balance, even the most favorable external conditions might fail to stir attraction.

Thus, the union sought between opposite polarities happens first in the subtle body, then moves inward to mind and heart, before manifesting outwardly in physical form. This progression elucidates why spiritual awakening often accelerates after marital union—energetic alignment ignites deeper states of consciousness.

While many pursue this connection externally, ancient yogis chose solitude, focusing inward to harmonize their energies independent of outside influence. Through profound inner work, they uncovered a hidden feminine aspect dormant within every masculine form, named Anima by Jung, and a masculine counterpart—Animus—lurking within the feminine. Awakening these latent energies reveals inherent androgyny.

This awakening is not a sign of weakness but a blossoming of creative, artistic, and transformative potential. Feminine energies pulse with creativity and vitality; masculine energies provide strength and structure. Balancing these polarities fosters extraordinary personal growth.

The sage Lao Tzu spoke to this truth: "The enlightened man knows the masculine yet sticks to the feminine." This balance may be cultivated through diverse means—dance and painting, discipline and structure—offering counterbalances to professional inclinations dominated by one polarity.

In the Himalayan tradition, conserving sexual energy for spiritual pursuits led yogis to carefully balance inner polarities through sadhana, eschewing sexual union. Worship of the divine feminine invoked vital energies that supported this balance, channeling power toward elevated states of consciousness.

Yet in society, imbalance between masculine and feminine roles disrupts harmony, fostering dominance of one side and causing psychological distress. Contemporary trends often blur these lines with boys encouraged toward feminine pursuits and women thriving in masculine spheres. Success is possible, but without true understanding, inner imbalance and confusion persist.

Grasping the nature of this polarity is indispensable for achieving harmony within, and ultimately, union with the ultimate reality.

What is sex?

Sex is the act of pleasure, and its influence upon our perception of the opposite gender is immense.From our earliest years, when left alone to wonder, our thoughts have been stirred by it. We remember the crushes we had in classrooms, the way we admired someone's delicate hands or someone's quiet bravery. We silently worshiped the one we loved, finding them perfect in every way. Even if they did the most terrible thing, they still appeared beautiful to our eyes. This kind of love—rooted in desire and pleasure—appears pure and innocent, yet it is false love. When we stand before a crush, our mouths fall silent, our hands tremble, our hearts flutter. What is this mystery of love and sex?It is the eternal attraction of opposites: the masculine drawn to the delicate feminine, the feminine enchanted by the confident masculine. Attraction awakens not through sameness but through curiosity in the other. Sometimes even the mind itself—the love of knowledge, of science, of creation—becomes an object of attraction. Yet beyond all these surface forms, we must ask: what do saints mean by love? They speak of unconditional love, a love which is no longer bound to the fleeting pleasures of the body but is instead a higher stage of self-development, a step toward spiritual ascendance.This love is utterly different from what we mistake as love in our worldly affairs. Sexual desire, however deep, is conditional. One says “I love you” to a partner, but hidden beneath those words is the longing for possession, for complementarity, for gratification. This attraction may stir our whole being—physiological, psychological, even intellectual—but it is not the love spoken of by mystics.

True love requires no other; true love simply is. In its presence, we see beings as they truly are, and in that seeing, we cannot help but love them, regardless of their faults or actions.Sex itself is simple science. It generates energy, it reveals the subconscious, it opens deep chambers of the mind —some radiant, others dark and destructive. It removes your boundaries and, at its peak, offers the pleasure of surrender. Yet here lies our error: we tell our sexual partner “I love you,” not realizing that more often we are in love with the part of ourselves reflected back in them. Sex is the union of two bodies, not necessarily of minds and souls. Only when minds also join can true friendship be born; only when souls unite can a divine relationship emerge—one founded not in desire or expectation, but in kindness freely given.Such a bond is possible only when one has transcended the restless pull of desire, when sexual energy is raised upward rather than consumed downward. In that transcendence, one sees others not as bodies but as souls housed in fragile vessels, each reflecting the infinite colors of the divine prism. How can two prisoners of flesh expect freedom through mere physical union? How can captivity be broken by yet another chain, however ecstatic? Yet paradoxically, sex also gives a fleeting glimpse of transcendence, because all centers of energy within us possess an ultimate, transformed state, and sex concentrates energy more intensely than anything. Its fruit is creation itself: the birth of human life, a seed carrying the potential of magnificence. This is no pastime. This is power.If misused, sex clouds the mind, casts illusions, and enslaves one to roles not of their choosing. A sexually deprived person often becomes lonely but sharp, detached and observant. A sexually indulgent person often becomes joyful but dull, sunk in comfort. With a partner, you exchange more than the body; you exchange energy, subconscious impressions, even identity.

That is why sex can enslave: it grants your partner invisible power over you, the ability to distort your self-image, to bend you into someone else's expectation. Yet no one can ever fulfill all expectations. To strive for that is to become untruthful to both the world and the self.The secret is this: do not seek to meet every expectation. Seek rather to be true according to your own understanding. If another accepts this, rejoice; if not, move forward, raising your energy upwards and inward. When sexual energy is conserved and transmuted, the mind gains clarity. Energy builds within, fueling creativity, discipline, and wisdom. One becomes a creator in both the worldly and spiritual sense.Sex as union is not evil. It offers joy, partnership, intimacy, even healing. But it also carries guilt, for it exchanges something unimaginably precious—vital energy—for a moment's release. If the mind transcends sexual urge altogether, it glimpses great purity. Such a mind may seem lonely to the world, but to itself it is suffused with clarity, holiness, and closeness to the divine.Sex, placed within marriage, becomes sanctified. Marriage offers context, and the mind thrives on context. With pure intention and hearts united, sex blossoms into something beyond desire, something sustained. Within such a bond, love is rooted not in fleeting attraction but in depth of commitment, becoming an eternal flowering.

When the sexual energy of such union is transmuted, it

gives rise to immense wisdom, creativity, and spiritual power: the human being turns from mere seeker of pleasure to co-creator with God.

Chapter 15

Accessing Intelligence—The Key to Higher Consciousness

Can intelligence be accessed consciously? Can it be summoned deliberately to its fullest extent?

Often, focusing concentration, such as creating tension between the eyebrows, is mistaken as a proxy for intelligence. This is simple awareness, yet intelligence encompasses much more. At its root, intelligence depends on the mind's capacity to comprehend and assimilate experience.

Among the remarkable distinctions separating humans from animals is the capacity for abstraction. Humans perceive a knife not only as a physical object but also as sharp —an abstract quality. This abstraction allows comparison, valuation, and imagination. Animals, even intelligent apes, wield tools but cannot refashion them into superior versions because their capacity for abstraction remains limited.

Is this capacity for imagination truly the essence of intelligence? Conventional views equate intelligence with mental agility, strategic problem-solving, or academic prowess, yet this view remains comparative and relative.

Every individual conceives intelligence differently: an athlete sees it as the ability to score strategically; a scientist, as problem-solving acumen; a mystic, as understanding the divine. These diverse definitions point to one common shortfall—an overreliance on comparison.

Life itself flows with intelligence. Plants instinctively perform their roles. The Earth obeys the sun's gravity without error. This immense wisdom sustains existence. Intelligence should foster sustainability and vitality, never degradation.

Yet humanity's current trajectory suggests a profound misunderstanding. As intelligence has increased, so has planetary destruction. This contradiction arises from mistaking intelligence for mere cleverness.

This chapter's focus is not on becoming "more intelligent," but on *accessing intelligence*: tuning into the universal mind beyond comparison.

Language shapes perception of intelligence. Each language constructs unique mental worlds. The richness of English—with its ever-expanding vocabulary, slang, and borrowed terms—continually renews itself, balancing structure with innovation. Yet it remains an imperfect vehicle for expressing the profound relationship between consciousness and intelligence.

In Indian philosophy, intelligence—or "Chitta"—is not merely a quality but a source. To truly understand such wisdom requires immersing oneself in language and culture, embodying their philosophy.

Multilingual experiences reveal how language alters perspective and humor, shifting entire cognitive landscapes. Language paints the canvas of consciousness.

To access intelligence is to attune consciousness to particular frequencies where ideas emerge naturally as solutions to problems. This process demands curiosity—a relentless desire to explore unknown realms.

History's most intelligent figures share this trait. The cunning politician masterfully leverages psychological understanding to gain power, but such intelligence is self-serving.

In contrast, true wisdom seeks no selfish ends. It listens to a deeper intelligence—the universal mind—guided by moral laws encoded in existence itself. Such intelligence calls for decisions that transcend personal gain, illuminating paths that uplift humanity.

Thus, intelligence emerges not as a competitive prowess but as a clear perception and alignment with universal needs, manifesting in elevated consciousness.

The Soul and the Intellect—A Great Dichotomy

The Enlightenment was hailed as the dawn of infinite progress. Philosophy and science began dismantling old dogmas, seeking truth through reason and evidence. Scientific methodology freed humanity from superstition, allowing clearer explanations of the universe.

But why did such rational thought emerge only recently? What caused humanity to accept flawed beliefs for centuries? Was the scientific revolution progress or the soul's demise?

Science demands intellect capable of abstract thinking—a distinctively human gift. Humans imagine sharpness, compare values, and dissect concepts to approximate truth. This intellect thrives on testing, falsifying, and refining explanations through experiment and logic.

Yet intellect carries a cost: it struggles to grasp the soul's mysteries. The soul dwells beyond objective analysis, eluding scientific capture. Many religions assert this, declaring the intellect powerless before the soul's essence.

Philosophers like Socrates hinted at the soul's immortality through reason but faltered in completeness. J. Krishnamurti and ancient sages of Advaita Vedanta championed *jnana yoga*—the path of knowledge—inviting seekers to "clear seeing." Stripping away mental veils reveals the pure seer underlying all experience, the soul itself.

Yet religious minds often vacillate, compensating for the intellect's limitations by embracing superstition: stars govern fate, gods dictate weather. Such beliefs offer comfort but resist rational challenge.

Science dismantles these myths. Through observation and verification, falsehoods fall away, often revealing truths aligned with ancient spiritual insight.

The soul's essence—pure subject devoid of objectivity—is often described as "nothingness." Raising consciousness awakens this essence but remains an unfamiliar concept for most.

Religious practices employ repetition, mantra, or ritual to quiet the mind, momentarily dissolving the suggestive ego and granting fleeting glimpses of elation or love. Yet the ego soon reconstructs explanations, reinforcing belief but obscuring true understanding.

Noetic science, exploring consciousness with tools and measurements, probes these phenomena, searching for objective correlates without denying subjectivity.

Ultimately, raising consciousness expands the soul's ability to perceive subjective realities, while the intellect provides the methodical framework to avoid superstition.

Practice—whether meditation, breath awareness, or sadhana—cultivates this dual insight. Scientific rigor balanced with experiential openness fosters genuine awakening.

Many intellectuals become trapped in cerebral pursuits, losing contact with the soul. Yet, existential thought suggests the answer lies simply in existence itself, transcending acquired qualities or labels.

Freeing Yourself from Time's Illusion

Time is the great deceiver. It sits silently in the background of every thought, every plan, every regret, shaping the way we live while pretending to be neutral. We treat it as something objective, something ticking out there on the clock, yet our entire experience of it is deeply personal, deeply subjective. Ask a child playing in the fields what time feels like, and he will say it doesn't exist. Ask a dying man, and he will tell you it is everything. Between these two extremes, we are all captives of its illusion.

The ancients understood this prison. In India, the sages spoke of *Maya* — the great veil that hides the real by binding us to appearances. Time was not a straight line for them but a wheel, the *Kalachakra*, endlessly turning. Every joy, every sorrow, every empire that rises will one day return to dust, only to rise again in another form. In Greece, Heraclitus said you never step into the same river twice, because both you and the river are in constant change. Augustine wrestled with the paradox of time: the past is gone, the future not yet, and the present vanishes the moment you try to hold it. And yet, somehow, time dominates us more than any tyrant ever could.

Modern physics confirmed what mystics whispered: time is not absolute. Einstein showed us that it bends, stretches, slows down with speed, and warps with gravity. The universe does not run on one universal clock; it is a shifting fabric, elastic and strange. If that is true, why do we still live as if the calendar and the wristwatch dictate reality? Perhaps because the illusion of time is not scientific but psychological. We are chained not by clocks but by memory and expectation.

This chain is heavy. Regret binds us to the past. Anxiety binds us to the future. Even pleasure is haunted by time, because the moment we enjoy something, we fear its passing. Our love becomes fragile, not because it isn't real, but because it cannot last forever. Our ambitions torture us because we are forever racing against the clock, trying to become something before the sand runs out. What is midlife crisis if not the recognition that we believed we had time, only to discover that time was laughing at us all along?

But what if time is not what we think it is? What if it is not a river carrying us helplessly forward, but a mental construct, a lens through which we interpret the eternal present? There are moments in life when time seems to dissolve — when we are absorbed in music, when we fall in love, when we are so present that hours pass like seconds. In those states, time does not vanish; it reveals itself as flexible, pliable, secondary. What remains is presence. What remains is the eternal now.

Eckhart Tolle built an entire philosophy on this insight, but it is not new. The Buddha sat under the Bodhi tree not to measure minutes but to dissolve them. To awaken is to realize that only the now is real, and that the past and future are shadows we carry in our minds. The *Bhagavad Gita* whispers the same when Krishna tells Arjuna that all beings are already dead, that their destinies have already unfolded — time itself is swallowed by the eternal.

Nick Bostrom, writing of simulation theory, suggests that perhaps our entire sense of temporality is coded into the structure of a simulation, a necessary condition for beings like us to evolve. If that is the case, then time is not the container of reality but one of its programs, one that could in theory be rewritten or bypassed. Daniel Schmachtenberger, in his systems thinking, often warns us that civilization itself is caught in a time trap: short-term incentives, quarterly profits, political cycles — all chasing immediate gains while ignoring long-term consequences. Humanity, he says, is racing against its own extinction, bound by a clock it refuses to acknowledge. In both cases, ancient and modern, mystical and rational, the message is the same: time rules us because we mistake its illusion for truth.

And yet, here we are, living in it. How do we free ourselves? To escape the illusion of time does not mean to deny clocks or abandon calendars. It means to break the psychological slavery. It means to live in such a way that time loses its teeth. The great saints and poets discovered this not by fleeing life but by entering it so fully that they touched eternity. Rumi writes that lovers do not count the hours; they are already in timelessness. Meister Eckhart says that the man who lives in the present moment lives in eternity.

To touch this eternity is not mystical escapism; it is the most practical revolution you can make. Imagine living without the weight of regret. Imagine acting without the chains of future fear. Imagine doing each task so fully that it becomes its own reward, without the restless need to move on. That is what the Zen masters mean when they say: "When drinking tea, drink tea." The simplicity is terrifying because it demands we surrender our addiction to control. To live in the now is to stop bargaining with the future.

There is a story of a monk who, when asked the meaning of enlightenment, said: "When I walk, I walk. When I eat, I eat. When I sleep, I sleep." The questioner, confused, replied: "But isn't that what everyone does?" The monk answered: "No. When they walk, their mind is already eating. When they eat, their mind is already sleeping. When they sleep, their mind is already walking." That is the bondage of time. The body is here, but the mind is elsewhere, forever leaping ahead or crawling back.

Science tells us we may one day stretch time — through technology, through cryonics, through genetic manipulation — but no invention will save us from the illusion until we change how we perceive. A man who lives a thousand years still suffers if his mind is never in the present. A man who lives a single day in true presence has already tasted eternity. Longevity without presence is merely extended slavery.

Thinkers like Bostrom look to the possibility of transcending biology, uploading consciousness, perhaps living in virtual realities where time could be paused, rewound, accelerated. These speculations dazzle the imagination, but they do not touch the core problem: even in a simulation where you could live forever, would you be free of regret, of longing, of fear? Or would you still suffer the illusion of time within a different frame? The real liberation is not technological but existential. It happens not by escaping the clock but by discovering that the self who fears the clock is itself a shadow.

For who are you, really? You are not the one bound to years and minutes. The child you once were is gone, and yet you feel continuous. The body you had ten years ago has dissolved and been replaced cell by cell, and yet you say, "I am the same." The continuity you cling to is not biological. It is consciousness. It is the awareness in which all change arises. And that awareness is timeless. It was present when you were a child, it is present now, and it will be present even in your final breath. To discover this awareness is to see that time is an appearance in you, not the other way around.

That is why the mystics smile at death. For them, death is not the end of time but the final unveiling of its illusion. The body falls, the years dissolve, but what you are has never aged. To know this while alive is liberation. To live this truth is to be free even while the clock ticks.

Look carefully, and you will see that time was never your master. It was your servant. It gave rhythm to your days, allowed you to remember and to plan. But somewhere along the way, you forgot its role and bowed before it as if it were a god. To free yourself is not to destroy the clock but to place it back in its rightful place — a tool, not a tyrant.

When you sit quietly, breathing, watching thoughts rise and fall, notice how each thought carries a timestamp: memory of yesterday, anticipation of tomorrow. Strip them of this temporal clothing, and you see them as what they are: clouds drifting through the open sky of awareness. The sky does not age. The sky does not hurry. It holds everything without being bound by any of it. You are that sky.

And so, the invitation is simple, though not easy. Step out of the hypnosis of time. Stop postponing life into the future or replaying it endlessly in the past. The present is not a thin knife-edge between two non-existent realms. It is infinite. It is the doorway to eternity disguised as this very moment. To enter it is to discover that you were never in time at all. Time was in you.

Chapter 16

Spirit

"Let the Spirit lead your life."

We are all made up of three essential aspects: the body, the mind, and the spirit. The body is responsible for survival—it manages its nourishment, excretion, and other functions naturally and unconsciously. You don't ask your liver to function in a specific way; it just does. The only role of the mind is to guide the body—providing energy and responding to signals when something feels wrong.

And indeed, we do. We know when something is wrong—when there's sickness approaching, when our bodies feel weak. We receive signals from our organs or nervous system indicating energy deficiencies in specific areas. But once the body is stable and healthy, it operates smoothly. If you provide it with proper nourishment, light, exercise, and maintain its temperature, it functions optimally.

However, the governance of the body can sometimes dominate, as in the case of overeating. In such instances, the body rules over the mind and spirit. The body craves satisfaction, urging for repeated indulgence in tasty food or substances like cigarettes, which temporarily relieve its desires.

Smoking, for example, gives a fleeting sense of relief that the body craves, compelling the mind and spirit to obey its commands.

The body is instrumental—a machine that requires care and maintenance. Properly utilized, it holds tremendous potential and can achieve extraordinary feats.

The Mind

The mind operates through desires. It is the realm of thoughts and emotions, but more importantly, feelings govern its functioning. You are what you feel in the moment. Anger prevents rational decisions, peace fosters calmness even in challenging situations, happiness brings positive thoughts, and sadness leads to depressive states.

The mind has many functions, especially conscious thought, which is the first layer we interact with. Thoughts are reflections of emotions, but they emerge from deeper levels. The mind can be classified into three parts:

The Unconscious Mind

This is the hidden, interconnected realm where processes occur without your awareness, much like your liver or kidneys functioning without conscious thought.

The Subconscious Mind

This is where your character resides—your likes, dislikes, habits, and predispositions. Changing a habit requires reprogramming the subconscious, as it operates differently from the conscious mind. It bridges the unconscious and conscious realms through habitual behaviors.The dreams you dream are the doorway to this subconcious, they are right before the Unconscious. One way to access this is to watch carefully the state of mind before you fall asleep, It is complete different functioning and appearance of the mind, it might even seem bizarre, but this bizzareness is where much of intetions fall deep into the Unconscious. This is the greatest time to for affirmations, and strong intended wills.

The Conscious Mind

This is what you interact with when you are "awake." It presents clear, real thoughts, constantly suggesting goals and desires, from material needs to emotional connections.

If you observe your dreams, you can tap into the workings of the subconscious. Dreams reflect your inner processes, often hinting at subtle changes in your personality or emotions. Even though days may seem repetitive, each day brings new manifestations from the unconscious, embedding deeper patterns into the subconscious. These, in turn, manifest as conscious thoughts and actions.

The Ego and the Spirit.

The mind's ego craves satisfaction. It seeks validation and expression. While not inherently wrong, unchecked egoic desires can lead to imbalance. The ego identifies with objects, ideologies, or abstract concepts like religion or nationality. Over time, this false identity creates attachment and ignorance. Lies, desires, and conflicts stem from the ego's relentless drive to expand "me" and "mine."

True contentment arises only when one recognizes the spirit—the essence of who you are. The spirit is the bliss body, the source of true joy and peace. All manifestations of the mind ultimately aim to fulfill this deeper desire for bliss. If an activity isn't enjoyable, you lack the energy to do it wholeheartedly.

The Alignment of Body, Mind, and Spirit.

Life's governance must center on nurturing the spirit. If the mind or body dominates, dissatisfaction inevitably follows.

For instance:

Letting the mind-ego govern life leads to endless desires and goals. Even technological advancements, born from the mind's ambitions, often create more problems than they solve.

Letting the body rule results in a life of hedonism, fixated on material pleasures, leaving behind morality, relationships, and true happiness.

When the spirit governs, conflicts of the mind subside. Lying diminishes—not due to imposed morality but from a natural desire for truth and enlightenment. The spirit's light fosters love, prosperity, and compassion for all creation.

True fulfillment lies in cultivating the spirit, which awakens everlasting contentment. It allows you to glimpse a greater intelligence behind life, fostering peace and harmony within yourself and with others.

Chapter 17

Religious Radicalism and Worldview

Most of us in our lives have at one point or another encountered religion in both positive and negative perspectives. In this chapter the discussion will center around radical religiousness and the psychology behind it.

What is Radicalism?

The beliefs or actions of people who advocate thorough or complete political or social reform.

Radicalism is not only religious or political; it can be non-religious and non-political too. Those who are against religion are also radical, as they believe in anti-belief.

The mind is a complex machine that works mostly as a problem solver. When the problem of purpose or existence is presented, the mind tries to solve it by acquiring knowledge and making conclusions—but crucially, the problem itself also arises from the mind. If the problem of existence is not raised, the mind will focus on other interpersonal or practical issues.

In the beginning of life, most circumstances are beyond individual control. Parents, educational systems, or the conditions into which one is born are seldom chosen. The mind, however, is highly adaptable and malleable like plastic or clay. It tends to accept whatever knowledge is given to it without much questioning. From this, the mind builds a worldview that feels coherent or is commonly accepted by the surrounding society.

A person exposed only to religious knowledge will

naturally build a religious worldview, while a person exposed solely to science will form a scientific worldview.

Belief: The Root Cause of Radicalism

Belief is a repeating thought pattern. When someone says they believe in something, an identity is formed around that belief. This identity often fuels rejection of opposing systems of belief. People are naturally drawn to others who share the same patterns, reinforcing and strengthening them over time. The cycle continues as individuals consume information from sources that confirm their beliefs and dismiss what challenges them.

When a belief system faces external challenges or collapses, the mind struggles. Imagine an iron dome of belief: whenever it cracks, the instinctive response is to repair it by seeking reassurance—through listening, reading, or reconfirming what feels "true." The mind is deeply uncomfortable with uncertainty, so it manufactures certainty through belief. From this vulnerability, radicalism emerges.

Everyone has some tendency toward radicalism. In fact, there are benefits in certain contexts—without scientific radicalism, modern science would never have advanced. It is worth remembering that scientists too were once considered outcasts or even dangerous.

Objective and Subjective Reality

The mind first attempts to understand objective reality, and then subjective reality. Objective reality is often filtered through education or sacred texts. For example, a Hindu may interpret objective reality through the Gita, just as a Muslim might through the Quran. Meanwhile, a person raised in a strictly scientific tradition perceives the world through scientific concepts.

Political, communal, and traditional beliefs are interwoven. An atheist, for instance, is often inclined toward communism, while an Abrahamic believer may lean toward monarchy or related systems. A person's spiritual or religious worldview tends to shape their community and political expectations.

Society adds another layer through hierarchy and money. People seek validation from leaders or celebrities, and wealth is equated with authority. The capitalist mindset reinforces a belief in "earning" not just material success, but even spiritual benefits. Intelligence is also often mistaken for truth, simply because it is admired.

Breaking Free from Belief Systems

Changing a belief system requires approaching truth as something to be directly sought and experienced, rather than blindly believed. Beliefs must be carefully examined. God should be understood, not merely believed in. Experiences of life should reveal interconnectedness rather than feed rigid personal, spiritual, or political frameworks.Becasue in life th emore rigid you become the more the temptation to break it all down arises.evry contraction will lead to an expansion and teh more you contract the more the force to expand.So become rigid and learn how to unwind slowly and carefully,becasue it might also happen that one expands too much going overboard.WIthout naming names we all know how repression manifest in religious organistions,through sexual abuse and domination.

Questions within objective reality must be asked deeply, while subjective reality should not be dismissed simply because of facts. The question "Who am I?" must be pursued with sincerity, without becoming trapped in one fixed identity.

To understand radicalism, one must also embrace compassion. Terrorists or deeply religious individuals too have their place in the larger human story. Without them, there would be no questioning of subjective reality. Prophets and spiritual leaders such as Muhammad, Jesus, and Buddha understood profound aspects of subjective reality, even if they lacked the scientific instruments for objective truth. Both dimensions must be explored without fear.

In experience lies truth—not in rigid knowledge, but in lived realization.

The mind is extremely moldable. I could make you sit in front of me and teach you a course while you are half-awake, barely listening. In that state, you are not fully conscious, nor are you questioning anything—you are passively taking in information. At the very least, your subconscious is constantly receiving, without the space or time to think for yourself. This half-awake state is a typical condition in which most education is received—whether religious or scientific.In such a state, I can penetrate your mind; it will be molded, and information will be absorbed easily. This process is what we call "brainwashing." If you hear the same thing repeated again and again for months, your mind will gradually become as rigid as concrete. Since you never questioned what you were taught, you accept it all uncritically, and when you enter the world, you perceive it through this concrete framework that has been fed to you.The mind is malleable, and if not challenged, it will accept whatever it is given.

The worldview you receive in childhood might be a half-truth, a cover-up, or intentional conditioning shaped by organizations. And these organizations, being unconscious themselves, have gone through the same unquestioned process. A fixed worldview implanted in the mind creates trouble both for the individual and for society, because conflict then becomes inevitable. At every step there is friction, since the world does not match the rigid "truth" one has been taught.What does a mind do then? It grows conflicted—or worse, it hardens itself further, creating boundaries to defend against the conflict. The inner conflict is thought to be resolved by erecting outer barriers. And we all know where that leads: nations are formed, religions expand, and radicalism spreads.A human mind is full of flaws. It is rarely 100 percent accurate in its judgments. In fact, an AI has more chances of being correct than a human brain. Whatever the human mind produces is never entirely perfect; there is always an element of error, something misplaced or inappropriate. Humans make mistakes. How many of you have ever achieved a perfect score in every exam you've taken? None of you. Why? Because even the most intelligent person you know has never aced an exam completely. Do you think the examiner himself would ace the exam he prepared? No. Even an examiner would fall short. If that is the case, how can we expect ourselves to always be right about the world?We cannot. We simply cannot.yet at the same time prana dictates our life

Pranic Levels

We can replicate minds because minds are artificially moulded. Our minds are a combination of terminologies and mindset systems we have gathered through our experiences. What is in our control is not the content of the mind, but our level of prana.

When prana is low in your body, you will have low-pranic thoughts. You will victimise yourself, blame others, and feel weak, with weak thoughts and expectations.When you are high in prana, you will have higher-pranic thoughts. Higher energy systems will work within you, raising your mindset and intelligence. Everything you see has a level of prana in it — a degree of livingness. Everything around you carries this.If you want to experience higher intelligence, a higher and more divine experience of life, you cannot achieve it merely by learning a more refined philosophy. The mind is nothing compared to what your life actually comprises. The mind is very tiny — a simple reflection of your feelings and knowledge accumulations. Yes, it has a utility and a purpose, but if you want to refine it, you must refine your prana, which is your practical life — the way you make decisions, the way you live, and the choice to neglect and ignore low-pranic thoughts that urge you to deplete prana.These low-pranic urges will always bother you, but if you keep resisting them, one day you will have built a great pranic system of energy for yourself. You will be almost kingly or queenly. Your taste will be of high quality, your level of being will be elevated, and you will vibrate at a completely different pulsation. Your mind will be utterly and obviously in your control.If you feel that your mind isn't in your control, it is because you have low prana, and you might also be living a life that scatters your energy. Identify all the activities that deplete your prana. You don't need to memorise a list of things to avoid — you simply have to see for yourself what is draining this energy. You already know what these are, because the aftertaste of such activities is guilt and weakness, which are low-pranic states.

Often, there are things we do that deplete us and make us feel guilty later. This guilt is a sign from nature, telling you that something is wrong. There is always a downward-moving urge in us, like gravity — we want to let go and fall. But if you keep falling, you will end up in hell. Heaven is when you have the highest prana in your body and life.Heaven cannot be reached by indulging in pleasures and activities that deplete prana. It can be reached by increasing prana within yourself. When you do, your consciousness and vision will be enhanced, and everything will naturally be psychedelic and joyful. Every moment will be blissful. But to move to that state, you will have to go through many inner demons and aspects of yourself that keep pulling you down. You must be your own guide. An external guide is not enough. People have been going to gurus for decades, yet they are not progressing because they keep repeating the same patterns.You must stop and nurture the small inner voice that leads you toward heaven. You already know this — this is just a reminder to increase your prana every day, in every moment. Religions have taught ways of living that increase prana within us. To go beyond religion, you must see the boundaries of its founders, see where they reached, and then climb beyond

.All past religions catered to a certain type of person — one who was lower in prana and intelligence than the average person today. We now have more intelligence, more knowledge, more access. This means we can transcend them by practising what they established and then going further — exploring other religions, esoteric teachings, and philosophies, all while aiming to reach heaven in this lifetime.Heaven is a state of consciousness. It is the bright recognition of love everywhere. It is light and joyous. It radiates and gives health, peace, and tranquillity. It is not what your mind imagines it to be — it is now. It is here, in your consciousness and in your prana.

The ultimate goal of all endeavors seeking the truth of our existence must be one. No matter which direction we choose to take, we must arrive at a single unity. This is something we intuitively feel to be right. We all know that the truth must be one, and there must be a way to understand it completely with no doubt whatsoever. Just as we experience intellectual clarity about a certain topic, we assume that somehow we can achieve a complete intellectual understanding of this universe as well. Our endeavors as scientists, philosophers, and spiritual practitioners are all aimed at this same goal: achieving complete clarity and understanding of the universe, leaving no doubts in our minds. We want to be so sure that all things that can be known are known so that, one day, when death comes, we can accept it with peace.

If you observe each person's endeavor to find this truth, you will be surprised at how individuals are capable of exerting themselves to tremendous extremes, and how this inner energy drives them to such extremes. A person in search of clarity becomes so focused that they embody the truth. Their sole ambition is to seek this answer, to seek their creator. Some of the most intelligent people are formed through the direction of this energy; they seek the truth with all their longing and utilize their intellectual power to understand its workings. The more a person thirsts for the truth, the more intelligent they become.

Physicists and scientists are particularly admirable because they have pushed themselves to understand abstract concepts and engaged in work with no other purpose than to find answers. An Einstein is not born intelligent; he becomes intelligent through his efforts to use his cognition to its limits, understanding himself, and then using his mind to push boundaries and develop theories. This is hard work. Conquering the mind is one of the hardest challenges one can undertake.

Begin by explaining the interconnections between modern physics research and the endeavors of Eastern mystics, including the striking coincidences not only in language but also in the paradoxes they produce. Fritjof Capra, in his book *The Tao of Physics*, explains these interrelations and coincidences in depth. He explores various traditions, including the highest Hindu philosophies of Non-Dual Shaiva Tantra, Buddhism, and the correlations with Chinese and Japanese thought, including Neo-Confucianism, which particularly interests me.

I have always believed in integration over specialization. While we have enough knowledge to specialize in a particular field and make advances within it, we often overlook the bigger picture. Our academics emphasize advancements and one-pointed focus, which can limit understanding of other aspects of this vast universe. Integration is crucial for reaching the Unified Theory that physicists strive for. Integrating different fields of knowledge is extremely important. As a writer and connoisseur of scientific knowledge, I appreciate my profession because it helps integrate various fields, leading to a deeper understanding of topics and their interconnections. Even a philosopher might be closer to the truth than a scientific experimenter, as they can see the grand picture—the grand mind.

Research in modern physics has led to several theories. Theories are solutions to specific sets of problems, and eventually, we aim to combine them to reach a Unified Theory. We have made remarkable progress over the past century in understanding matter and its workings. We have learned that matter is both a particle and a wave. In layman's terms, it appears as a particle and
" behaves" like a wave. Like Shiva, consciousness behaves like Shakti, nature. The particle's "nature" is to act like a wave.

Maxwell and Faraday, who were great experimenters of the past century, provided us with the complete theory of electromagnetism. This led us to conclude that the fundamental "unit" of the universe is not merely billiard balls colliding, as assumed since Newton, but something called force fields. This conclusion led Einstein to reject the notion of "ether" and view electromagnetic fields as physical entities in their own right.

Relativity theory and atomic physics shattered our Newtonian worldviews. According to relativity theory, space and time are interconnected and form the four dimensions of a continuum called "space-time." Gravity, according to Einstein, bends space and time, creating curvature; the greater the gravitational force, the greater the bend.

Quantum theory has shown that the properties of atoms arise from the wave nature of electrons. The "solid" property we perceive is actually a consequence of typical quantum effects.

The main books I want to highlight for those interested in understanding the world through a modern physicist's eyes are

Fritjof Capra's works, Tom Campbell's *Big Theory of Everything*, and other recent research articles in consciousness and physics. Current research shows striking coincidences with some Eastern mystical thoughts. Reality increasingly resembles the mystical worldview the closer we examine it. Reading modern physics research articles and the Upanishads, I sometimes find it difficult to differentiate between the two.

The mystical insight or event known as Enlightenment in a spiritual seeker's life is a complete merging into the "source" of the universe. Mystics describe life on Earth as paradoxical—some say it is Maya, while others describe it as simultaneously full and empty. These paradoxes are similar to those found in quantum physics through the uncertainty principle and Schrödinger's experiments.

Understanding consciousness has been a quest for humanity for ages, with ancient texts discussing it, though often obscured by religious context. Indian culture, however, was known for its openness and transcendence of certain ascetic seriousness. A spiritual person is seen as one who experiences and understands the facets of this universe, capable of being both a warrior and a lover.

The Upanishads present direct truths about the nature of consciousness, referring to this ultimate ground that is not graspable yet can be felt as a closeness. They describe existence as the essence of life, without which the world would not exist.

Recent research in physics and consciousness, notably the Penrose-Hameroff theory (ORCH- OR), posits that consciousness is a product of quantum computations in the brain's microtubules. In my opinion, this explanation is unsatisfactory. The Western mind, now increasingly engaging with Eastern thought due to media coverage, attempts to resolve the world's complex nature by reducing it into smaller problems and training individuals to advance in specific fields. While this
approach has been crucial in medicine, it has also been counterproductive in many ways. There is a fascinating term called "metacrisis," reflecting our rapid move toward it, with current systems running on reductionist thought processes. Daniel Schmachtenberger and other anthropologists have predicted this, and the best we can do is to "bend" the curve, reducing the delta region.

My point is simple: we should utilize the knowledge we are gaining about the universe through modern physics to improve its survivability. We need to view the universe as a living entity, which it is proving itself to be and understand the larger picture of our actions and their consequences.

The Cosmic Dancer is in tune with this basic nature of Reality. He respects his counterpart his nature which is none other than himself. He desires the Ultimate desire preservation of his own nature which is what makes him the most Intelligent Being.

Chapter 18

Integration of Archetypal Psychology and Yoga of Dreams

"Dreams and Their Mysteries"

Man is prana and prana flows from one direction to another at all times. When at rest, energy is properly flowing throughout the system. In dreams, for example, energy continues to move through the body, and each part of the body conveys a certain message to the mind. The conscious aspects of a dream reflect this energy movement. Dreams are, of course, fascinating, but if we really observe our energy while asleep, we may notice that restful sleep is often accompanied by "good" and pleasant dreams.

Buddhist monks, who spend years in retreat simply observing the happenings of the body and mind, have discovered that the content of dreams is also significant, as it can inform our decisions in waking life. Waking life, too, is dreamlike in the sense that there is less control in the "normal" sense. This control can be cultivated by being more aware and mindful. This effort is different from the ordinary effort we make to accomplish tasks; naturally, we only pursue what stimulates us, which leads to fatigue. Mindfulness and awareness, which are distinct from ordinary concentration, help you enhance your clarity of life as you perceive it in the moment.

Right now, you are perceiving something by reading it, which creates fluctuations in your mind and stimulates you both intellectually and energetically. The stimulation we so often crave is the root of all energy movement; we constantly want either to receive or give energy, or to transform it into something else. Most of us do this unconsciously: each system or chakra that requires energy simply takes it without our awareness, and we fall into this trap repeatedly. If we look at our lower instincts, such as hunger and sexual desire, we see how powerfully they drive us—and our societies often revolve around these patterns of energy movement, leading us toward food, money, or sexual entertainment.

Movies are designed the same way; each film draws us into the protagonist's experience, stimulating our senses in an indirect manner. Every movie leaves a karmic imprint on the mind and may even trigger latent karmic traces, eventually leading to confusion and misery. Dreams operate similarly, though the process is reversed: here, stimulation occurs directly through inner energy, and the mind simply reflects scenarios we may have experienced before.

Dreams can be a fascinating reflection of the state of the mind and the karmic traces that have been triggered. In response to these triggers, we might make decisions throughout the day. A layer of subconscious background often veils our waking life, slowly fading but persisting throughout. Hence, many meditation practitioners aim to gain control over their dreams.

Dreams also reflect fears, the hidden or repressed aspects of oneself. Everything is somehow balanced in sleep: energy nourishes various organs through the nervous and digestive systems, rejuvenating the whole being. Deep sleep is an optimal state of total rest, when energy relaxes in all parts, no longer moving—and the experience is tranquility and calm. Upon waking, such freshness lingers, and that lightness can make your day more meditative.

We often believe our dreams are beyond control, but if we understand the dynamics of energy—how it moves through centers and causes the impressions of each center to emerge—we can observe this movement and gently learn to guide it. There are many dream practices that rely on focusing on specific centers while sleeping, gently directing energy there for healing or calming effects.

Dream content varies from person to person, according to culture, tradition, and experience, but the essence of dreams remains similar. That is why we must talk about symbolology, emphasizing interpretation over literal conceptions of dream content. For example, seeing a ghost in a dream does not mean ghosts exist—it may indicate a deep fear, because energy is stuck in the heart region where this emotion is held.

You can dream of something you have repressed throughout the day. Anger, for instance, may find room to vent in the deep unconsciousness of your sleep. Sometimes even a slight mention of something—a passing reference to your cousin or a relative, a fleeting name that flickered across your consciousness—can trigger an entire dream centered on that person.Dreams emerge because, during sleep, your mind is resting and "going with the flow." It accesses a layer beyond the conscious realm—a layer that tries to "make sense of everything." This realm is random and chaotic, often making little sense to your waking mind, but to your subconscious it is perfectly natural. The subconscious creates intricate, hidden maps within itself, and dreams are one way they surface.Therefore, it is crucial to get a good night's sleep—and to dream big, at least while you are unconscious.

Every center responds in dreams. Only in deep sleep is everything tranquil; healing, a process occurring in sleep, often takes place within dreams. Through slow practice, dreams can gradually be changed.

There are three important things one must observe in oneself to properly control oneself:

1. Where the energy is being diverted.

2. Being aware of the movement of consciousness and energy throughout waking life, which aids in looking more deeply into dream life.
3. Recognizing that each person has different impressions unique to their individuality.

It is difficult to give conceptual guidance, but by consciously moving your own energy, meaningful change can occur. This is a critical error in the self-help industry: believing things will change by understanding them conceptually alone. Things never change that way; in fact, the state may even worsen.

However, thinking energetically—using the system of chakras, nadis, and conscious direction of energy and thought—makes it possible to act by activating dormant parts of yourself. When waking life is brought under greater conscious control—through active tools like writing, imagination, and conscious meditation—dreams can also be brought under control. This leads to lucid dreaming and the ability to change aspects of dreams.

Greater awareness and residing in one's true nature should become more natural before proceeding further. Visualization can help guide energy and consciousness; people may use different symbols for various chakras. Don't be confused by the diversity of symbolism—create or adopt a symbol that attracts you and stick with it. Once the symbol is internalized, you will no longer need it. You will feel the energy center as simply as you feel the back of your hand.

Initially, these centers work on an as-needed basis, but as you become more conscious of them, they will activate and be more available. You may notice changes in various life areas: from career choices to where you live. Things may become uncomfortable, as alignment and control increase.

We often get stuck in unnatural patterns, with habitual energy consumption focused in certain centers, leading us to react instinctively over and over. Instinct arises from the lower centers, and the more instinctual a person is, the less intellectual and aware they become. Intuition, on the other hand, comes from deeper, more refined awareness. It can emerge in dreams or with mindfulness. Intuition also comes from observing the causes and effects in dreams and mental patterns. A wise person—deeply intuitive—can sometimes predict life events by seeing the causal cycles at play.

Dreams, too, can be predicted intuitively, and through dreams, waking life can be predicted. This requires years or decades of careful observation of dreams, reactions, and actions, with sustained awareness and mindfulness.

Intuitive growth is something different—what we generally call wisdom. Wise words come from intuitive growth, developed through striving for the kind of intelligence Spinoza defined: analyzing causes and effects, formulating theories and predictions, and seeking universal laws.

Relying on intuition is tricky, because often what you mistake for intuition is nothing more than superstition. This occurs especially in religious and spiritual circles, where someone may believe they are receiving an intuitive warning that something terrible is about to happen—when in reality, it may simply be what scientists now humorously call a "brain-fart," yes, that is the actual term.However, if a healthy person is balanced, aligned within themselves, and has enough experience and knowledge, their intuition can serve as a reliable guide. Intuition, in such cases, is not a magical process but rather a combination of logical prediction and subconscious reasoning. For example, mothers often sense things about their children, and fathers naturally feel protective instincts about theirs. Yet only parents who are genuinely healthy—emotionally involved and present in their children's lives—are able to accurately sense, anticipate, and gently guide the directions their children may be heading toward.The more you understand your own mind, the greater your ability to understand the minds of others.

Dreams and their mysteries are many—philosophers, psychologists, and analysts have spent lifetimes exploring them from varied perspectives. Tibetan Buddhists and Bon monks have not only interpreted and predicted dreams but have also learned to manipulate and change dreams at will through diverse dream and sleep practices, uncovering physical, mental, and astral secrets.

If, for example, you dreamed of ice cream one night, it is likely you will decide to eat ice cream the next day—or at least consider it.

In *The Tibetan Yogas of Dream and Sleep* by Tenzin Wangyal Rinpoche, the author describes in detail the mechanisms of dreams and how to experience different kinds of states in the dream or astral world.

Our dreams are patterned; they are not just random imaginings. There is a clear-cut way of understanding and even predicting what you might dream about each night. Your dreams can also affect your decisions during the day, both consciously and unconsciously. If you keep a dream journal, you may notice how your daytime thoughts are connected to nighttime dreams.

We all dream by day and by night—often, we dream more during the day if we are not working or concentrating. If we are not mindful or present, we are lost in daydreams from various centers: dreams of security, of family, of being respected, or of overcoming a rival. Life is a dream, but only for those who are awake. every moment of distraction is a kind of dream—dreams of complex things, of teaching, or of concepts. Life truly happens only when we are awake and mindful of our dreams.

Not all dreams come true; in fact, only a small fraction will ever be realized in physical life. Whatever happens is still somehow unsatisfactory, often because we link happiness or satisfaction to it, but in reality, it is just the relief of a burden from the mind's shoulders.

Suppose one realizes that life is a dream—what then? If this is realized, we become more careful with our dreams, seeing patterns of cause and effect and acting according to laws that offer lasting results. For example: if you earn a large sum of money and dream of spending it on a lavish house to prove your worth, you will spend and enjoy, hosting relatives and friends. After the celebration, you will continue to dream —perhaps dreaming of greater fame or respect. This is not to belittle spending, but to highlight that, upon achieving a dream, you merely relieve yourself of one burden and take on another.

Why not relieve yourself of the burden of dreams in this moment? Recognize the futility of endless dreaming. Instead, perhaps dream of goodness, of investing in knowledge or helping others. Yet even these acts can arise from ego, which is never satisfied. As Osho says, if you dream of goodness for egoic reasons, you are still dreaming. Only when you have shed the burden of tomorrow's dreams are you truly awake.

Nighttime dreams relate to archetypes: if you examine myths and stories from human culture, you will notice patterns in main characters and protagonists —the psychologist Carl Jung called these universal aspects archetypes. Each of us, in different life phases, strives to fulfill the desires of these archetypes. A beggar dreams of being a king, a king dreams of renouncing it all; a saint dreams of pleasures in heaven, and a husband dreams of solitude.

If we fulfill these desires consciously, there is a chance to accomplish and satisfy each archetype within us, but if unconscious, we are likely to remain dissatisfied with whatever we achieve.

The dreams you experience at night present scenarios and past impressions. The difference between daydreams and nighttime dreams is that, during the day, you are partly aware of your dreams and desires and can rationalize them; at night, you are not aware of dreaming, yet you continue to act in the dream according to your psyche's impressions. Prana moves through the body while you sleep, healing and clearing your energy.

Sigmund Freud noted that dreams often reveal what is repressed during the day, and while this is not the whole truth, it's true that a lot of energy released occurs in dreams at night.

Practical Takeaway :

Dream practise:

- Concentrate on the throat chakra before sleep, imagining a bright red lotus. As you drift off, the dreams you experience in the first two hours of healthy sleep will often relate to the throat, perhaps involving communication.
- Wake up after two hours, visualize a white light at the third eye center, go back to sleep, and observe your dreams, keeping the visualization vivid.
- Wake up two hours later, imagine a black void at the heart center, do a brief breathing practice to clear your energy, and observe your dreams as you go back to sleep.
- Wake up a final time two hours later, visualize a black void in the sexual chakra, and observe the dreams that arise as you return to sleep.
- Practice this sequence for at least three months, until you are able to have a lucid dream. (Lucid dreaming is not described in this book, because sometimes explanation hinders experience.)

Questions for self:

What do you observe about your patterns of thought during these four phases?

How is this practice changing the way you see sleep and

dreams?
Which archetypes do you encounter most during this phase of your life?

Chapter 19

Why We're Never Really Free (Until We Are)

Freedom is the word humanity loves most, yet understands least. We chant it in revolutions, we write it into constitutions, we carve it into monuments, and still, it eludes us. Every age imagines itself freer than the one before, and yet the chains change form rather than disappear. The slaves are unshackled but remain prisoners of poverty. The citizens vote yet remain bound by propaganda. The worker signs his contract willingly, but wakes each morning with the same invisible yoke of necessity across his shoulders. We call ourselves free because no king commands us, and yet our lives are dictated by forces far subtler: fear, desire, time, biology, society.

True freedom is not political. It is existential. You can live in a democracy and still be a slave to your own thoughts. You can wander across continents and still be caged by your past. You can have every choice available in a marketplace, yet never know the joy of being unconditioned. The deeper truth is that freedom is not about options, but about essence. It is not about doing whatever you want, but about realizing who you are beneath the wanting. Until then, we are never really free.

Look at the way the world conditions us from birth. The infant, pure and unshaped, begins to absorb language, identity, culture. Before he can speak, he has already been named. Before he can choose, he has already been told what he is: boy or girl, rich or poor, this religion or that. The family, the nation, the culture — they pour into him like rivers into a vessel, filling him with stories of who he should be. What we call personality is often this cargo of conditioning. We walk through life with the weight of voices not our own, repeating them so often that we think they are ours. Where is freedom in this?

Even when we break away from our parents, we are captured by society. Advertisements whisper into our subconscious, politics shape our fears, social media manipulates our desires, algorithms study our habits better than we do ourselves. The modern man boasts of being autonomous, yet his tastes, moods, and beliefs are engineered by forces he cannot even name. He imagines he is free because he chooses the brand of shoes, the flavor of ice cream, the color of his car. But these are not choices. They are pre-packaged scripts. We live in a vast theater of suggestion, mistaking the actor's mask for our own face.

Freedom, then, cannot be granted by law or taken by another. It must be discovered within. Sartre was right when he said that man is condemned to be free — that no matter how much we try to avoid it, the burden of choice presses upon us. But Sartre also missed something: choice alone is not freedom. Choosing between cages is not liberation. Choosing between distractions is not awakening. The question is not *what* do you choose, but *who* is the chooser? If the chooser is still a bundle of conditioning, then every choice is just another repetition of the past.

Look more closely and you will see the subtler chains. We are bound not only by culture but by our own biology. Hunger, lust, fatigue, hormones — they pull at us invisibly, directing our moods and actions. Neuroscience tells us that by the time you decide to lift a finger, the brain has already made the decision milliseconds earlier. Free will, then, may itself be an illusion. Spinoza hinted at this centuries ago: man believes he is free because he is conscious of his desires, yet ignorant of the causes that compel them. You feel free when you smoke the cigarette, but you are in fact a puppet of the craving. You feel free when you chase success, but you are enslaved to a story planted in you long ago.

So where does that leave us? Are we doomed to be prisoners forever? Here lies the paradox: we are never really free until we are — and the moment of awakening shatters the entire illusion. For there is a level of being deeper than conditioning, deeper than thought, deeper than even biology. The mystics called it the soul, the Self, the Atman, the witness. It is the dimension in you that is not touched by circumstance. The storms of desire and fear may rage, the narratives of culture may echo, the hormones may surge, and yet beneath them, there is a stillness that does not move. That stillness is the true ground of freedom.

When you touch it, you realize freedom is not something to gain, but something you always had. The cage was never locked. The prison bars were made of smoke. The self that believed itself bound was itself the illusion. Krishnamurti once said, "It is no measure of health to be well-adjusted to a profoundly sick society." To be free is to step out of this sickness, not by rebellion alone, but by awakening to the timeless presence that precedes all conditioning.

Think of the prisoner who sits in his cell, dreaming of escape. Every night he imagines breaking the bars, digging tunnels, climbing walls. Years pass in this fantasy, until one morning he touches the bars and realizes they are made of paper. The prison dissolves the moment he sees through it. This is the secret of freedom: you do not escape the prison; you awaken from it.

But this awakening is not cheap. It requires the courage to look deeply into your own chains. To see how much of what you call "myself" is borrowed. To see how your so-called choices are patterned responses. To see how fear manipulates you, how pleasure entraps you, how memory dictates you. Most people cannot bear this sight. They prefer the comfort of believing in their own freedom, even if it is false. To pierce this illusion is painful, but it is the first step toward liberation.

And what happens when you taste this freedom? Life changes in texture. You still act, but your action is no longer mechanical. You still think, but thought no longer binds you. You still feel, but emotions flow without owning you. You still play the roles of society, but you wear them lightly, like garments you can take off. You can be a parent, a worker, a citizen, and yet in the core of your being, you remain untouched.

Nietzsche dreamed of the Übermensch, the one who creates his own values, who is free from herd morality. Yet even this vision is incomplete, for it is still bound to the will, to the act of creating. True freedom is even simpler. It is not the power to invent new chains but the recognition that you are the sky in which all chains appear and vanish. You are not the actor, nor the role, nor the script. You are the silent witness of the play. To realize this is to be free even while you walk in chains.

So let us not deceive ourselves. Until we awaken, we are not free. We are guided by forces unseen, repeating scripts written before our birth. But this truth is not despair; it is invitation. The very recognition of bondage is the beginning of release. The moment you see the illusion clearly, you are already stepping beyond it. Freedom is not far away. It is here, closer than breath, waiting to be remembered.

And when it comes, it comes not as a conquest, but as a homecoming. You do not seize it; you surrender to it. You do not acquire it; you awaken into what you always were. Then the paradox dissolves: we were never really free, until we are — and once we are, we see we always have been.

Chapter 20

The Path of Love: Bhakti Marga

Love is the oldest path and yet forever new. It is the force that has built civilizations, toppled empires,created religious conflicts, carved poetry into the bones of language, and drawn mystics to the edges of madness. Every religion, every philosopher, every poet has circled it like moths around a flame, and yet none have ever captured it fully. Love is too vast to be contained, too intimate to be defined. The moment you try to hold it, it slips through your fingers. And yet, without it, life is dust and ashes.But undderstanding that the path of love is full of irrationality , you will be freed from it and all teh misery it has brought in the form of emotional pain.

From the beginning, love whispers into our being. The child clings to the mother's warmth before he knows the word for it. Lovers discover in one another not just companionship but a window into the infinite. Artists, musicians, mystics — they all return to the same truth: that love is the only experience that dissolves the boundary between self and other. In love, you are no longer confined to your small island of identity. You expand, you flow outward, you become larger than yourself.

Plato spoke of love as the ladder that leads us from the beauty of the body to the beauty of the soul, and from the beauty of the soul to the beauty of the divine itself. What begins with desire, if followed truly, does not end in possession but in transcendence. It is as if love were the rope thrown down by eternity into time, inviting us to climb. Yet most of us remain tangled in the lower rungs, mistaking infatuation for the whole. We clutch at forms, fearing their loss, and miss the essence that calls us beyond.

The mystics knew this secret well. Rumi danced in circles, intoxicated not with wine but with the Beloved who could never be named. His verses tremble with a longing that is both earthly and divine: the aching for the touch of the beloved's hand is inseparable from the yearning for union with God. To love truly, he tells us, is to be consumed, to burn until nothing remains but love itself. Simone Weil echoed the same truth in her quiet way: love, she said, is the consent to distance, the willingness to let the other be, even if that other is God withholding Himself. Love is not grasping, but surrender.

And yet, in our time, love has been domesticated, packaged, reduced to a product. We swipe right, we market ourselves, we measure affection by utility. Love becomes a transaction, a fragile contract between two egos negotiating terms. It is no wonder that so many feel hollow in their relationships. Love cannot be manufactured, it cannot be bargained. It is a fire, not a commodity. And fire, by nature, consumes. It does not ask permission. It does not consult the clock.

But what does it mean to walk the path of love? It is not merely romance, though romance can be its spark. It is not merely affection, though affection is its fragrance. The path of love is the willingness to be vulnerable, to be pierced, to be broken open. To love is to risk pain, because only what is fragile can reveal what is eternal. Every heartbreak is a doorway if you dare to step through. For in heartbreak, you discover that what you loved was not the form, but the essence shining through it — and that essence cannot die.

This is why love is the greatest teacher. It strips away illusion faster than philosophy ever could. You may think yourself detached, wise, unshakable — until you fall in love. Then suddenly you are vulnerable, needy, alive in ways you cannot control. Love humbles you. It teaches you that freedom without devotion is emptiness, that knowledge without tenderness is cruelty. To love is to finally understand that the other is not an object in your story, but a universe in themselves. To love is to bow before mystery.

In this way, love and death are twins. Both dissolve the ego. Both force you to confront the limits of control. Both strip away your certainties and throw you into the unknown. Perhaps this is why so many traditions intertwine love and death. The Sufis speak of *fana* — annihilation in the Beloved — which is nothing less than the death of the separate self. Christ speaks of losing oneself to find oneself, and his final act on the cross is the supreme expression of love through surrender unto death. The Hindu bhakti saints wept and sang to Krishna not because they wanted possession but because they wanted dissolution. To love is to die into the other, and in that death, to discover eternity.

But the path of love is not sentimental. It is fierce, uncompromising, often cruel in its honesty. True love does not flatter the ego; it dismantles it. True love does not confirm your stories; it burns them away. To walk this path is to risk everything — your pride, your certainty, your safety. That is why so few dare to truly walk it. It is easier to remain in transactions, in comforts, in arrangements dressed as love. But those who dare discover something astonishing: that love is not only about the beloved, but about awakening the heart itself. The beloved is the mirror; love is the revelation.

Even in its ordinary forms, love teaches this truth. The parent who loves a child discovers a capacity for sacrifice they never knew they possessed. The friend who loves another learns to share their pain, not out of duty but out of genuine resonance. These are glimpses of the deeper truth: that love dissolves separation. It is not about two becoming one in some cliché sense. It is about discovering that the two were never separate to begin with.

The philosophers of modernity often distrusted love. Nietzsche warned against it as weakness, Schopenhauer dismissed it as the will-to-life manipulating us to reproduce. And yet, even in their cynicism, love haunted them. For if life has any meaning at all, it reveals itself most powerfully in love. Not in theories, not in calculations, but in that sudden breaking open when you realize another being's joy or suffering is as real as your own. Love is the collapse of solipsism. It is the proof that we are not alone in our consciousness.

And so the path of love is not merely a human drama. It is cosmic. The physicists tell us that gravity bends space and time, pulling stars and galaxies into relation. Perhaps love is the inner echo of this cosmic gravity — the pull that brings souls together, the attraction that binds the universe into a single fabric. To walk the path of love is to align yourself with this gravity, to allow yourself to be drawn into union, even at the cost of your separate self.

But let us not mistake love for perpetual sweetness. Love wounds as much as it heals. To love God is to endure His silence. To love humanity is to suffer its cruelty. To love another is to risk betrayal, loss, change. But would we prefer safety over this? A life without love is not safety — it is death by suffocation. Better to be burned by love than to remain unlit. Better to risk heartbreak than to die without ever having dissolved into another.

When you walk this path to its end, you discover something extraordinary: love was never between you and the other. It was always the ground of being itself. The beloved was the doorway. What you loved in them was the spark of eternity shining through their form. And once you see this, you realize that love is not confined to romance, to family, to friendship.

It pervades everything. The trees breathe it, the stars pulse with it, every creature carries it as its hidden essence. Love is not one path among many; it is the path. All other paths — knowledge, meditation, art, discipline — are only fragments of what love accomplishes in full.

To live in love is to live in truth. Not the truth of definitions, but the truth of being. It is to awaken each day not asking, "What can I take?" but "How can I give myself away?" It is to live not in fear of loss but in wonder at the endlessness of connection. It is to see the world not as separate objects but as faces of the same beloved.

And perhaps this is the final paradox: love makes us most human, and yet it is also the force that carries us beyond humanity. To love fully is to step out of the little self and into the vastness where all beings meet. It is to realize that the heart is not an organ in the body, but the center of the universe itself. And once you know this, you understand why the mystics sang, why the poets wrote, why the prophets wept. They were not exaggerating. They had seen it. Love is not a metaphor. It is reality.

So let us walk the path of love. Let us risk its dangers, surrender to its fire, allow it to dismantle everything false in us. For at the end of this path, there is no end. There is only the endless opening, the eternal embrace. We were never meant to merely survive. We were meant to burn, to dissolve, to be consumed — until nothing remains but love itself.

The Beautiful Emptiness

In the heart of silence lies a fullness—a paradoxical beauty that emerges not from having, but from the clarity of nothingness.
We are often taught to fill ourselves—with achievement, knowledge, validation—but seldom are we shown the power of emptying out.

Emptiness, in its purest form, is not a lack. It is a womb. A space of quiet possibility. It is where ideas are born, where truth echoes, where the self listens rather than speaks. When you are no longer trying to be someone, you become everything.

A Mirror Called Nothingness

Nothingness is the greatest mirror. It reflects without judgment, without distortion.

When the noise quiets, the roles dissolve, and all distractions fade—you're left face-to-face with the raw self.

And what you see there may not always be pretty. But it is real.

In that stillness, the ego withers. The illusions peel.

And the soul, for once, breathes. This mirror is not empty—it is infinitely full. Full of your becoming.

The Abstract Flow

There is a rhythm to existence. One that isn't bound by logic, or language, or structure.

It flows like a river—abstract,
shapeless, knowing. To
control it is to suffer. To follow
it is to dance.

The wise don't grip life tightly. They attune. They listen.

They let the current carry them, not to where they want to go, but where they must. In surrender, they find direction. In chaos, form. In mystery, truth.

Spiritual Insights

The Light Inside the Cave

We often search for truth outside—books, teachers, rituals.

But the most radiant light is often found in the darkest, quietest places. The cave within.

It takes courage to go inward. To leave the safety of systems and enter your own wilderness. Yet it is there that the sacred fire burns the brightest.

Meditations with No Name

Some meditations aren't guided. They aren't structured. They don't follow a script.

They happen in a moment of breath. A gaze into the sky. A touch of wind on skin.

These unnamed meditations are the ones that transform us the most—because they find us when we're not looking.

Chapter 21

Pranayama – A Technique to Increase Life Energy

"A Step Into Samadhi"

Breath is the most intimate bridge between body and spirit. Before thought arises, before even the first stirrings of desire, breath is already moving—silent, unnoticed, constant. From the moment of birth to the final sigh, it remains our faithful companion. And yet, though it is the ground of life itself, we rarely pause to explore its mysteries.

The ancient yogis of India did not make this mistake. For them, the breath was not merely the mechanical act of inhaling oxygen and exhaling carbon dioxide. It was the doorway to higher consciousness, the vehicle through which one could influence the currents of thought, emotion, and even destiny. They called this science **pranayama**—the expansion and regulation of life energy through conscious breathing.

Sri Yukteswar Giri, the guru of Paramahansa Yogananda, wrote in *The Holy Science* that pranayama elongates life by slowing the decay of the body. Oxygen renews cells, he explained, but the deeper secret lies in the way controlled breathing harmonizes the nervous system, balances the vital forces, and quiets the restless mind. A life lived with conscious breath is not just longer—it is deeper, clearer, more luminous.

The Yogic View of Breath and Consciousness

In the *Yoga Sutras*, Patanjali outlines the eightfold path (ashtanga) leading to **Samadhi**, the state of direct union with the Absolute. After moral disciplines (yamas and niyamas), physical postures (asana), and before meditation (dhyana), comes pranayama. This sequencing is no accident. Without mastery of the breath, the mind remains turbulent, unfocused, unable to enter the still depths required for meditation.

Breath and thought are bound together like two wings of a bird. When one is disturbed, the other is agitated; when one is calm, the other settles naturally. Observe yourself: when you are angry, breath is rapid and shallow; when relaxed, it is slow and deep. The yogis discovered that this relationship is reciprocal—by **regulating the breath**, one can immediately influence the mind.

Thus, pranayama is not merely about health (though it undoubtedly strengthens the body). It is about **liberating consciousness**. Each cycle of breath becomes a movement inward, peeling away distractions, inviting silence, preparing the soil for meditation.

Life Energy: The Currency of Action

Consider for a moment what we mean by "life energy." It is that subtle vitality which animates thought and action. When abundant, we feel enthusiastic, creative, capable of transforming ideas into reality. When depleted, we procrastinate, fall into inertia, or succumb to destructive habits.

Every choice we make either conserves or squanders this energy. Poor diet, restless sleep, addictions, and toxic emotions drain it rapidly. Meanwhile, practices like mindful movement, fasting, silence, and above all, **conscious breathing**, replenish it.

Pranayama is, in this sense, an economy of energy. Each

measured inhalation is a deposit into the bank of vitality; each calm exhalation releases impurities and wasted tensions. The practitioner begins to notice subtle reserves of strength, clarity, and willpower that were previously inaccessible.

Flow, Samyama, and Sahaja Samadhi

Modern psychology speaks of the state of *flow*, described by Mihaly Csikszentmihalyi, where one becomes fully absorbed in an activity—whether painting, reading, or playing music. In such moments, the sense of a separate "self" dissolves into pure doing. Time stretches, effort vanishes, and joy arises naturally.

The yogic tradition calls this state **Samyama**, the fusion of concentration (dharana), meditation (dhyana), and absorption (samadhi). But yoga distinguishes between unconscious flow and conscious absorption. Watching a film, for example, can also dissolve self-awareness, but we emerge with new desires and impressions imprinted on the mind. This kind of flow binds us further to samsara—the cycle of craving and attachment.

True yogic Samyama, however, is a **lucid absorption**. The practitioner enters deeply, but without being stained by impressions. This is the doorway to **Sahaja Samadhi**, the natural state where calmness pervades action itself. Work, art, and even relationships become free of grasping and clinging. One acts out of fullness, not lack.

Love and Breath: The Subtle Union

Love, too, is intimately connected to breath. Think of moments when you are deeply attuned to someone you cherish—you unconsciously synchronize breathing patterns. You sigh together, laugh together, pause together. In such moments, boundaries soften. Their joy feels like your joy, their sorrow like your own.

Breath is, therefore, the **physiological root of empathy**. By cultivating awareness of it, we expand our capacity to connect—not just with people, but with all beings. A yogi in deep pranayama feels the pulse of the universe in his lungs, as if the trees themselves are breathing through him.

Why Breath Leads to Freedom

Philosophers have long debated what it means to be free. Is freedom the absence of external constraint, or is it inner mastery? For the yogi, true freedom begins when one is no longer enslaved by the unconscious rhythms of body and mind.

Most people live at the mercy of their breath. It quickens with anger, it shallows with fear, it halts with shock. They are pulled like puppets by unseen strings. The yogi, by contrast, learns to cut those strings. By consciously directing the flow of prana, they step into a sovereignty deeper than any political or social liberty: the sovereignty of the self.

This is why Sri Yukteswar emphasized that pranayama can elongate life—not merely by prolonging years, but by granting a quality of time otherwise inaccessible. Each controlled breath is a taste of eternity, a sip of timelessness.

Practical Takeaways: Pranayama Techniques

Below are foundational techniques. Practice with patience, never force. A calm, steady approach yields the greatest results.

1. Observation of Natural Breath (Anapana)

- Sit comfortably, spine erect.
- Simply observe the natural rhythm of your breath at the nostrils.

- Notice coolness on the inhale, warmth on the exhale.
- Do not control—just witness.
- *Benefit:* Sharpens awareness, calms the wandering mind.

2. Equal Breathing (Sama Vritti)

- Inhale for a count of 4, hold for 4, exhale for 4, hold for 4.
- Continue for 10–15 rounds.
- Gradually increase count to 6 or 8 as capacity grows.
- *Benefit:* Balances the nervous system, induces tranquility.

3. Alternate Nostril Breathing (Nadi Shodhana)

- Close the right nostril, inhale through the left.
- Close the left, exhale through the right.
- Inhale through the right, exhale through the left.
- This is one round. Practice 5–10 rounds.
- *Benefit:* Purifies energy channels (nadis), harmonizes hemispheres of the brain.

4. Victorious Breath (Ujjayi)

- Inhale slowly through the nose while gently constricting the throat, creating an oceanic sound.
- Exhale with the same constriction.

- Practice for 5 minutes.
- *Benefit:* Builds internal heat, sharpens focus, deepens meditation.

5. Cooling Breath (Sheetali)

- Roll the tongue into a tube (or place tip at roof of mouth if difficult).
- Inhale through the mouth, exhale through the nose.
- Repeat 8–10 times.
- *Benefit:* Reduces anger, heat, and restlessness.

6. Kapalabhati (Skull-Shining Breath)

- Sit tall, exhale forcefully by contracting the abdomen.
- Let inhalation happen passively.
- Do 20–30 pumps, then rest. Repeat 3 rounds.
- *Benefit:* Cleanses lungs, energizes body, awakens mind.

7. Deep Exhalation for Instant Calm

- Inhale gently, then exhale twice as long as the inhale.
- Example: inhale 4 counts, exhale 8 counts.
- Continue for 5 minutes.
- *Benefit:* Reduces anxiety, prepares mind for meditation.

Closing Reflection

Pranayama is more than technique. It is an attitude of reverence toward life itself. Each breath reminds us: we are not separate, not isolated fragments, but expressions of the same vast rhythm. Inhalation receives the gift of existence; exhalation returns it. Between the two lies the still point, the silent witness, the eternal self.

Practice begins with breath, but it ends in freedom. Through pranayama, the yogi steps not only into longer life but into **timeless life**. Each breath becomes a prayer, each pause a doorway into the infinite. And in that doorway waits Samadhi—the realization that everything has always been alive, and so have you.

Chapter 22

The Position of Art in Our Lives

Art has always been with us. Long before we learned to count, before we carved laws into stone, before we built cities or engines or machines, we painted on the walls of caves. We sang to the stars, we drummed the pulse of the earth, we danced in firelight. Why? Not because survival demanded it. The body needs bread, but it does not need poetry. The body needs shelter, but it does not need paintings of bison leaping across stone. And yet humanity has never lived without art. Perhaps because the body survives by bread, but the soul survives by beauty and worship.

We often imagine art as entertainment, as luxury, as something for museums or concert halls. But art is more primal, more necessary than this. It is not a hobby; it is a hunger. Without it, the human being shrinks. Art does not merely decorate life; it reveals it. It opens dimensions of experience that logic cannot touch. It is how the invisible becomes visible, how the unspoken finds a voice.

The philosophers wrestled with art uneasily. Plato, suspicious of poetry, banished the poets from his Republic, fearing that art deceives us with imitation, drawing us further from truth. And yet, paradoxically, it is Plato who gave us myths so enduring that they outlive every technical argument — the cave, the charioteer, the ladder of love. Even he could not escape the power of story, for story is the way truth enters not only the mind but the marrow. Aristotle, more forgiving, called art a catharsis, a purging of emotions. Nietzsche crowned art as the highest affirmation of life, the marriage of Dionysus and Apollo, chaos and form. For him, when philosophy grows dry, only art can carry us into the fullness of being.

And so it is. For art is the bridge between reason and mystery. It does not argue; it unveils. A painting does not prove anything, yet it changes the way you see. A poem may be nonsense in logical terms, yet it pierces deeper than a library of treatises. Music has no meaning you can pin down, yet it moves armies, heals grief, ignites prayer. Art bypasses the intellect and goes straight to the root. It is the soul recognizing itself in form.

Great literature like the Quran is born not through logical interpretation of the truth but through a muse a poetry woven in divinity.

Think of the way music can take you out of time. You sit in a room, your heart heavy, the world gray — then a melody arises, and suddenly the walls dissolve. You are transported, not to another place, but to a deeper layer of this one. The grief is still there, but now it has shape, dignity, beauty. You can bear it, because the music bears it with you. This is art's secret power: it redeems suffering by giving it form. What was chaos becomes rhythm, what was mute becomes song. And in that alchemy, you are healed.

This is why the mystics have always been artists. Rumi did not only preach; he sang. The Psalms of David are not essays but poetry. The Upanishads unfold not in arguments but in hymns. Even the silence of the Zen masters is a kind of art — a gesture, a performance, a koan sculpted into the air. Religion, at its highest, is inseparable from art. The cathedral is a sculpture of prayer in stone. The temple bell is philosophy melted into sound. The calligraphy of the Qur'an is truth dancing in letters. To seek the sacred without art is like trying to breathe without air.

And yet, our modern world has shrunk art into commodity. We buy it, sell it, hang it as decoration, consume it as distraction. We scroll through images without seeing them, play songs as background noise. We have forgotten that art is a discipline, a devotion, a doorway. True art requires vulnerability. To create it is to strip oneself bare. To receive it is to surrender, to let go of defenses. That is why true art feels dangerous — it can move you in ways you cannot control. It can break you open.

But this breaking is necessary. For art, like love, dissolves the illusion of separation. When you look at Van Gogh's swirls of starlight, you are not merely looking at paint on canvas; you are entering his vision of the cosmos, his anguish, his wonder. When you read a poem by Rilke, you are not alone in your longing; you are joined by another human being who, across centuries, felt the same fire. Art is the proof that our inner lives are not isolated islands but one great ocean, flowing through countless forms.

There is another dimension to art: it teaches us how to see. Most people move through the world half-blind, seeing only what is useful. The tree is timber, the river is water supply, the sky is weather forecast. But the artist sees differently. The tree is not lumber; it is a cathedral of living veins. The river is not utility; it is a song written in liquid motion. The sky is not data; it is infinity gazing back. To learn to see like an artist is to awaken to the miracle of existence itself. And you need not paint to do this. To live artfully is to live attentively. To cook, to walk, to speak with presence — this too is art.

Art is not only aesthetic; it is ethical. It demands honesty. A false painting, a dishonest poem, may trick the mind but never the soul. We recognize the authentic because it resonates. Great art is never propaganda, never manipulation, because it emerges not from agenda but from necessity. The artist creates not because he wants to impress but because he must. It is the overflowing of being. And this necessity awakens necessity in us. It calls us to live more truthfully, more vulnerably, more beautifully.

Consider also how art shapes memory. A civilization is remembered not by its GDP or its armies but by its art. The Greeks live on in their tragedies, the Indians in their epics, the Persians in their poetry, the Africans in their drums, the Chinese in their calligraphy. When empires collapse and nations vanish, what remains is the art — fragile, yet indestructible. To make art, then, is to defy time. It is to inscribe eternity into matter.

But perhaps the deepest role of art in our lives is not even expression or memory, but transformation. To encounter true art is to be changed. You cannot walk out of a cathedral the same as you walked in. You cannot read Dostoevsky without feeling your conscience stirred. You cannot hear Beethoven's Ninth without glimpsing the grandeur of the human spirit. These experiences do not entertain; they awaken. They tear the veil of the ordinary and let us glimpse the real.

And so, the position of art in our lives is not peripheral but central. It is not the luxury of the few but the birthright of all. To live without art is to live without full humanity. To restore art to its rightful place is to restore ourselves.

Perhaps this is why Dostoevsky once said, "Beauty will save the world." Not beauty as fashion, not beauty as indulgence, but beauty as revelation. For in beauty we recognize harmony, order, love. Beauty is the fingerprint of the eternal upon the transient. To live for beauty is not escapism; it is resistance against despair. It is to affirm that life, despite all its darkness, is worth the song, worth the dance, worth the painting.

So let us return to art not as pastime but as path. Let us allow ourselves to be pierced by it, broken open by it, healed by it. Let us create, not to impress, but because the soul demands it. And let us see the world itself as art — the dawn painting the sky, the wind composing music in the trees, the human face a portrait of infinity. When we live this way, every moment becomes a masterpiece. And perhaps then we will realize that the highest art is not on canvas or stage, but in the way we live our lives.

For to live is to create. To breathe is to sculpt time. To love is to compose eternity. And in the end, when all paintings fade and all songs fall silent, what remains will not be our possessions or our achievements, but the art we made of our souls.

Religion: The Highest Form of Art

Religion is not what most think it is. We inherit words, rituals, doctrines, commandments, yet the heart of religion is not in these. Religion, at its essence, is art. Not art in the sense of decoration, but art in the highest sense: the creation of beauty, the shaping of form from formlessness, the attempt to express the inexpressible. Where the painter uses color and canvas, where the poet uses words and rhythm, religion uses life itself. Its medium is the human soul, its canvas the heart, its sculpture the transformation of being.

But look at what has happened. The gallery has become the prison. Religion, in most places, is reduced to repetition, fear, and power. It has become an institution that demands conformity rather than a living art that awakens the soul. The priest replaces the poet. The ritual replaces the song. The rules replace the vision. People cling to the form and forget the formless truth it was meant to reveal.

Yet all the great founders were artists of the spirit. Moses, hearing a voice in fire and stone. Christ, speaking in parables like a poet. Muhammad, receiving verses that flowed like music. The Buddha, walking barefoot under trees, sculpting silence into insight. None of them offered dead rituals; each created a living art form — a way of shaping human consciousness toward the divine.

Religion becomes art when it is lived, not when it is memorized. It becomes art when prayer is not recited but sung from the marrow, when ritual is not repeated but re-inhabited, when myth is not dismissed as falsehood but seen as metaphor pointing to realities too vast for reason alone. Religion becomes art when it lifts us into wonder.

But how easy it is to mistake the form for the essence. There is an old story of Mulla Nasrudin.

One day, he was sitting outside the mosque with a bowl of yogurt, scooping it into his mouth with a grin. A pious man approached him, scandalized.

"Nasrudin! You cannot eat yogurt here. This is a sacred place!"

Nasrudin looked at him calmly and said, "Tell me, friend — if I eat yogurt in the mosque, does it make the yogurt holy? Or does it make the mosque ordinary?"

The man had no answer.

The point is simple: holiness does not reside in the place, the form, the object. Holiness is in awareness. A ritual performed without awareness is nothing. Eating yogurt with awareness may be more sacred than bowing mindlessly in prayer. Religion as art is not about what you do, but *how* you do it. The quality of presence is everything.

This is why true religion is the highest art — because it demands not just skill of the hand or cleverness of the mind, but totality of being. The artist of the soul cannot be half-present. He must pour himself fully into the act: into prayer, into compassion, into silence, into awe. Every brushstroke of the day becomes a gesture of creation. Washing dishes becomes a sacrament, if done in presence. Walking becomes a pilgrimage, if walked in awareness. Speaking becomes prophecy, if spoken from truth.

In this way, religion rescues life from banality. It reveals that nothing is ordinary. The stone is alive, the river sings, the stranger carries the face of God. Religion, as art, is the refusal to reduce life to mere function. It is the insistence that everything — eating, breathing, mourning, loving — can be turned into beauty, into offering, into sacred performance.

But just as art can be counterfeited, so can religion. There is art that is lifeless — mechanically painted, copied, mass-produced. And there is religion that is the same — lifeless, mechanical, inherited, repeated. The difference is not in the outward form, but in the inner fire. When fire burns in the artist, the work glows. When fire burns in the devotee, the prayer soars. Without fire, it is dead wood, dead canvas, dead words.

The challenge is that fire cannot be commanded. It must be kindled. And it is kindled by contact with mystery. This is why every authentic religion emphasizes silence, solitude, the encounter with the vastness beyond words. Without silence, fire dies. Without mystery, art becomes craft and religion becomes bureaucracy.

The tragedy of our age is that religion has largely lost its art, and art has lost its religion. Religion, stripped of mystery, becomes moral policing. Art, stripped of transcendence, becomes decoration or commodity. But the two are meant to be lovers. True religion inspires art; true art nourishes religion. Both spring from the same source: the human hunger for beauty that points beyond itself.

The task of our time may be to reunite them. To let art remind religion of beauty, and let religion remind art of depth. To let the poet and the mystic sit together again. To remember that the temple was always a gallery, and the gallery always a temple.

Religion as art does not ask you to believe but to create. It does not ask you to conform but to risk. It asks: *what will you make of your soul? What shape will your life take? What beauty will you offer the world?* You do not need canvas or marble. Your days are the canvas, your gestures the brush, your choices the sculpture.

And perhaps this is why the greatest saints and sages also laughed like poets and sang like children. For they knew that religion without art is heaviness, and art without religion is emptiness. Together, they become dance. Together, they become song. Together, they become a way of being in which every act, no matter how small, is radiant with meaning.

So let us not reduce religion to dogma. Let us live it as art — trembling before mystery, shaping beauty out of our finite lives, offering each moment as a work of creation. For when we do, we may find that the highest form of art is not a painting or a poem, but a human being fully alive.

Practical takeaway:

Explore other religions,dare to go an sit in their prayer halls,talk to them and befriend them.

The Agony of Seeking.

What is it that we are seeking and why is it that we realize too late the inherent nature temporariness of this world and its belongings.why is it that we don't see the plain stupidity of seeking things outwards sooner and when we actually reach a point of finding a building a world for ourself why don't we ever stop to consider that everything we have gathered in this materialistic world has led us to death.that eventually death is going to make everything we worked for vanish in just a moment.every amount gathered every brick placed will not longer be in our experience as we have now left the plane ,now we have left the plane of the living and crossed the bridge ,which the living cannot grasp and as long as we have a living mind we ourself will never really been able to grasp.Is this vanity?is this reducible dust that we worked hard for just going to blow away ? What matters must be the impressions that we have carried that we have built ,that we have yearned and worked hard for so long to inculcate.these discipline this mindset this control?is that what matters then ? are the glimpses of God for a moment's time ,the spacious clarity by which things resounded are those enough are those enough ?the agony of the seeker is that he wants to gain the eternal the eternal ungraspable with his limited mind and in this process loses his own mind his own sanity.this is agony to search God is to search infinity to search God is to search for something ungraspable and in this search end up on the streets under his roof with a bowl on your hands and an ego so big that even begging you don't beg you look down.whoever talked about ecstacy is lying ,whoever talked about the real is saying the truth ,the real is not mystical it is the garbage that you see on the streets it is the father who traumatises his son ,it is the mother who suffers the burden and it is the poor son who can never fulfill their expectations.It is the politician that lies it is the organization who never cared for the employee it is the hurt inside the father's heart when he knows that his child needs food yet has no job to bring him his food.God is a joke he tricks you and you always fall for it.you always fall for one thing that you always are thirsty for, hope.

The Divinity in Goodness.

" Nature Rewards Kindness "

Is life not psychedelic enough? Is life, at its most boring, fundamental experience, not raw and awe-inspiring? I believe it is. Life is psychedelic, nature is awe-inspiring, and the relationships we have with each other, the small psychological games that play inside our minds, the acts of kindness, and the momentary feeling of upliftment you feel when you look at the sunrise are enough to make you understand that life is awe-inspiring, great, and fundamentally the most exquisite experience one can have. This experience brightens when we do good. I don't mean do good from a political perspective or from a place outside our minds; I mean goodness from the heart.

> Nature is divine because look at how it rewards goodness with positivity, with fresh chemicals releasing inside you, making you more healthy and returning that act of goodness with happiness. That is the divinity in goodness. A healthy person strives to do good; they make others feel safe, give the weak a pillar to stand on, and give the poor strength because they are connected to the source. They are empathetic, understand others' hearts, and comprehend how their hearts are capable of hurting them. So goodness done from the heart, from a place of emotion, is so rewarding and original. The rewards are immediate and come

like a wave to the edge of an ocean; they come from the depths and manifest themselves slowly before going back into the depths.

The Source acts in mysterious ways and works harmoniously with depth. Its rewards are profound and so thoughtful and intelligent that sometimes, or most times, they are imperceptible due to their intelligent depth.

So give that good remark you are holding on to, say those kind words, help those poor souls, and make them see the depths of the Source. Acts done out of love and kindness are something one will remember on their deathbeds. Acts done with goodness of heart will, in fact, be the only things whose memory will brighten and refresh you. So don't miss opportunities; serve this nature as much as you can, and it will reward you with fruits of divinity and bliss. It will reward you with love, and you will become a source of love. You will shower it on others and see the profundity and depth in your actions.

The Mechanisms of Influence: The Aspects That Brainwash Any Unaware Person.

"You need to know this."

There are forces acting on your mind every single day—quiet, invisible, and powerful. Most people walk through life unaware of them, and that is exactly why they are so easily influenced, persuaded, and sometimes outright manipulated.

To protect yourself, remember this acronym:

AAALCCSSR

- **Automatic Response**
- **Authority**
- **Association**
- **Liking**
- **Contrast**
- **Consistency**
- **Similarity**
- **Social Proof**

- **Reciprocity**

These nine levers of influence—what Robert Cialdini famously calls the *"Weapons of Influence"*—are the psychological handles through which compliance is extracted. Once you begin to see how they work, you'll start noticing them everywhere: in sales calls, political speeches, social interactions, religious groups, relationships, and even subtle family dynamics.

Most people don't need to master all nine. Many become exceptionally good at just one—like projecting authority, or creating instant liking—and that alone becomes enough to shape another person's decisions.

At the heart of it, influence is the art of achieving a *"yes."*
A yes to a purchase.
A yes to a request.
A yes to someone's worldview, ideology, or leadership.

Let's break these down—not just as theories, but as psychological mechanisms that run your life if you're unaware.

Automatic Response: The Mindless Yes

The human brain is fast, lazy, and economical. It is designed to save energy, and therefore, it automates as much as possible. This is useful for survival, but dangerous in a world where others understand these reflexes better than you do.

Automatic responses work like hidden switches. Certain cues trigger certain behaviors without conscious thought.

Think of how you choose a café.

You don't analyze systematically. Instead, you respond to cues:

- the warmth of the lighting
- the friendliness of the waiter
- the familiarity of the cups
- the background music

One cue feels slightly better than another—and your brain says yes.

Marketers intentionally design this automation. They know that if they can trigger a familiar emotional cue—comfort, nostalgia, excitement—you'll follow through with a purchase while thinking you made the decision freely.

This mechanism gives birth to another powerful trigger: **scarcity**.

Scarcity: The Illusion of Urgency

"Limited edition."
"Only 2 left in stock."
"Last 24 hours of sale."

You have seen these a thousand times. They work because scarcity links directly to our survival instincts. What is scarce feels valuable, even if it isn't.

When a product becomes "rare," your mind inflates its worth automatically. Scarcity pressures the automatic response system, not the logical one. It creates a fear: *"If I don't act now, I lose."* And humans hate losing more than they love winning.

Cialdini didn't theorize this from a distance—he infiltrated sales floors and marketing departments to observe

how people are manipulated on a daily basis. His conclusion?
We are far easier to fool than we think.

Association: Becoming Valuable by Proximity

Humans are symbolic creatures. We don't just see people for who they are—we see what they are connected to.

Marketers understand this deeply:

- If you admire a celebrity, their endorsement transfers positive qualities onto the product.
- If a friend tells you about a service, their trust rubs off onto it.
- If someone aligns themselves with a respected idea or institution, they automatically seem more credible.

Association hijacks your judgment.

Have you noticed how often companies ask for referrals?
They want your *identity* to become their marketing tool.

Even on a personal level, adults often use association for subtle influence:

- Mentioning shared values
- Aligning with your interests
- Referring to mutual friends
- Signaling that they are "like you"

Sometimes it's innocent.
Often, it's calculated.

Reciprocity: The Debt You Never Asked For

This is one of the most powerful weapons ever discovered.

When someone does something for you—no matter how small—your body sends a message:

"You owe them."

Even if you never asked for the favor.
Even if the gesture meant nothing to them.
Even if the intention behind it was manipulation.

Salespeople use this constantly:

- A free sample
- A complimentary consultation
- A small "gift"
- A discount "just for you"

These gestures create a psychological imbalance. And most people cannot tolerate the discomfort of not giving back—so they comply.

Politicians use it.
Corporations use it.
People in everyday life use it.
Often with full awareness.

When someone gives, observe their intention. Benevolence exists, but so does strategic kindness.

Understanding These Mechanisms Is Self-Defense

Influence is not inherently evil. It can be used ethically —to inspire, guide, or help. But when left unchecked and undetected, it becomes a tool for exploitation.

Once you understand the mechanisms behind persuasion, something remarkable happens:
the spell begins to break.

You pause before saying yes.
You question your impulses.
You recognize when a person is using one of the nine levers on you—softly or aggressively.

Awareness is the only real antidote. If there is one truth worth remembering, it is this:

You are most influenceable when you are unaware of the influence.

The world will always attempt to shape you—your beliefs, your choices, your desires. Influence is not something you eliminate; it is something you learn to navigate consciously.

The more you notice these nine mechanisms, the more power you reclaim over your mind. You begin making choices from clarity, not compulsion. You stop being manipulated by scarcity, swayed by authority, or guilt-trapped by reciprocity. You become a person who says yes when you mean yes, and no when you mean no.

Awareness is liberation.
Influence becomes harmless the moment you see it clearly.

And once you master this, you won't just resist manipulation —you'll begin to understand human behavior with a depth that few people ever reach.

Rhetoric and its Use to Manipulate the Truth

"Concerning what really affects the minds of the masses."

Many people fall victim to carefully crafted statements that appear truthful but are inherently manipulative. Examining the writings and speeches of great orators and leaders reveals a certain style they use to express hidden opinions and desires. This language appeals to the masses, while their personal agendas are often overlooked and accepted. This is a key concept for any philosopher trying to uncover the truth within these words, to see if any of the works are truly honest or blatant lies cleverly disguised to produce power and respect.

In fact, the statistics can be truly shocking.

One manipulative technique used by many orators and leaders is the use of rhetorical statements that appeal to emotions, tapping into hidden thoughts that the masses have but are afraid to express. This skillful manipulation of human emotions allows the writer to understand the emotional state of the masses and grasp the internal dialogue that a group of civilians is having with themselves. Ultimately, dictators, orators, and religious leaders have all used such techniques to conform to the ideals of a certain group and utilize the power of words and poetry to appeal to the emotions associated with those ideals.

Many people use such statements in their orations and writings, including political campaigns and war propaganda. Those unfamiliar with these tactics are more susceptible to falling for them, especially since these ideals are often placed amidst believable and seemingly harmless statements.

There are obviously many clever manipulative techniques that these people use, but I want to focus on one psychological aspect that can help us understand when someone is manipulating us using rhetoric. These methods are frequently used by salespeople, businesspeople, politicians, dictators, and even family members to manipulate children or partners. It's important to understand a few things about these statements.

Of course, there are certain genuinely innocent people who have no inclination towards such manipulation, and being constantly on the lookout for potential suspects is not advisable either.

Let's look at a technique based on breathing. That's right, breathing and observing the breathing mechanism of our bodies can help us understand the nature of our minds. There are three things that happen in a breath: the inhale (acceptance, intake, inward movement), where you take in something foreign from the environment you exist in and hold it for a few moments. The more you take in this environment, the more you become a part of it, the more you inhale its essence and meaning, the more open you are to being influenced.

The mind works in a similar way. Let's look at an example. Imagine that you are happy. Imagine it for a while, tell yourself that you are happy. Wouldn't you, after a while, actually start to believe in happiness? Wouldn't you really be happy? It's a kind of trick that we know works sometimes instantly, of course, it requires a little effort and power to hypnotize your own mind.

But this is exactly the kind of technique that orators use. They use certain slogans which, when repeated, will be ingrained in our minds, making us see the statements as truths even though they might mean very simple things. They might use certain statements before and after their speeches which are obviously carefully designed using a ton of other rhetorical devices to make the mind believe in certain ideals. People might even use techniques or actions in which the whole body and mind participate. Now you are fully in their grip, truly participating, and of course, participation and action strengthen beliefs and give value to such beliefs. Once you value these statements more and more, you try to see that your mind derives intense pleasure from acting according to those values and beliefs. The worst part is that the participant doesn't even know they are under a spell. Rhetoric is such a powerful tool.

So be aware of what you take in, the company you keep, and the associations you make. Make certain "self-imposed" values your top priority, or at least give high priority to your own values instead.

The Buddha always stressed the importance of understanding the nature of the mind. Once you start to be aware of certain attitudes the mind takes in certain regards, you start to see how easily malleable it is, how easily it conforms to the environment, and how easily and intensely it desires approval from those in its environment. Mimicking is how children learn, and if you are a learner and not a careful one, you are open to manipulation.

This leads us to the second part of the breath, the stable part between the inhale and the exhale, the part where you are restless, where you stop but can't wait for the exhale. Of course, this is where oxygen is turned into carbon dioxide, and where processing happens in the still, silent space where you are stuck between two actions: to inhale or to exhale, that is the question. This is where you are in a dilemma, where decisions are made, and things are digested.

So, how does the mind react to the information it has received? How does it react to the fresh new values, new perspectives, new hopes, and new expressions of their inner thoughts? Someone has said something they've thought about for years. Now, this guy, they understand him, they believe him because he and they are similar. They bond with him because he uses the same language and expresses himself in a way they could never have imagined.

You then make a decision: vote for him, go to his rally where he will speak more about the thoughts and ideals that approve your values and beliefs. This is where the job is done, and you exhale a long sigh. You act.

And always be aware of the "breath."

The Dichotomies of the Mind

"The mind creates dichotomies that cause us to suffer."

The first step on any spiritual journey, even full religious conversion, is realizing that you are not your mind. The mind is constantly playing games, and we've been blind enough to believe it is us, moving without any choice to examine its contents and its games. These games are designed to acquire certain hits, see certain things, or experience things.

My journey began with this realization: that I might not be who I take myself to be. I then delved deeper into the mind's games. It constantly craved and complained. If it wasn't doing that, it began playing these games with false dichotomies: Do I believe or not believe? Do I act or not act? Do I behave morally or immorally? Of course, at some point, the trap of dichotomy becomes so obsessive that we write whole essays on a simple decision of whether to do something or not.

So, what is the mind? Is it a constant mechanical chatter that tries to optimize one personality or the other, or does it constantly try to achieve one thing or another? How can we truly get rid of these dichotomies of decisions that seem so real to us that we have no choice but to choose? What then should we do when we find ourselves in a dichotomy?

Sales and Marketing: Masters of Manipulation

Sales and marketing people can teach us a lot about social psychology. They constantly manipulate us using different techniques that put us in a dichotomous situation. They try to trap us into choices that don't even exist and can be easily ignored in the first place. They make us believe we don't have a choice by forcing us to choose.

I was once fooled by this tactic when a friend who lived in the US asked me one day, "Do you want to talk tomorrow at 4 pm my time or 6 pm your time?" Without even considering that I had the option to not talk in the first place, I replied, "6 pm my time." So, what happened here? I realized that I was given an illusion of choice while I truly had no choice in another decision.

Contemplate on a few other sales and marketing

techniques that you might have encountered.

Transcending False Dichotomies

So, how can you really transcend these false and unproductive dichotomies?

Look at the Bigger Picture: Looking at a problem from a broader perspective can always help you understand and see different choices and options that are hidden within those apparent choices. Remember the rule: "There are no two choices. There is always a third, a fourth, and a fifth." Look for those options and then decide.

Stay Calm Under Pressure: This is something I had to cultivate over time. I have to admit that spirituality and meditation really helped me understand that being calm can make your mind make wiser decisions, even in crowded marketplaces where salespeople are using different techniques to put pressure on you. If you stay calm and know for a fact that time is an abstract concept, you can extend the decision-making process and decide on something from a calmer, wiser place. This applies not only to sales tactics but also to general life decisions. Wait, and you will see that there are usually more options, and things can be approached more wisely. Even for the abstract dichotomies that the mind lays upon you, there is always time to make your decision. There is no hurry, even in religious or spiritual matters.

Trust: Trust fate. Once a decision is made, trust in a higher power and understand that what is done is done. It is better to trust in the universe and the judgment your mind makes. After all, remember that you are something transcendent, something beyond nature. You are what, in Tantric terms, is called "Bhairava" or "Shiva," the eternal divine consciousness that transcends all things observable, even your mind.

Seek Help: Remember to identify false dichotomies and understand that when you are in conflict, you can seek an opinion from someone else to gain more options and choices, instead of trapping yourself in a dichotomous situation.

How to Not Take Offense at All

Once you recognize that being offended is a natural fight-or-flight mechanism, it makes sense that it arises when your identity or some aspect of it feels threatened. However, taking offense isn't bad; it's the reactive response that can be problematic. Reacting offensively often leads to bad decisions and arguments. So, let's delve deeper into what happens when we take offense.

The Dichotomy of Flight and Fight

First, we need to understand the natural fight-or-flight response and our inherent bias towards one of these reactions. We all have a tendency to react to situations head-on or by escaping them.

These tendencies depend on conditioning patterns and past experiences. If you've found that fighting has solved problems in the past, that will be your natural inclination. Conversely, if escaping situations has proven valuable, that will be your go-to response. We've all encountered people who tend to gossip or avoid direct confrontation. This might be us too in certain situations. Regardless of judgments, it's best to recognize these natural tendencies and patterns. Certain situations or influences can trigger these different mechanisms. For example, a usually quiet person can become violent under the influence of alcohol. Observing others' reactions in stressful situations can also help us understand normal human responses. A normally confrontational person might have avoided a fight altogether by simply ignoring the provocation.

The first step is to identify your own tendencies. You can escape a situation and still be offensive by gossiping or complaining behind someone's back.

Go Beyond the Dichotomy

Once you recognize your tendency, look for other options. You can escape and then confront the person later, or there might even be a completely different approach. A wise person understands that transcending the natural fight-or-flight response is possible. You could allow the other person to react first and observe their behavior, or completely surprise them with an unexpected response. There are many options; experiment and see what works for you. Maybe even try (in a controlled setting) offending someone and see how they react to assess their normal behavior.

The most important realization here is that taking offense, especially if it's a verbal reaction, often stems from insecurity about a specific issue. The less insecure you are, the less likely you are to be offended. People who are close to us often know how to push our buttons, and confrontations can involve a lot of button-pushing. Sometimes, they'll target your insecurities. Don't reveal your sensitivities readily. As you grow older and more mature, you should aim to reduce your insecurities over time. Pay attention to what offends you and the things that trigger you. Try to work on them. People often see our insecurities more clearly than we do ourselves, so be open to receiving constructive criticism, even if it's delivered poorly. When someone is enraged, they are often

vulnerable and reacting unconsciously, revealing their hidden wounds.
You might be doing the same, especially with your partner.

Acting and Confrontation

If you truly want to work on yourself, remember this rule: there's always a role you choose to play in front of others, and nobody is truly their complete selves with anyone. You'll eventually realize this as relationship facades start to drop. We often vent our anger on those closest to us, whether it's our parents, partner, or siblings. It's hard to truly transcend anger, but acting or confrontation can be helpful strategies. If you're inexplicably angry at someone, try acting out the anger. You'll see that your brain can take the signal inversely and make you feel the opposite way you're acting. However, if there's a legitimate reason for your anger, confrontation might be the best course of action.

Repressed Anger vs. Releasing Anger

Repressed anger is worse than expressed anger. Unfortunately, we're often taught to suppress anger because society views it as unacceptable. This can lead to a lot of repressed anger, particularly in young men. It builds tension and creates a false sense of coping. If repression is a typical reaction, try the other way around. Try letting go and actually expressing your anger. Act it out, give it your all, and be aware of how you're reacting. See what comes up, what hidden issues are revealed. This way, you'll be able to deal with anger more effectively.

Remember, you'll never be entirely free from anger. It's not inherently bad, but it can be painful and irrational. However, as you deal with your insecurities and do the necessary self-work, you'll be able to confront anger more effectively and with a clear mind.

How to Achieve a Euphoric State Without Drugs.

"It requires discipline. Not going to lie."

Drugs or any mind-altering substance are used only when you're not content with your normal state of consciousness. When your usual state feels boring, too "normal," or sober, you might feel the need to change your environment a bit. The easiest way for some adults is to buy alcohol or any drug that can instantly and

確実に(kakutei suru - Japanese for "certainly") alter their state of consciousness.

There's a 100% chance you'll feel instantly better. You don't really have to do anything for it; you just inhale or drink, and it takes you to "another" dimension.

Obviously, there are different things we do to change our experience. Sex is also one way to induce certain feelings and give you a different kind of "high" that's obviously different from your normal state of consciousness.

So, this constant chase to escape a normal state of consciousness is what leads us to drugs in the first place. We basically want cheap ways to have fun and guaranteed ways to instantly escape into another random episode of life. Happiness needs to be guaranteed, and if it is, it works well. If it's not guaranteed, it doesn't work well or even sell.

Obviously, there are ways to be healthily happy, but for most drug users, including those who use nicotine or cannabis, healthy methods don't really induce a high that meets their expectations.Usually, healthy approaches require a lot of resilience, patience, and "work." The effects, even then, aren't "psychedelic" or mind-altering.

Now, let's understand this need to change the state of consciousness. Consciousness always wants to experience something brighter, exciting, and spiritual. It wants to feel higher emotions, compassion, and oneness, which is the highest experience it can feel. All the mentioned drugs certainly guarantee that, but things that are cheap and easily bend your mind's experience usually come at a cost. Things that are short-term and guarantee certain ecstatic feelings come at a long- term cost.

Someone who has done drugs will understand the withdrawal symptoms that follow. Someone who has been addicted to something knows the problems of recovering from addictions. The whole neural system of the brain changes due to these drugs, and everything that changes the state of normal consciousness and the way life is led is also changed. Knowingly or unknowingly, our ambitions change, our minds desire those hits, and all of our life revolves around acquiring those hits.

So, what then is the natural way? What then is a way to attain peace and tranquility of enormous proportions without the need for drugs? The whole philosophy needs to be changed. The way life is perceived needs to be changed, and things that are true and closely related to the substratum of the universe, things that are free from delusions, need to be adopted.

Philosophical or intellectual aspirations of any kind can do that. Once a person recognizes how intellectual endeavors give the mind a healthy perspective on learning and exploration, it becomes a remarkable thing. Exploration, not only in the sense of physical movement but also the mental exploration that is curiously undertaken, can start a chain of exploratory thoughts that lead to real exploration of the mind. This is more challenging and rewarding. Of course, it seems very boring at first, as is usually the case with any healthy endeavor. This must be understood regarding the universe as a rule, almost a law: things manifest at a cost and expenditure.

If you are ambitious and desire to do something great in this life, it usually requires a tremendous amount of sacrifice in the short term. But don't be too quick to lose hope because this "sacrifice" isn't really a sacrifice. The mind's ability to adapt to routines and habits is tremendous. You will be surprised at how the mind is capable of altering and becoming truly one with the routine or activity.

So, exploration of any intellectual kind is a practice that can change not only your own perspective but eventually change the way things are perceived in this world. You're able to understand things in a much broader manner. You're able to empathize and look at lives through the inner lens, a lens that is closely related to reality and the substratum of the universe. Through interconnectedness and movement, you will be able to glimpse and raise your consciousness not only through gaining knowledge but also through service and understanding how the mind works.

All spiritual activities are mind-altering activities. The prayers our ancestors used to do, the different kinds of practices like compassion and gratitude, and understanding the nature and attributes of the Universal Mind can help one attune to the natural frequency of this universe. By understanding and following these rules or invocations, you can certainly experience a mind- altering and spiritual experience.

Of course, there is a short-term cost. Purification requires constant practice. Once you start to purify yourself, you'll begin to see that life becomes simpler. You'll catch the pulse of life and stay with it until you become pure enough to blend in with the world, to raise your consciousness through these practices of meditation and contemplation. This endeavor is truly about understanding and connecting with yourself, understanding the nature of mind and looking at its varied aspects. The universe rewards these endeavors in mysterious ways. It leads anyone to understand the workings that are closely related to the subtle realm and the mental realm, which are accessible through the subtle body and the mental body. These realms are usually only accidentally and unknowingly accessed by drug users.

Purification requires a taste, and meditation does exactly that. Once a person starts to taste something of a higher nature of consciousness in meditative states (which happen rarely for those beginning this endeavor), the spiritual journey begins. This journey is completely psychedelic in nature. Once you start to glimpse the reality of who you are, you'll seek this reality more and more. You'll want it so much that I've seen people leave their homes for some glimpses of it.

However, you don't need to leave home for the spiritual journey. It's not a sacrifice; it doesn't work that way. You need to stay exactly where you are and be able to listen where the universe is taking you. You need to be aware enough to catch that voice within you and follow the path (and there are many paths, of course). Once the path is seen clearly, the glimpses will begin to increase, which is a good sign. This actually leads you to higher states of being. Sometimes the signs are subtle, but instinctively the voice keeps pushing you towards perfection.

You'll see that all the bad behaviors are dropped because they only lead to an illusory fluctuation, not a real conscious fluctuation. You'll see that life becomes more natural and in tune. You'll see that wherever your heart takes you, it takes you towards the growth that's required in a certain area.

The more you indulge in these explorations, the hard work doesn't seem so hard anymore. In fact, it keeps becoming more and more interesting. Eventually, you'll figure out certain creative endeavors that you're naturally attuned to, something that you see potential in. Then it's a matter of disciplining and constantly evolving that skill. The whole process of learning can actually be very interesting, and things are usually very explorative in learning. You start to see the big picture of how things are connected, and you start to have fun at whatever it is that you're doing. Just start to enjoy and be at peace with yourself. The more you connect with the inner child's wonder, the more you see how explorative life can become even in normal states of consciousness.

You'll start to intuitively understand how you can induce certain states of consciousness, certain flow states, by doing certain creative activities or even physical exercise. These flow states will then help you evolve as consciousness to a higher and higher state of consciousness. These will lead you to exploring even more and understanding these different realms of consciousness and these different states.

Hence, there is a natural, healthy way to induce or get a "higher" state of consciousness purely through meditation, pursuit of any art or philosophical investigations, and trying to satisfy your intellectual curiosities. Obviously, the rewards are even higher as every aspect of your life is improved: mental health, financial health, relationships, and overall spiritual growth.

Everything You Need to Know About Increasing Cognitive Function.

Cognitive decline is something we all inherently dread. In a world where intelligence is valued more than anything, where being intelligent is desirable, and being alert and cognitively sharp is the most precious thing we all want, I can give you some suggestions on how to stay cognitively active and train your mind to handle effortful tasks effortlessly.

What Can Increased Cognitive Ability Do for You?

Cognitive ability is the capacity to overcome mental barriers to perform effortful activities. Cognitive tasks require more effort and expend more energy; they are slow and deliberate by nature and require concentration and focused attention.

An increase in cognitive ability means not only improving your capacity to face "effort," which is uncomfortable by nature, but also increasing your tendency to experience effort more frequently. Usually, the struggle is mostly internal when it comes to achieving and manifesting the dreams you aspire to.

The struggle is with the mind that craves comfort and does not want to improve or bear the burden of effort.

This internal battle is a constant, day-to-day

struggle that never truly stops. If you desire growth in professional, financial, physical, or any other area of life, you need to understand that growth is uncomfortable. It involves shedding a certain personality and creating a new one; it means moving forward and changing yourself.

Growth is extremely difficult, and we all know this. But if we have a longing to achieve something in this world, we must confront this uncomfortable nature and overcome it. The more we overcome the tendency to give up, the more we are able to face the next challenge and continue to grow.

The decline in cognitive ability is often marked by the mind's attempt to surrender. When you notice that your mind is trying to give up, it is a sign that your cognitive function is decreasing.

Our intuitions are quick, and we often rely on them to make decisions. While intuition is effective for quick decisions, it can become a "default state" of thinking, leading us to rely on it exclusively. However, intuition is not always reliable. Cognitive ability involves the mind's capacity to make decisions slowly and deliberately, considering all options. We must train ourselves to think this way. Intuitive thinking has its uses but is often exploited by sales and marketing professionals to make a sale. Those who do not engage their cognitive minds may end up making poor decisions in many areas of their lives. Differentiating between these modes of thinking is essential for cognitive improvement.

This process is experiential, and you can interact with your mind to understand its "default" mode. A slow thinker is often very smart because they carefully consider their decisions. We often think that someone who makes quick decisions is smart, but usually, it is the deliberate thinker who makes the right decisions. Fast thinking is intuitive, and while intuition can be developed over time, it requires a foundation of slow, deliberate thinking and good decision- making.

Hence, cognitive work and effortful thinking are essential for growing into a good decision-maker and eventually a good intuitive thinker.

For example, if you take a class on lets say Data structures and algorithms, the universities follow a structure where you learn over a few months. During this time, you engage in effortful thinking or cognitive work. When there is a test at the end of the course, it requires "intuitive thinking," based on the cognitive work you did previously. The more cognitive work you put in, the better you will perform on the test.

This principle can be applied to relationships as well. The more you invest in cognitive thinking about your relationships and decisions, the more you will find that your intuitive decisions improve. Those who frequently experience conflicts and emotional outbursts are often cognitively weak, unable to consider the consequences of their actions, and struggle with the discomfort of fast intuitive thinking. A rise in conflicted relationships can also be a sign of cognitive decline.

How Can You Actually Improve Cognitive Ability?

Cognitive decline is partly due to old age. However, spiritual endeavors can be helpful in overcoming this decline, as many spiritual activities focus on understanding the mind itself. Many psychologists who are great meditators gain insights into the mind and its workings. What I'm sharing here is "general wisdom" that people eventually realize on their own.

Successful businessmen and politicians often understand and apply techniques that boost their success.

Dictators exploit this understanding, highlighting the lack of wisdom among the masses.

So, what are the main techniques to improve cognitive ability? Cognitive ability is a practice that requires constant maintenance and engagement. You can't miss a few months and then expect to catch up. The type of work you do also affects this. If your work is cognitively challenging, you might need to understand how to unwind from constant cognitive activity. This phenomenon is known as ego depletion, marked by a significant drop in blood glucose levels. In a remarkable study, psychologists found that jurors were more likely to grant parole after meals, suggesting that cognitive functioning requires glucose. A drop in glucose can lead to frustration and even health issues. Therefore, exercising regularly and checking in with your doctor are basic practices to maintain cognitive ability.

If you're not doing challenging work, you are more likely to become cognitively slow. Both the body and mind are like muscles or containers that need continuous work. There are many practices you can adopt, such as meditation to focus your attention, solving multiplication problems, and using techniques like the ADD-3 method described byDaniel Kahneman in his book *Thinking, Fast and Slow*. For instance, if you start with a number like 5439 and repeatedly add 3 to each digit, you exercise cognitive skills like memory and calculation.

Memorizing things and performing small challenges, like remembering a grocery list or a few dictionary words, can also improve cognitive function. Avoiding alcohol, intoxication, and smoking is crucial for maintaining cognitive ability, as these substances have irreversible negative effects on the body and mind.

Exercising and challenging yourself cognitively daily can help you make better decisions and improve intuitive thinking. Remember, it's all about mindset. Practical wisdom is only useful when applied with effort and cognition.

Reading:

Thanks for reading. Reading is another important activity to keep yourself sharp. There are three things I do while reading, inspired by German psychologist Reuven Feuerstein:

Input: Understand the knowledge thoroughly. Repeat sentences, seek explanations online, and try to grasp even the technical details of a book.

Elaboration: Expand on ideas by adding your own thoughts, interrelating concepts, and creating a big picture. Explaining what you've learned to yourself can be a cognitively challenging task.

Tests: Testing yourself helps fix information in your mind. Write essays, answer questions, and review content to recognize and correct errors. You don't need a professor to do this; ask yourself questions and judge your understanding.

These are just some tools I've shared. You will discover your own tools tailored to your tastes and goals, which will be more effective because they are personal.

The Practice of Brahmacharya

The Gold Within

"Raso Vai Sa" declares a verse in the Rig Veda. It literally denotes one of the highest spoken truths mankind will ever hear. It reveals the root cause of why Adam and Eve were brought down to Earth—after they were seduced by the serpent in heaven and ate the fruit of desire, they were metaphorically brought down to this plane of Earth from the heavens where they had been enjoying everlasting bliss and spontaneity.

We, as humans, fall down to Earth in this life sometimes. And this Earth is grounded; it is real. It has its needs, it is mundane, and it is filled with never-ending desires. This Earth is suffering. We fall, where once we were in heaven —if we remember our childhood. I don't mean the things you had in childhood; I mean the *consciousness* you had when you were a child—when you were seeing the world as it was meant to be seen. You fell when you ate the fruit of desire, and kept falling again and again.

But it is not your fault. You are not to be blamed. The adults around you are to be blamed—the adults who are still in this endless battle of desire. But even they should not be blamed, because many of us do not understand eternity. Only some who have dared to continue the battle until the end have understood that fight. And they have seen that they are reaching closer and closer to eternity.

Eternity is within us. It is when we leave the short-term gratifying things in search of the eternal that we find heaven lies within. We see that all of this sacrifice of desires is worth it, even for a moment's glimpse of our eternal nature. Searching for eternity helps you step into what we in India call *brahmacharya* — a practice that endows man with supreme power, wisdom, and character that is strengthened only through this discipline.

Brahmacharya means being firmly established in "Brahman." But how will you achieve that? By believing in yourself? By reading books and scriptures? By meditation? No. By practically resolving to be in Brahman at every moment of your life—to actually identify with and act as the Brahman, as the pure consciousness that you are—and to not be deluded by *vasana*, the desires that will keep creeping up again and again throughout your life.

Your entire life is capable of transformation; you are capable of transforming your entire existence if you understand this one simple phrase: "Raso Vai Sa."

Your *veerya* is your God. Your inner sexual power can be transmuted into perfection and into *siddhis* of the body and mind. Your intellect can grow stronger only through your *veerya*. You lose it when you experience an orgasm.This is not gender-specific, and it is not only for men, because we are not merely bodies. Archetypically, every human being embodies both masculine and feminine principles. There is no man or woman in this world in an absolute sense—every human contains both, and can experience both manhood and femininity.

This practice of *brahmacharya* purifies the mind and allows it to reach a state of character where your whole body and mind radiate the supreme consciousness within you.

Without control over your veerya, you are constantly falling down from the mountain. Only those who have complete mastery and control of their *veerya* will be able to reach the epic peak of the mountain; all others will fail to climb.

To be as Brahman is to act as Brahman. To be pure consciousness is to become more conscious, and this heightened consciousness will dissolve the desires of the mind.

This short chapter, though placed at the end of part one of this book, is actually the beginning of your *practical spiritual journey*. It contains the highest truth, which everyone shall realize one day if they are sincere enough to strive to live for God and God alone.

Without going into further details, remember this: all perfection can be attained through the control of the sense organs.

Practical takeaway:

Practice brahmacharya — celibacy, purity.

Question to self:

"What talents have you lost since you lost your veerya ?"

And now yoga...

Chapter 23

The knowledge of the soul is a pivotal event in our lives when we awaken to our true nature. This true nature, which reflects our life and personality, is suddenly revealed, and we realize that we possess a transcendent aspect. In that special moment, we understand that we are not what we thought we were for most of our lives. We recognize that we were bound to a changing, conflicted mind, flitting from idea to idea, moving wherever it led us. But when we receive this knowledge of the soul, things start to become clear. We realize that we are not this impulsive, fiery mind. Once we understand that we are like clear water, the turbidness of the mind reveals itself to us. We see that this turbidness comes and goes of its own accord—it arises when we crave clarity and dissipates when we desire nothing.

This is the turbidness I am referring to, the kind embedded in our hearts and subconscious. It stems from the patterns of the subconscious, shaped by our repeated, often unnoticed habits. These habits repeat daily, yet we remain unaware of them. But one day, it hits us like a flash of insight: this is what was blocking me; this is what was causing my turbulence. If we are courageous enough, we can overcome it. The moment we become aware of it, we are on the path to overcoming it. Perhaps it's a small gesture you've held onto since high school, a recurring thought while brushing your teeth, or a habit you know you should abandon but continue anyway. These are the things you want to overcome; you inherently know that something inside you says you shouldn't indulge in them. Oddly, these are not societal impositions but rather the voice of your future self, formed every time you daydream or desire to be like someone else.

The nature of desire changes, and what you once desired is now forgotten, replaced by new desires. Understanding this nature can free you because this is Samsara, the cycle that keeps going. Is there a way to completely transcend all desire? Is there a way to completely remove this turbidness? Is there a clarity that will instantly clear it all? And what would your life be like after attaining such a state of desirelessness? It's hard to imagine, right? Even in imagination, we never truly envision freedom; whatever we imagine binds us. What binds us creates suffering, which demands transformation. Transformation is not necessarily bad; through it, we create and free ourselves, shedding a little and moving forward. Life is like that.

In transformation, there is also clearing. When you prioritize this clearing above all else, recognizing that while outward desires have their allurements, you desire inner clearing and freedom more and more. You start to feel it and see the signs. Just as the future self-created from past desires evolves, a new future self emerges—an archetypal figure of the Superman in Nietzschean terms or the Sage in Jungian language. This future self guides and signals where change is needed, pointing out faults. If you are courageous enough, you transform and gradually find a clearing, residing more often in your soul's true nature, experiencing immense pleasure from the Buddha nature. You transcend desires and dwell in the ever-still, precious lake.

Whenever you find this clearing, grasp it even in mid-conversation, for it may be the last memory before death.

Yoga is union — the union of body, mind, and soul. It brings balance to the life of the practitioner. It balances all sides of the mental psyche as well as the physical aspects. A yogi is very balanced in life and also in their perspective on life. It brings the practitioner to a view that is more adaptable. Like everything in life, it makes one intelligent — and by intelligence, I mean adaptable to the environment. The capability of observing and applying experiential wisdom to assess the environment, the situation, and to solve problems enhances in a yoga practitioner.

The credit goes to the great Rishi Patanjali, who in his lifetime wrote extensively on Ayurveda and Yoga. His eightfold path to Samadhi (enlightenment or the highest state of consciousness) is undoubtedly a clear-cut path that gives no confusion and illuminates the way forward. The only prerequisite to approaching yoga is resilience or a strong affirmation — an intention to go through the entire path without distraction. Patanjali never talks about God. He talks about the mind, about how to remove the *kleshas* (afflictions), and about purification, but he never mentions God — neither did the Buddha. Because God is a tricky thing to talk about. God to Patanjali is the highest state of consciousness that man himself can reach, and has reached several times, in the form of the Buddhas who come, the Mahaviras, and the many saints who have attained this state of perfection and oneness.

The *Yoga Sutras* are among those texts that have been commented upon by many yogis. I myself have read several of these commentaries by Swami Vivekananda, Swami Nirjanananda, Swami Satchidananda, and so on — the list goes on and on. But this book is written by a Muslim, a Muslim who happened to find his way to Yoga and Buddhism because the talk of God had not made sense to him. A Muslim will surely relate more to Yoga because the practices in Islam are not very different. Islam, in fact, is an organized and inclusive form of Yoga. Islam includes God, and the path is one of deep surrender to God.

When a Muslim prays *namaz*, he stands obediently before God — whoever or whatever form that might be. With belief in the one who created him, he stands and keeps his eyes lowered in a posture of reverence, performing *namaz* with his body. He prostrates in a manner pleasing to God, as taught by the prophets. He sits obediently before God, reciting all the prayers and words that hail Him. In this whole process, the mind and body — both involved in *namaz* — gain a certain sense of unity, and the soul illumines. This illumination, however, is limited because it is not Yoga; it does not purify the whole body.

But if we practice Yoga in the same spirit as a Muslim prays *namaz* — with reverence to the highest consciousness there is, with attentiveness to the breath and postures, using the body to surrender to that consciousness — Yoga can take us to the highest state very quickly. It will also keep us healthy, and our minds will grow sharper. Yoga is not merely about postures. We often tend to adopt what is physically beneficial for us, but Yoga's ultimate goal is not better posture, beauty, or sharpness — though it brings all these benefits. The true goal of Yoga is to reduce the fluctuations of the mind and to sit in meditation with one-pointed concentration on the object of meditation until we dissolve in the bliss of Samadhi.

The preparatory process is what keeps many of us stuck in Yoga practice. All Yoga postures are meant to make the body strong and healthy enough to sit for long periods of meditation — to allow the *kleshas* of the mind to resolve themselves, and to help one glimpse, and eventually merge into, the ocean of bliss that is our true nature. The whole process is also a process of mind training — constantly purifying the mind and nervous system, and striving to create an environment conducive to meditation. The path of Yoga therefore concerns every aspect of life — sexual desires, ambitions, financial situations, relationships — every area has an impression upon the mind and creates memories of the past or imaginations of the future. These memories and the pathways to them are observed during meditation or contemplation.

In the previous part of this book, a brief overview was given so that you, the reader, understand the many aspects that can help you attain this higher state. Of course, the Yoga described by Patanjali leads us to something called *Savikalpa Samadhi* or cessation of thoughts. There are also different kinds of *Samadhis* prescribed by different saints. The state of *Sahaja Samadhi* is similar to what a mindful person experiences when practicing constant mindfulness throughout the day — something much sought after today, as it keeps one in this state continuously without losing it.

The point of Yoga is to access this state again and again, with more ease and control. For this to happen, one must have control over the mind.

The next part of this book concerns itself with the step-by-step guide to *asanas*, *pranayama*, and the various other techniques of Patanjali's eightfold path.

It is also important to understand that the goal is not in the future — it is here and now. We simply cannot see it because we are asleep. If we awaken, and see for the first time what Yoga can truly do for us, we will understand much about ourselves, our minds, and the universe itself.

Yoga is purely scientific in its approach. Apart from Patanjali, there have been many Yogic texts like the *Shiva Samhita* and the works of Gorakhnath. These texts, in addition to the complete system of Patanjali, are especially helpful in this age as they incorporate practices in greater detail. Nonetheless, the *Yoga Sutras* of Patanjali remain the cornerstone of all other Yoga texts.

People take from Yoga whatever they need at their stage of life — postures for strengthening the body, purification techniques for cleansing the system — but Yoga is a complete process. The more one stays in the process, the more one evolves into higher states of consciousness. It supports mindfulness practice throughout the day and keeps the mind in a state of *sattvic* balance.

If one cannot maintain mindfulness, the purification practices and simple *asanas* can help clear the *pranic* blockages in the body and mind, allowing energy to flow and sustain mindfulness through the day. The more we are awake and mindful in our daily lives, the more control we have over the mind during meditation.

It often happens that meditation becomes ritualistic, while the rest of the day is spent in unawareness — this does not bring real progress. The point of Yoga, meditation, and contemplation is to remember that you are consciousness itself. Even if you meditate for an hour but forget awareness throughout the day, it leads to little improvement.

Of course, it requires energy and mental control to remain mindful every moment, day and night. Yoga's processes help build that energy and strengthen both body and mind to attain the state of *Sahaja Samadhi*. Many people may reach this state without yogic practice — there are many paths to the goal — but eventually, every path converges here. The eightfold path of Yoga is the most precise and procedural method, showing progress in all areas of life. It leads to balance and ever-growing intelligence.

There are many delusional paths too, and though some people may have attained high states of consciousness through them, a true yogi is never delusional. A yogi is clear and performs daily duties without losing touch with the outer world.

Clarity improvement is a sign of progress in a yogis mind, when clarity dawns your mind, when everything you see is clear and shining your consciousness is optimal, and you are seeing things as they are.

And there is no other way to improve clarity than the purification practises that are taught by the yogis ,some of which are mentioned below, all asanas improve the strength of your nervous system and if practiced regularly can cure internal diseases and blockages in your system,.Practices are now mentioned below, practise which aim to bring light upon the chakras in your body and practices that are available in every Yogi's toolset ,this practice will give you a system of living that is the best way to live life,It enhances all aspects of your life equally and gets you closer and closer to perfection.

Chapter 24

The Science of Inner Fire

Why the Fire Is Within

Yoga begins as a whisper in the human heart: a quiet remembrance that the mind is not the master, but a doorway. In the silence between breaths, a soft flame burns — subtle, alive, patient. This flame is not symbolic; it is the same fire that sustains the cosmos, now coiled within the spine of a single human being.

The sages called it *Agni*, the sacred fire, and they saw in it both life and awareness. Every practice of *Haṭha Yoga*, every breath drawn in *prāṇāyāma*, and every gesture of *mudrā* is an offering to this inner fire.

The ancient texts do not treat yoga as philosophy alone. The *Śiva Saṁhitā* calls the body *a city of ten gates*, through which the soul experiences the world and, through discipline, may re-enter the center of its own being. The *Haṭha Yoga Pradīpikā* declares that the purpose of all physical and breath practices is to awaken the sleeping energy — *kuṇḍalinī śakti* — and guide it upward through the central channel, *suṣumṇā nāḍī*.

But before that ascent, the practitioner must learn the language of energy. To light the inner fire without understanding its nature is to play with lightning in the rain.

The Principle of Prāṇa

Everything that lives, moves, and transforms is animated by *prāṇa*, the universal current of life. It is not mere oxygen, nor a concept of vitality, but the intelligent motion that bridges the body and the mind. The *Śiva Saṁhitā* says, "As long as *prāṇa* dwells in the body, there is life. When it departs, life ends."

The sages divided *prāṇa* into five major expressions — *prāṇa*, *apāna*, *samāna*, *udāna*, and *vyāna* — each governing a distinct movement of energy.

Prāṇa-vāyu moves upward from the heart to the throat, fueling inspiration, enthusiasm, and the intake of air and impressions.

Apāna-vāyu moves downward from the navel to the perineum, responsible for elimination, grounding, and release.

Samāna-vāyu resides at the navel, harmonizing the upward and downward currents, digesting both food and experience.

Udāna-vāyu rises from the throat to the head, expressing speech, will, and subtle perception.

Vyāna-vāyu permeates the whole body, maintaining cohesion, circulation, and balance.

When these five currents move in harmony, the mind becomes luminous and steady. When they conflict, the mind fragments into tension, desire, and fatigue. Haṭha Yoga begins by restoring the original rhythm of *prāṇa*, so that awareness can expand without resistance.

To work with *prāṇa* is not to force it but

to listen. One cannot command the wind; one aligns with its direction. Through breath awareness, postural stillness, and disciplined living, the practitioner becomes sensitive to the interior climate.

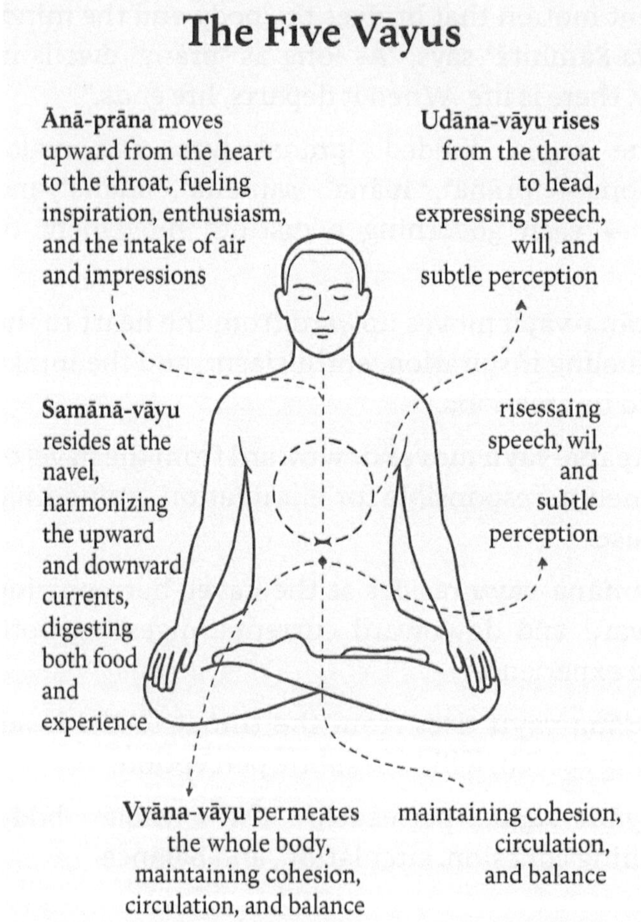

The Network of Nāḍīs

The body of energy is woven through with channels known as *nāḍīs*. The *Śiva Saṁhitā* and *Haṭha Yoga Pradīpikā* agree that there are seventy-two thousand of them, though only three hold primary importance: *iḍā*, *piṅgalā*, and *suṣumṇā*.

Iḍā nāḍī, beginning at the left of the spine and flowing to the left nostril, is lunar in nature — cooling, reflective, and connected with the parasympathetic rhythm.

Piṅgalā nāḍi, starting on the right, is solar — warming, active, and stimulating.

Suṣumṇā nāḍi, the central channel, runs through the spinal axis, connecting the base of the spine (*mūlādhāra*) to the crown of the head (*sahasrāra*).

The Three Nādis

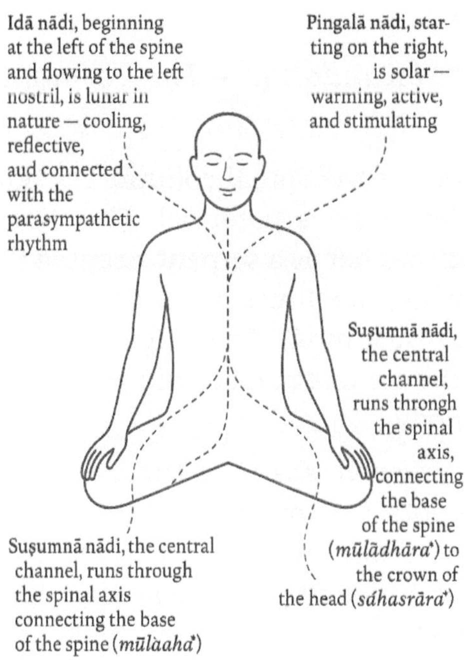

The two side channels weave around the central column like serpents, crossing at six primary junctions that correspond to the *cakras*. These crossings create the pulsations of duality — day and night, inhale and exhale, logic and intuition. When *iḍā* and *piṅgalā* are balanced through *prāṇāyāma* and ethical discipline, *suṣumṇā* awakens, and the current begins to rise.

In the language of the *Śiva Saṁhitā*, "When the breath flows equally in both nostrils, the mind becomes steady, and the path of the middle opens."

Balancing these channels is the preparatory work of *Haṭha Yoga*. Without this balance, higher practices are like pouring pure ghee into a wet log — the fire sputters and dies.

Śakti and Kuṇḍalinī — The Dormant Power

At the root of the spinal column lies *kuṇḍalinī śakti*, the coiled creative potential. The *Haṭha Yoga Pradīpikā* describes her as a serpent sleeping three and a half times around the *liṅga* at the base, blocking the entrance to the *suṣumṇā*. The language is symbolic: *kuṇḍalinī* is the contraction of infinite consciousness into the finite body.

When awakened, she rises through the centers, piercing the knots (*granthis*) that bind perception to material, emotional, and intellectual identifications. This ascent is not violent; it is the gradual ignition of higher awareness.

Each *cakra* she passes through is a mirror of the universe: the survival instinct transforms into creativity, desire into purpose, emotion into devotion, intellect into silence. To awaken *kuṇḍalinī* safely, the practitioner must refine the instrument — body, breath, and mind — until they vibrate at the same frequency as her awakening.

The fire imagery of yoga points not to destruction but to purification. Fire removes the dross from gold. Likewise, disciplined practice burns inertia (*tamas*), restlessness (*rajas*), and ignorance (*avidyā*), revealing the still radiance of consciousness itself.

Balancing the Solar and Lunar Currents

Before attempting to raise energy upward, the two poles of the vital system must be harmonized. This is the science of *Haṭha*, literally "sun and moon."

Haṭha Yoga Pradīpikā explains:

"When the breath moves through *iḍā*, the body becomes cool; when through *piṅgalā*, it heats. When both flow equally, balance arises, and *suṣumṇā* becomes active."

The simplest and most direct way to regulate these flows is through alternate-nostril breathing, or **nāḍī-śuddhi prāṇāyāma**.

Basic Practice — Nāḍī Śuddhi

1. Sit in a steady posture, the spine erect, the face relaxed.
2. With the right hand in *viṣṇu-mudrā*, close the right

nostril with the thumb and inhale through the left for a slow, measured count.

3. Close both nostrils; hold the breath briefly in stillness.

4. Open the right nostril and exhale smoothly.

5. Inhale through the right, hold, and exhale through the left.

6. This completes one round. Begin with 6–12 rounds daily.

The purpose is not retention but rhythm. Each inhalation feeds the lunar current, each exhalation feeds the solar. Over weeks, the practitioner begins to feel subtle shifts: a clearer mind, steadier mood, and a faint warmth in the spine.

Advanced versions introduce *kumbhaka* (breath retention) and ratio, but the beginner's aim is simply to equalize. The scriptures insist that only when the currents are balanced can *suṣumṇā* open and meditation deepen.

Basic Practice – Nâdî Suddhi

1 Sit in a steady posture, the spine erect, the face relaxed.

2 With the right hand in viṣnu-mudrâ, close the right nostril with the thumb and inhale through the left for a slow, measured count

3 Close both nostrils; hold the breath briefly in stillness

4 Open the right nostril and exhale smoothly

5 Inhale through the right, hold, and exhale through the left.

6 This completes one round. Begin with 6-12 rounds daily.

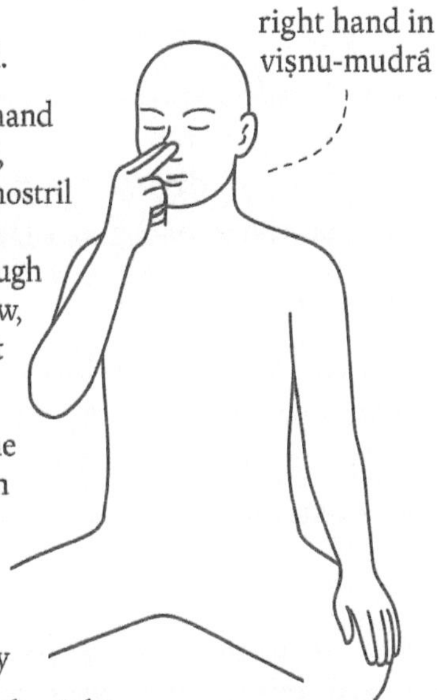

Preparation for Practice

To step onto this path is to adopt a certain way of living — not moral dogma, but sensitivity. The body is the first altar; the breath, the first mantra.

1. Environment

Practice in a quiet, clean place with fresh air. Early morning, before sunrise, is ideal — the atmosphere carries stillness, and both *iḍā* and *piṅgalā* naturally balance.

2. Diet

Choose foods that lighten rather than dull the usesenses: fresh fruits, vegetables, grains, and clean water. Avoid heavy, fermented, or intoxicating substances. The fire of digestion mirrors the fire of awareness; if one is disturbed, the other dims.

3. Discipline of Time

The body learns through repetition. Fix a regular hour for practice, even if only thirty minutes. The *Śiva Saṁhitā* says, "As a stream shapes the rock, so daily practice shapes destiny."

4. Attitude

Do not practice to achieve an experience. Practice to become more conscious of what is already moving within you. The true miracle of yoga is not ecstasy, but steadiness.

5. Rest and Observation

After each session, rest in *śavāsana*. Let the energy redistribute. Keep a small journal: note changes in breath, dreams, digestion, and temperament. These are signs of the body adjusting to higher voltage.

Purification and the Six Acts (Ṣaṭkarma)

The classical yogic view begins with a clear premise: a disturbed body cannot host a quiet mind. The *Haṭha Yoga Pradīpikā* opens its second chapter by prescribing six cleansing acts—*ṣaṭkarma*—to clear the channels of *prāṇa* before advanced practice. These methods are not religious rituals but physiological tuning mechanisms designed to free the nervous and glandular systems from habitual obstruction.

1. **Dhauti** — Internal Cleansing*

Gentle stomach cleansing, using water or controlled swallowing, tones the digestive tract and neutralizes excess mucus. For the modern practitioner, the spirit of *dhauti* may be expressed through fasting, mindful eating, and conscious hydration. The essential principle is to maintain a digestive field free of stagnation so that *samāna vāyu*—the harmonizing current—functions without strain.

2. **Basti** — Yogic Enema

In classical texts this refers to cleansing the colon with water while seated in a squatting posture. Its modern parallel is simple intestinal hygiene and the cultivation of elimination at regular hours. Clean intestines reflect a clean mind; irregular elimination subtly agitates *apāna vāyu* and anchors attention in discomfort.

3. **Neti** — Nasal Purification

Saline cleansing of the nasal passages, performed gently, purifies the airways and the subtle link between breath and thought. When the nostrils are clear, the alternation of *iḍā* and *piṅgalā* flows becomes perceptible.

4. **Trāṭaka** — Steady Gaze

Though placed among cleansing acts, *trāṭaka* is a bridge to concentration. Gazing at a single point stabilizes the optic nerve and steadies the oscillations of the frontal brain. In time, it purifies vision itself—the habit of looking outward without seeing.

5. **Naulī** — Abdominal Churning

Circular rotation of the abdominal muscles massages the internal organs and strengthens *manipūra cakra*, the seat of personal will. Its true effect is psychic digestion: the ability to assimilate experience without residue.

6. **Kapālabhāti** — Cleansing the Frontal Lobe

Rapid, rhythmic exhalations expel stale air and stimulate cerebral circulation. The term literally means "shining skull"; when done correctly it brightens perception and prepares the brain for *kumbhaka* (breath retention).

The *ṣaṭkarma* are not ends in themselves. Their value lies in clearing the instrument so subtler forces can be sensed. To adopt even one or two of these practices with care and consistency refines the field in which higher yoga unfolds.

Foundational Āsanas

After purification, the body must be trained to remain motionless without tension. The *Śiva Saṁhitā* teaches that the posture should be "firm and pleasant." Stability without rigidity is the mark of readiness.

The Haṭha Yoga Pradīpikā lists fifteen principal postures; four are essential for meditation:

1. **Siddhāsana** — The Accomplished Seat

The heel presses the perineum, creating a mild *mūla bandha* naturally. It unites the base and the crown through the central line of the spine.

2. **Padmāsana** — The Lotus Posture

Symmetrical and grounded, it balances *iḍā* and *piṅgalā* instantly. When the spine aligns effortlessly, breath and thought follow suit.

3.**Svastikāsana** and **Sukhāsana** — Simple Cross-Legged Seats

For those with less flexibility, these maintain the same intention—spinal verticality and open chest—without strain.

4. Śavāsana — The Corpse Pose

Not merely rest, but a rehearsal for surrender. Conscious relaxation resets the nervous system and dissolves compulsive control.

Each posture is a conversation between gravity and awareness. The earth pulls downward, consciousness lifts upward; equilibrium between the two produces stillness.

Regular practice of a few postures—held long enough for breathing to become fine and effortless—builds the physical resilience needed for internal work. Flexibility is not the goal; neutrality is.

Bandha and Mudrā — Lock and Seal

When posture becomes steady, the practitioner learns to redirect energy through specific muscular and neural locks called *bandha*. The purpose is to prevent *prāṇa* from dissipating and to encourage its ascent through *suṣumṇā*.

1. **Mūla Bandha** — Root Lock

Gentle contraction of the perineal muscles draws *apāna vāyu* upward. This act transforms the descending current into ascending force. It is the first step in reversing the ordinary expenditure of life energy.

2. **Uḍḍīyāna Bandha** — Abdominal Lift

Performed after exhalation, it creates a vacuum that draws energy toward the heart. Physiologically it massages the diaphragm; psychically it teaches uplift without tension.

3. **Jālandhara Bandha** — Throat Lock

The chin rests near the chest, regulating pressure between head and heart. It guards the brain during breath retention and turns awareness inward.

Together these form *Mahābandha*, the "great lock." The *Haṭha Yoga Pradīpikā* notes that their coordinated use stills the fluctuations of *prāṇa* and mind simultaneously.

Mudrā, literally "seal," extends the same logic to the entire psycho-energetic system. *Mahāmudrā*, *Mahāvedha*, and *Khecarī* are advanced expressions, uniting all three *bandhas* with mental focus. Their real function is symbolic integration—the sealing of body, breath, and awareness into a single field.

The Science of Prāṇāyāma

When the channels are clean and the posture firm, the next step is conscious regulation of breath. The term *prāṇāyāma* joins *prāṇa* (vital energy) with *āyāma* (expansion). It is not breath-holding; it is the measured expansion of life's rhythm until it mirrors the stillness of the spirit.

Purpose

1. To balance *iḍā* and *piṅgalā*, enabling the flow of *suṣumṇā*.
2. To steady the autonomic nervous system, reducing physiological noise.
3. To make the mind transparent, capable of sustained attention.

The Śiva Saṁhitā advises beginning only after the body feels light and the appetite moderate. Breath control performed on a gross foundation leads to disturbance rather than clarity.

Stages of Practice

1. Awareness of Natural Breath

Simply observe inhalation and exhalation at the nostrils. Note which side is dominant; note the pauses. Observation itself begins purification.

2. Equalized Breathing Sama Vṛtti

Inhale and exhale for the same count. This smooths the wave pattern of *prāṇa* and teaches evenness of temperament.

3. Alternate-Nostril Breathing Nāḍī Śuddhi

Already introduced earlier, this remains the central method for balancing solar and lunar flows.

4. Retention (Kumbhaka)

Introduced only after months of smooth breathing, *kumbhaka* stabilizes consciousness between the polarities of in- and out-breath. In that pause, *prāṇa* and *manas* rest upon each other.

5. Extension and Subtle Breath

Eventually the breath becomes so refined that physical movement ceases; awareness breathes itself. This is called *kevala kumbhaka*, spontaneous suspension.

Precautions

* Never strain or force ratio.

* Practise on an empty stomach and calm mind.

* If warmth in the spine or dizziness arises, return to natural breathing.

Consistent prāṇāyāma generates internal heat (*tāpa*). This is the "fire" that the title of this chapter refers to—not a physical burning, but the subtle combustion of inertia into clarity. The practitioner learns to sustain this fire without exhaustion, transforming metabolic energy into luminosity of awareness.

A Daily Sādhana Framework

A practical framework integrates the above methods into a single, digestible routine. The aim is regularity, not intensity. The following sequence synthesizes classical principles for a 60- to 90-minute morning practice:

1. Quiet Arrival 2 hours before Sun rise (5 min)

   Sit, establish intention, allow breathing to settle.

2. Neti and Kapalabhāti (5 – 10 min)

   Clear nasal passages; perform gentle rounds of 30–60 exhalations.

3. Foundational Āsanas (20 min)

   Choose 3–5 postures emphasizing spinal verticality. Remain in each until breathing slows naturally.

4. Bandha Practice (10 min)

   Light *mūla bandha* on exhale; brief *uḍḍīyāna* after exhale; maintain *jālandhara* during retention.

Integrate awareness of all three as comfort allows.

5. Prāṇāyāma (20 – 30 min)

Begin with 12 rounds of *nāḍī śuddhi* at equal ratio. With time, introduce gentle retention.

6. Meditative Stillness (10 – 15 min)

After breathing, remain seated, eyes closed, observing the after-currents of *prāṇa*. Awareness may rest at *ājñā cakra* or the heart center.

7. Śavāsana (5 min)

Lie supine, releasing effort completely. Let the residual warmth spread through the limbs.

This routine is not rigid; it is a template. The spirit of haṭha lies in constancy and self-study. Adapt timing to health and circumstance, but never omit the beginning and end: arrival and stillness.

The Silent Evidence

Every technique in yoga is an instrument of inquiry. *Haṭha Yoga* is often described as the "ladder to Rāja Yoga," but it is also a mirror held to life itself. The postures reveal our habitual resistance; the breath reveals our concealed fears; the locks and seals show where energy leaks through distraction.

Philosophically, these observations rest upon a single principle from the *Śiva Saṁhitā*:

"As is the microcosm, so is the macrocosm; as is the breath, so is the movement of worlds."

When the individual rhythm becomes aligned with the universal rhythm, action and stillness merge.

This is the hidden aim of the science of inner fire—to harmonize the metabolic, emotional, and mental fires into one clear flame.

Practitioners often ask when results will appear. The answer is paradoxical: transformation begins the moment observation becomes consistent. The outer signs—flexibility, calmness, wakefulness—are reflections of an inner re-ordering already in motion.

The *Haṭha Yoga Pradīpikā* closes its section on *prāṇāyāma* with the statement, "When the breath is unsteady, the mind is unsteady. When the breath is steady, the mind is steady, and the yogī attains stillness." The text does not speak of visions or powers, only steadiness. That is the measure of the inner fire: a quiet, unwavering awareness burning through the noise of time.

Summary of Principles

1. Purify before intensifying.
2. Stabilize posture before controlling breath.
3. Balance the solar and lunar flows before awakening the central channel.
4. Observe effects; never rush process.
5. Let warmth arise, not heat; clarity, not excitement.

Closing Thought

Fire is both creative and destructive. The difference lies in the vessel that contains it. *Haṭha Yoga* fashions that vessel out of muscle, nerve, breath, and awareness so that the same power which ages the body can illuminate the mind. In disciplined hands, the flame becomes a lamp, not a blaze.

Chapter 25

The Body as Temple

"The Sacred Architecture of Flesh"

The ancient masters never saw the body as an obstacle to spiritual life. They saw it as the temple where the Infinite hides in plain sight. Every cell, every nerve, every quiet rhythm of the heart is a stone laid in that invisible architecture. The human frame was designed to host awareness. When neglected, it becomes a cage; when refined, it becomes a shrine.

The *Haṭha Yoga Pradīpikā* opens its discussion of āsana by declaring that the first step toward higher consciousness is to steady the body. The *Śiva Saṁhitā* goes further, stating that through the body one gains the knowledge of the cosmos. Matter itself is consciousness in condensed form, and when treated with reverence it reveals its original luminosity.

To call the body a temple is not a metaphor of devotion only; it is a scientific statement of interdependence. The temple of yoga is built from three materials—*anna* (the food-born body), *prāṇa* (the vital movement), and *citta* (the luminous mind). When these three align, spirit becomes tangible.

Why the Physical Disciplines Matter

Modern seekers often wish to leap straight into meditation, bypassing the humbler tasks of posture, diet, and cleansing. But the fire of attention cannot remain steady in a vessel that leaks. Without a purified nervous system and regulated breath, awareness scatters. The ancients insisted on bodily discipline not from obsession with health but from experiential necessity. They understood that consciousness expresses itself through the medium of physiology; if the instrument is discordant, the melody of awareness is distorted.

The āsanas strengthen the spine—the central mast of perception. Balanced muscles free the nerves; open joints free the currents of *prāṇa*. A tranquil stomach produces a tranquil brain; this is not poetry but biochemistry. The cleansing rites and moderation of diet remove the constant background noise of metabolic struggle. In that silence, subtler intuitions appear spontaneously.

The *Haṭha Yoga Pradīpikā* calls āsana the "first limb of haṭha." It is said that without mastery of posture, the practice of breath and concentration cannot be sustained. The same law applies in life: when the body wavers, the mind follows. Stability of form generates stability of perception.

The Body as Field of Awareness

The *Śiva Saṁhitā* teaches that within the body exists a miniature universe—a web of rivers, suns, and winds. The skeletal structure forms its mountains, the bloodstream its tides, the breath its wind, the heart its sun. Every sensation, pleasant or painful, is a message from that inner landscape. When we treat the body merely as an object to be shaped or decorated, we lose its sacred vocabulary.

Yoga reverses that forgetfulness. Each posture becomes a verse of scripture written in muscle and bone. When we stand in balance, we are literally reading the text of creation through our own alignment.

To feel the body deeply is to discover that awareness is not confined to the head. It pervades the entire organism. The feet perceive the earth, the spine perceives the sky, the skin perceives the air. When these perceptions harmonize, an inner resonance arises—a hum that the yogins call *nāda*, the sound of the subtle body alive.

Āsana — The Still Form

The scriptures list many postures, yet their aim is singular: to cultivate steadiness and ease. The still form of the body is the crucible in which restlessness burns away. The practitioner learns that motionlessness is not deadness but equilibrium.

When one holds a posture without strain, observing breath and sensation, the duality between mover and moved dissolves. This is meditation through the body itself. The geometry of āsana trains the brain to dwell in symmetry; the longer one abides in that symmetry, the clearer the mirror of mind becomes.

Philosophically, āsana demonstrates a profound law: consciousness shapes matter, and matter in turn refines consciousness. Every deliberate alignment of limb and spine is a declaration that spirit is choosing order over chaos.

Cleansing and Moderation

The *ṣaṭkarma* practices described earlier are the first purification of the temple. Equally important is the daily discipline of moderation—eating only what nourishes, sleeping only what restores, speaking only what uplifts. These simple acts maintain the temple's purity far more effectively than occasional austerities.

Moderation (*mitāhāra*) is repeatedly praised in the *Haṭha*

Yoga Pradīpikā. Excess of any kind—food, speech, emotion, even austerity itself—creates turbulence in *prāṇa*. The middle path is not compromise; it is precision. The balanced flame gives light, the excessive flame consumes its own wick.

Cleansing and moderation also possess a psychological meaning. They train the mind to recognize sufficiency. In a world driven by accumulation, the yogic act of "enough" is revolutionary. Each time we eat with awareness or rest without guilt, we reaffirm that inner freedom does not depend on indulgence.

Bandha and Mudrā — The Sealing of Energy

The locks and gestures of yoga are subtle reminders that energy must circulate in harmony, not dissipate aimlessly. Philosophically, *bandha* represents containment —the recognition that power without direction becomes chaos. By symbolically drawing the vital forces upward, the practitioner rehearses the inward return of consciousness toward its source.

Mudrā means "seal." To seal energy is to close the circuit between body, breath, and awareness. In ethical life, this corresponds to integrity—the refusal to let intention and action drift apart. Every time the practitioner aligns inner feeling with outer gesture, a mudrā is formed in spirit if not in muscle.

Prāṇa and the Architecture of Vital Energy

The human being is an electrical organism. Every heartbeat, every neural impulse, every thought is a movement of current. *Prāṇāyāma* refines that current by introducing rhythm and pause into the involuntary. It is the art of teaching nature to breathe consciously through us.

The importance of this cannot be overstated. Breath is the hinge between the visible and the invisible. If it remains mechanical, awareness remains mechanical; when it becomes mindful, awareness awakens. A few minutes of measured breathing can reverse hours of mental agitation because the nervous system listens more quickly to breath than to reason.

When practiced with patience and respect, the regulation of breath becomes self-therapy. It equalizes the two hemispheres of the brain, calms hormonal tides, and opens the door to intuitive understanding. Thus the physical act of breathing becomes a direct philosophical statement: that life can be guided without coercion, that control is best exercised through harmony.

Ethics of the Body

To treat the body as a temple implies reverence in every contact—food, sexuality, labor, rest. The *Śiva Saṁhitā* hints that the very same forces that create bondage, when honored consciously, become liberation. Therefore, bodily ethics is not suppression; it is sacred economy. We do not waste the currents of life on compulsion or neglect.

This reverence extends to others. The yogin who perceives the body as a shrine begins to see every being as a shrine. Violence, exploitation, and indifference lose their ground. What begins as self-discipline ripens into compassion; what begins as cleanliness ripens into transparency of heart.

Discipline and the Gradual Ascent

The temple of the body is constructed slowly. No genuine transformation is sudden. Even the burning of impurities follows the laws of physics—heat must be applied steadily. The *Haṭha Yoga Pradīpikā* cautions that overexertion is as harmful as laziness. The yogic way is not heroic strain but constant presence.

Each day's practice is a small offering to the inner altar. Some days the flame leaps high; others it merely glows. The wise practitioner learns to honor both, understanding that continuity itself is the highest austerity. The fruit of such steadiness is not performance but insight—the quiet recognition that every movement, from blinking to breathing, can serve awakening if done with awareness.

A Framework for Daily Practice

A stable rhythm sanctifies the temple. Morning remains the best time for most seekers, when the mind is least cluttered. Create an order that the body recognizes as sacred repetition: a few minutes of stillness, gentle movement, observation of breath, silent sitting. Keep the same corner of the room, the same mat, the same prayer of intention. This constancy weaves the ordinary into the extraordinary.

No external schedule can replace sensitivity. Illness, fatigue, or emotional turbulence are signals to simplify. True discipline listens; it does not impose. The measure of progress is not duration or complexity but the clarity that follows practice. If the rest of the day carries a fragrance of balance, the temple is being well kept.

Reflections — The Body as Philosopher

The disciplined body becomes its own teacher. It reveals directly the truths that philosophy only describes. When digestion improves, one understands interdependence; when breath steadies, one experiences impermanence; when posture aligns, one feels the union of heaven and earth. These are not metaphors but embodied insights.

The body, long scorned as base, turns out to be the philosopher itself—a silent sage that has been teaching since birth through the language of sensation. Pain warns of imbalance, pleasure hints at harmony, fatigue counsels rest. Yoga trains us to interpret these teachings correctly, neither clinging to comfort nor fearing discomfort.

To keep the body pure, strong, and serene is an ethical act as well as a spiritual one. In the temple of yoga there is no separation between hygiene and holiness, anatomy and revelation. Every heartbeat recites the mantra of existence; every exhalation is a brief surrender to eternity.

Closing Thought

The practices of haṭha are not minor preliminaries; they are the pillars on which higher perception rests. Without them, meditation floats in abstraction. Through them, the infinite learns to stand upright in human form. The body, properly understood, is not an obstacle to transcendence but the very doorway through which transcendence enters the world.This has been the theme of the book throughout.

To neglect it is to leave the temple dark and unvisited. To honor it through daily discipline is to keep the flame alive, so that when consciousness awakens fully, it finds its home already prepared.

Chapter 26

The Breath as Bridge

"Between Two Worlds"

Every life begins with an inhale and ends with an exhale.

Between those two tides, everything we call *experience* takes place. The ancients saw in this rhythm the most immediate expression of the cosmic pulse. The body and the mind may seem separate, but they move to the same metronome of breath.

When the breath is hurried, the mind becomes fractured; when the breath is steady, thought becomes lucid. This is not mysticism but intimate physiology. The diaphragm is the lever that swings open the doors between sensation and consciousness.

The *Śiva Saṁhitā* says, "As long as the breath is in the body, life abides." The *Haṭha Yoga Pradīpikā* adds, "When the breath wanders, the mind is unsteady; when the breath is still, the mind becomes still." Across centuries the message remains unchanged: whoever masters awareness of breath masters awareness itself.

The Intelligence of Prāṇa

To breathe is to invite *prāṇa*—the universal vitality—into personal form. Every inhalation is a handshake between the individual and the infinite. Air is the vehicle, but *prāṇa* is the passenger. The lungs move, yet the true movement occurs in subtler dimensions where thought and feeling circulate.

Prāṇa is not an inert force; it is conscious energy. It knows how to mend wounds, regulate heartbeat, and weave thought into language. It animates attention itself. When that intelligence is respected through gentle rhythm, it cooperates; when neglected through strain, it rebels as anxiety or exhaustion.

Understanding *prāṇa* transforms one's relationship with health. Instead of fighting the body, one learns to negotiate with its currents. Fatigue, restlessness, even mood swings reveal the quality of *prāṇa* moving through the system. A calm day corresponds to an even flow; a chaotic day to an erratic one. The yogin studies these tides not to control them but to move in harmony with them.

Rhythm and Awareness

Breath is the only physiological process that is both voluntary and involuntary. This dual nature makes it a bridge between the conscious and the unconscious. When you hold your breath, you feel both your power and your limits: you can guide the rhythm, yet life soon demands its own pace.

Every emotion alters this rhythm. Fear shortens it; joy expands it; grief pauses it. The mind may lie, but breath never does. It is the body's truth-teller. To become intimate with one's breathing is to develop emotional literacy at the deepest level.

Philosophically, rhythm is order. A rhythmic breath means life arranged around balance. When breathing becomes erratic, awareness fragments; when rhythm returns, the pieces gather. For this reason, traditional yoga treats breath observation as the foundation of meditation rather than a mere prelude to it. To witness breath is to witness the play of impermanence within the permanence of being.

Kumbhaka — The Pause that Reveals

Between inhalation and exhalation there is a pause—a brief silence. The texts call it *kumbhaka*, the "pot-like" state that holds *prāṇa* in stillness. Biologically it is a moment of equilibrium; spiritually it is a glimpse of eternity.

Every pause is an invitation to taste what exists when movement ceases. In that gap, the mind is neither gathering nor releasing—it simply is. The wise observe this natural pause rather than manufacture it. Over time it lengthens on its own, as though awareness wishes to rest longer in its own company.

This simple recognition changes the way one experiences time. Life no longer feels like a sequence of events but as a continuous wave, cresting and falling into silence. *Kumbhaka* teaches that the essence of action lies in rest, and the essence of rest lies in readiness.

Sound and Silence

The movement of air through the nostrils produces sound. At first it is merely physical—a soft hiss. With awareness, that sound becomes mantra. Many traditions describe hearing a subtle vibration—the *So-Ham*, meaning "I am That." Whether or not one names it, this inner resonance is the signature of life.

Listening to breath as sound refines perception. The ears turn inward; attention becomes circular. Outer noise diminishes. Eventually the sound fades into its own origin, leaving pure silence. This is not absence but fullness, a silence dense with presence. In that silence, the distinction between listener and listened dissolves.

The philosophical meaning of this practice is profound: all forms arise from vibration and return to it. To trace the sound of breath back to silence is to participate consciously in creation's cycle. Every exhale is dissolution; every inhale, genesis.

The Subtle Psychology of Breath

The breath is a barometer of consciousness. Its patterns reveal not only physical state but the structure of personality. Fast, shallow breathing corresponds to a mind preoccupied with control; slow, steady breathing belongs to a mind inclined toward reflection. Observing these tendencies with patience—not judgment—gradually alters them.

From a psychological viewpoint, the habit of attention that arises through breath awareness strengthens equanimity. One learns to witness impulses as they form rather than after they erupt. The pause before exhalation becomes the space in which choice replaces compulsion.

Breath also teaches empathy. When you truly listen to your own breathing, you begin to sense the breathing of others —the fatigue of a friend, the tension in a room, the collective sigh of a crowd. Compassion is born from this shared rhythm. In breathing together, humanity remembers its unity.

The Cosmic Dimension

The Upaniṣads call the breath *prāṇa*, the horse on which the soul rides. Each personal inhalation mirrors the inhalation of the universe; each exhalation mirrors its dissolution. Scientists speak of stellar winds and cosmic background radiation; the yogin perceives the same principle through lived experience. The macrocosm breathes through the microcosm.

When awareness of this correspondence becomes steady, a quiet reverence enters every act. Eating, walking, even speaking feel like part of one continuous respiration of the universe. The notion of "my breath" dissolves. There is only breathing. There is only life expressing itself through temporary form.

The Breath of Daily Life

The highest application of breath awareness is not limited to the mat or cushion. It extends into work, conversation, and solitude. A balanced breath during argument preserves dignity; a slow exhale before decision brings clarity. In moments of beauty, deep breathing prolongs gratitude; in sorrow, it anchors the heart.

The practical yogin uses breath as feedback. If it grows ragged, he knows the mind has strayed; if it flows smoothly, he knows alignment has returned. Thus every situation becomes a classroom, every breath a lesson in returning home.

When breath awareness becomes habitual, the ordinary gains a luminous texture. Walking down a street feels rhythmic, typing becomes musical, listening becomes devotional. The bridge no longer connects two worlds—it reveals that there was only one world all along, seen now through the lens of presence.

Ethical Implications of Breath

To control one's breath is to influence one's behavior. A calm breather rarely harms; a labored breather easily reacts. The discipline of gentle breathing cultivates patience more effectively than moral argument. Because respiration and emotion share the same nervous pathways, tranquility of one ensures tranquility of the other.

The practitioner who understands this takes responsibility for the atmosphere they create. Their steady breath becomes medicine for others. In meetings, households, or classrooms, a composed breather unconsciously regulates the group rhythm. This is silent leadership—the governance of energy rather than opinion.

Philosophy of Letting Go

Every exhale is an act of surrender. Inhalation gathers; exhalation releases. Together they form the eternal dialogue of holding and letting go. To breathe consciously is to participate willingly in impermanence. Each breath rehearses the art of dying peacefully and being reborn without fear.

The more one observes this cycle, the less one clings to fixed identities. The breath teaches impermanence not as loss but as rhythm. It whispers that continuity does not require permanence—only balance. This realization softens ambition and dissolves regret. The practitioner becomes simple, transparent, available to the moment.

Framework for Practice in Daily Rhythm

The following is not a prescription but a conceptual framework—a rhythm for living with awareness of breath rather than controlling it.

Morning:

Begin the day by noticing the first conscious breath after waking. Let that breath set the tone for attentiveness. During washing or walking, sense how the body begins to synchronize with daylight.

Work Hours:

Return to awareness at transitional moments—before opening a door, answering a call, or sending a message. One calm breath changes the texture of action.

Evening:

As daylight recedes, observe the natural deepening of exhalation. The body's wisdom prepares for rest without command. Align with it rather than fight it.

Before Sleep:

Lie still and feel ten breaths travel through the body without interference. Let thought disperse with the last exhale. Sleep then becomes an extension of meditation.

This rhythm requires no schedule and no strain—only remembrance. The bridge remains intact whether one sits in meditation or walks in the marketplace.

The Breath as Teacher

The breath is the most faithful companion of human life. It asks for nothing and remains until the end. It accompanies joy and despair alike without judgment. To become conscious of this companionship is to feel supported by existence itself.When one truly listens to breath, its sound resembles compassion. It enters without demand and leaves without resistance. To imitate that quality in thought and action is to live the essence of yoga.

The philosopher inquires into reality through words; the yogin inquires through breath. One seeks to define; the other to embody. Both aim at understanding, but the path of breath leads through intimacy rather than abstractionUltimately, the bridge of breath does not connect two separate lands. It reveals that body and mind were never apart. Breath is the evidence of their unity, the living mantra whispered by creation to remind itself of itself. When that is realized, every inhale becomes a hymn of gratitude, every exhale an offering of peace.

Chapter 27

Awakening the Centres – Part I

"The Map Beneath the Skin"

The ancients drew a map that no surgeon could find, a map not etched in blood or bone but in breath and awareness. They called it the *subtle body*—a field of intelligence woven through every atom, shimmering between thought and sensation. To understand the mind, one must also learn to feel this body of light.Modern psychology calls it energy, affect, or nervous regulation. The yogis called it *prana*. It is the bridge between consciousness and matter, thought and action, soul and form. When you breathe with awareness, you touch this bridge.

Every thought alters your breath; every breath shapes your thought. Observe a mind in fear—its breath is shallow and sharp. Observe a mind in peace—its breath is wide and fluid. The breath is the messenger of the mind, but it can also become its teacher.

In this chapter we explore what the ancient masters called the *centres of awareness*—not organs to be found, but doors to be opened. Through them the river of consciousness rises, from instinct to insight, from the coil of survival to the expanse of freedom.

To awaken these centres is not to chase mystical lights or visions. It is to refine the nervous system into a transparent instrument of awareness, to learn the art of listening to energy as one listens to music. It is the psychology of the subtle body —the science of self-transformation.

The Serpent and the Stairway

In the root of the body sleeps a serpent—not a creature of scales but of potential. She is *Kundalini Shakti*, the coiled force of life. The sages spoke of her in symbols: she lies dormant at the base of the spine, guarding the passageway to higher consciousness. When she awakens, she does not ascend like lightning; she rises like dawn.

To awaken the serpent is to awaken the totality of life within you—the power to create, to feel, to act, to know, to love, and finally to merge with the vast silence beyond mind. But she cannot be forced awake. Like the earth itself, she stirs only when her seasons are ripe.

Patanjali hinted at this in his concise statement: *"Yogaḥ citta vṛtti nirodhaḥ"—Yoga is the cessation of the fluctuations of mind.* When the restless waves settle, the lake of awareness becomes still enough to reflect the inner sun. Then the energy that once scattered outward begins its natural movement inward and upward.

The *Shiva Samhita* calls this the "path of the river Saraswati," the invisible current flowing through the centre of being. The *Hatha Yoga Pradipika* warns that before this current can flow, the channels—*nadis*—must be purified, the body stabilized, and the mind balanced. Awakening without purification is like sending a flood through a narrow pipe; it breaks more than it nourishes.

So, the first movement toward awakening is not ascent, but preparation. The serpent does not climb a shaky reed; she seeks a still spine and a quiet heart.

The Science of Still Energy

Between the skin and the soul flow countless rivers of prana, subtle channels called *nadis*. Of the 72,000 said to exist, three form the central triad: *Ida*, *Pingala*, and *Sushumna*.

- **Ida**, beginning at the left of the base, spirals upward to the left nostril. She is lunar—cool, receptive, inward. In psychology, she manifests as imagination, empathy, rest, and the parasympathetic calm.

- **Pingala**, rising to the right nostril, is solar—warm, active, outward. She governs logic, vitality, focus, and the sympathetic drive to move and do.

- **Sushumna**, the central channel, lies between them. When Ida and Pingala are balanced, the central river opens, and awareness flows without division.

When one nostril is dominant, the corresponding hemisphere of the brain becomes more active. Ancient yogis noticed this long before neuroscience did. They used breath regulation (*pranayama*) to balance these flows, to harmonize mind and energy.

Practice 1: Nadi-Shodhana (Balancing Breath)

1. Sit with spine upright, shoulders relaxed.

2. Bring the right hand to your nose. Gently close the right nostril with the thumb, inhale through the left.

3. Close the left with the ring finger, exhale through the right.

4. Inhale through the right, close it, exhale through the left. This is one round.

5. Continue 7–12 rounds, keeping the breath smooth and unhurried.

6. Feel how the mind begins to settle into balance—neither sluggish nor restless.

Psychological note:
Each cycle trains the mind to hold two polarities together—effort and ease, control and surrender. Over time, it builds the mental quality Patanjali called *samatvam*, evenness.

When the dual currents are balanced, the body feels symmetrical and the mind luminous. This is the first taste of awakening—not ecstasy, but equanimity.

The Seven Fields of Awareness

The ancients spoke of **seven primary chakras**, or *centres of consciousness*. Each is both an energy field and a psychological state—a mirror where consciousness sees a specific aspect of itself. To awaken them is to integrate the layers of being.

Let us explore them not as exotic symbols but as living experiences within the psyche.

1. Muladhara — The Root (Foundation)

Location: Base of spine
Element: Earth
Psychological function: Safety, stability, belonging

This is where life anchors itself in matter. When stable, you feel grounded, confident, capable of meeting the world. When blocked, fear and insecurity cloud perception.

Practice:
Stand barefoot. Feel the soles meet the ground. Breathe down,

not up. Imagine roots descending from the spine deep into the earth. With each exhale, release fear; with each inhale, draw steadiness.

> Ask yourself nightly: *What did I fear today? Did I breathe through it, or contract against it?*

2. Svadhisthana — The Sacral (Flow)

Location: Below the navel
Element: Water
Psychological function: Emotion, pleasure, creativity

Here prana begins to move. When open, it gives birth to spontaneity and joy; when obstructed, life feels dry and mechanical.

Practice:
Sit or stand with soft knees. Circle the hips gently as you breathe. Let the movement become fluid. Imagine emotions as tides—neither clung to nor resisted.

> Journaling cue: *What emotions did I suppress today? What would it mean to feel them fully without acting them out?*

3. Manipura — The Solar Centre (Will)

Location: Navel region
Element: Fire
Psychological function: Confidence, transformation, purpose

When this fire is balanced, you act with clarity; when excessive, you burn others; when weak, you doubt yourself.

Practice:
Sit tall. Inhale to the navel, exhale as if fanning a flame there. Feel warmth build. Then hold stillness, sensing the glow spread through the torso.

Reflection: *Where did I spend my energy today? Was it aligned with my deeper purpose?*

4. Anahata — The Heart (Union)

Location: Center of chest
Element: Air
Psychological function: Compassion, connection, acceptance

This is the meeting point between the lower centres of survival and the higher centres of understanding. When awakened, love ceases to be emotion and becomes presence.

Practice:
Sit quietly. Bring attention to the heart area. With each breath, imagine inhaling gratitude, exhaling tension. Recall someone who evokes warmth. Feel that warmth expand beyond the body.

Affirmation: *I let myself be seen, and I let others be.*

5. Vishuddha — The Throat (Expression)

Location: Throat
Element: Ether
Psychological function: Communication, authenticity, truth

This is where inner experience finds voice. Suppressed expression congests energy here, leading to anxiety or self-doubt.

Practice:
Chant a long *AUM* or simply hum softly. Feel vibration spread from throat to skull. Let unspoken words dissolve into sound.

Reflection: *Was I honest today? Not brutally so, but lovingly so?*

When these five centres begin to harmonize, the body becomes a temple of flowing awareness. Emotions integrate with clarity, instinct fuses with understanding. But the journey upward requires purification—the clearing of what blocks the current.

5. Purification Before Ascent

In every ancient text, before the awakening comes the cleansing. The *Hatha Yoga Pradipika* speaks of *shatkarmas*—six purificatory acts to cleanse the body. The *Shiva Samhita* repeats: "The body is the bow, the mind the arrow, the soul the target; but the bowstring must be strong and clean."

In psychological language, purification means facing the shadows we avoid—the emotions, habits, and attachments that bind prana. Without this inner hygiene, energy magnifies imbalance.

Patanjali described this as *tapas*, the inner fire of disciplined self-observation. It is not harshness but honesty—the willingness to stay present with discomfort until it teaches what it must.Just as a river clears when its flow is unblocked, consciousness clarifies when suppression ends. Every practice in yoga psychology begins with purification—not to reject the world but to make perception transparent.

Practice 2: The Rooting Ritual

1. Sit on the ground.

2. Place palms on the earth. Feel its quiet strength.

3. Whisper silently: *I am supported. I am safe enough to see.*

4. Recall a recent fear or tension. Instead of analyzing it, breathe it into the earth through your palms.

5. Wait for the exhale to lengthen naturally.

6. End with gratitude—thank the earth for holding what you release.

Practice 3: Witness Meditation

1. Sit comfortably, spine tall.

2. Close the eyes. Let the breath settle.

3. Begin to watch thoughts like clouds. Don't name them.

4. Each time you notice identification—"I am thinking"—return to simply *seeing*.

5. Continue for 10–15 minutes.

> *Purpose:* To establish *sakshi bhava*—the witness attitude—where awareness learns to observe mind without merging into it. This attitude keeps energy stable as deeper centres awaken.

Purification is not moral cleansing; it is energetic alignment. When the body is steady, breath rhythmic, and emotions acknowledged, the current that sleeps at the base begins to stir. Not violently, but like the first tremor of spring beneath frozen soil.

Chapter 28

Awakening the Centres – Part II

The Inner Fire and the Breath of Transformation

Energy changes form through heat. In yoga this heat is called **Agni**, the fire that transforms both food and thought. When you digest experience well, it turns into wisdom; when you don't, it turns into residue—resentment, tension, fatigue. The third centre, *Manipura*, is the furnace of that digestion.

In the language of the body, it lies around the navel and solar plexus. In the language of psychology, it is your sense of agency—how you act, decide, and assert your direction. Most people either under-use or over-use this fire. Too little, and life feels dull or passive; too much, and it burns into anger or control.

The goal is not to extinguish the fire, but to make it **steady and usable**—like a stove that cooks instead of a flame that scorches.

Practice 4: Breath of Transformation (gentle Kapalabhati)

1. Sit upright, relax the belly.
2. Inhale normally, exhale with a short, firm pulse through the nose. Let the inhale happen by itself.
3. Do ten pulses, rest. Work up gradually to three rounds of twenty.

4. When finished, sit quietly and feel the warmth in the abdomen.

5. Observe how the mind becomes clearer and more decisive without aggression.

If strong emotions arise afterward, don't interpret them—let them move through the breath until they quiet. The practice activates both energy and emotional residue; observation completes the burn.

A few minutes of this every morning before food clears dullness and sharpens focus. It is not about mystical fire—it's metabolic and psychological regulation.

When you begin to trust this centre, action becomes cleaner. You stop over-explaining yourself and simply do what needs doing. The intellect no longer argues with the will.

7. The Heart as the Bridge

When energy stabilizes below, it naturally moves toward the chest.
The **Heart Centre (Anahata)** is not sentimental—it's integrative. It joins the instinctual drive from below with the insight from above. If the lower centres are survival-based and the higher ones are abstract, the heart is the translator between them.

Emotion becomes intelligence here. Instead of being pushed by feeling or suppressing it, you begin to **understand emotion as information**: what it is signaling, what it needs.
Most imbalances in yoga practice come from skipping this level—chasing light or visions while the heart remains armored.

Practice 5: Coherent Breathing

1. Sit or lie down comfortably.
2. Inhale for five seconds, exhale for five seconds. Keep this rhythm.
3. While breathing, place one hand on the chest and one on the abdomen.
4. Feel both rise and fall together.
5. Continue for five minutes.

This rhythm synchronizes breath, heart rate, and nervous system. The mind often quiets by itself. After a week of daily use you'll notice reactivity reducing; compassion arises as a physiological fact, not an ideal.

Philosophically, this centre represents **acceptance of polarity** —love and detachment, joy and sorrow, giving and receiving. The yogic texts describe it as *Anahata*, the "unstruck sound"—the harmony that exists before conflict begins.
In practice, it means learning to hold opposite experiences without collapse.

A simple reflection: when a situation feels heavy, place your attention in the chest and breathe until the sensation softens. Don't analyze; let the breath interpret it for you.

8. The Eye and the Crown

As the current continues upward, the mind becomes both quieter and sharper.
The **Ajna centre**, between the eyebrows, governs perception, intuition, and inner direction. It's where thought organizes itself into insight. The **Sahasrara**, at the crown, is not a

physical point but a state in which awareness recognizes its own vastness.

These stages are often over-described. In reality, awakening here is not fireworks; it's **clarity without strain**. You start to see the structure of your own mind: how thought forms, how emotion attaches, how attention moves.
That observation itself is the awakening.

To stabilize it, bring precision to focus.

Practice 6: Steady Gaze (Trataka, simplified)

1. Sit facing a small candle or a black dot on the wall, at eye level.
2. Keep your eyes steady on the point for one minute.
3. Close the eyes and visualize the same image between the brows.
4. Repeat three times.
5. End with eyes closed, noticing the after-image fade.

Do not strain; the goal is steadiness, not endurance. Over weeks this strengthens concentration and reveals how attention behaves—wandering, resisting, returning.

Once concentration steadies, shift to **internal observation**: watch the thinker itself. When a thought arises, ask, "Who noticed this?"
That question isn't for an answer; it breaks identification. Awareness begins to recognize itself as separate from content.

Patanjali called this *viveka khyati*—discriminative insight.
It's not mystical; it's the same clarity that allows you to step out of a dream once you realize you're dreaming. The difference is

that now the dream is waking life.

Common signs of stability:

- You notice thoughts earlier.
- Emotional spikes shorten.
- Decisions come from calm clarity rather than tension.

Avoid glorifying these experiences. Treat them as improvements in cognitive hygiene. The purpose of higher centres is better functioning, not spiritual performance.

9. Integration: Living the Centres

Real progress is seen not on the mat but in the day.
When the centres begin to work together, you feel **a sense of inner economy**—less wasted energy, fewer contradictions. Sensation, feeling, and thought communicate instead of compete.

Awakening does not mean staying in heightened states; it means **being able to move through all states consciously**.
On some days, grounding is needed; on others, expression; on others, silence. The art is to know which layer to inhabit at a given moment.

A short daily sequence can help maintain that balance:

Practice 7: Full-Body Awareness Scan

1. Sit quietly, eyes closed.
2. Bring awareness to the soles of the feet. Inhale attention up the legs to the pelvis; exhale down again.
3. Continue through abdomen, chest, shoulders, arms,

throat, head, and crown.

4. At each region, pause for a breath, sensing warmth or vibration.

5. End by feeling the whole body at once, breathing naturally.

This practice teaches the nervous system to perceive itself as a unified field. Over time it removes the "compartmentalization" that keeps the psyche split—thinking one thing, feeling another, doing a third.

In conversation, notice from which centre you're speaking.

- From the root: you seek safety.
- From the solar plexus: you assert or defend.
- From the heart: you connect.
- From the brow: you clarify.
  That awareness alone begins integration.

Integration also means **simplicity**: eating when hungry, resting when tired, listening more than speaking, working without hurry. Yogic psychology is lived through ordinary decisions, not special rituals.

10. The River Returns to the Sea

Eventually the practice matures into naturalness. You no longer "work" on centres; you live with an **ongoing sensitivity** to energy and attention.
The breath becomes self-adjusting, the mind self-correcting.

In the old texts this is described as *Sushumna awakening*—the central current of awareness flowing freely through the system. In modern terms, it's an integrated nervous system: flexible, responsive, resilient.

What follows is not perpetual bliss but **a stable baseline of clarity**. You can feel deeply without drowning, act strongly without aggression, rest completely without inertia.

At this stage, formal meditation and daily life merge.
Walking, speaking, or eating can all be done with the same attention you once reserved for sitting practice.
This is what the Yoga Sutras mean by *kaivalya*—freedom in participation, independence in the midst of connection.

Closing Thoughts

The work of awakening the centres is the work of **knowing yourself through every layer**—body, breath, emotion, thought, awareness.
Each practice is a feedback loop: observe, adjust, observe again.
Over months and years, the system learns to stay aligned by itself.

If there is a single guiding principle, it is this:

> **Do nothing violently—neither suppress nor force.**
> Observe honestly, act moderately, rest regularly.

Transformation is not an act of conquest but of cooperation between consciousness and its vehicle. The more you cooperate, the more life begins to function as an intelligent whole.

And that wholeness is the true awakening—not a mystical event, but a daily competence in living with depth, precision, and peace.

Chapter 29

The Kriya Currents

1. The Movement of Energy

In the stillness of deep meditation, most practitioners eventually feel something begin to move inside—a pulse, a vibration, a current that seems neither physical nor imaginary. This is the first sign that awareness has started to touch its own energy.

Yoga calls this current *Kriya*—movement arising from within.Kriya is not an exercise; it is an **energetic event**. The word comes from the root *kri*, "to act." But here action is spontaneous, not willed. It is the movement of consciousness through its channels.

The practices of **Kriya Yoga** are structured ways of **guiding this movement**—turning it from random surges into an organized evolution.

Hatha Yoga purifies, Raja Yoga stills, but Kriya Yoga **connects**—it bridges purification and stillness by awakening the **dynamic intelligence of prana**. It does not suppress the mind; it **transforms its energy pattern** by circulating awareness through the spinal axis, through the six psychic centres, or chakras, until consciousness perceives itself as flow.

---

2. What Kriya Yoga Is—and What It Isn't

Much of what is called Kriya Yoga today has been diluted into techniques for relaxation or visualization. In its classical sense, as presented by the Nath and Tantric yogis and elaborated by Swami Satyananda Saraswati, **Kriya Yoga is an integrated system** that includes:

- **Pranayama** — breath regulation that steadies the pranic field.
- **Mudra and Bandha** — gestures and locks that direct pranic flow.
- **Concentration on chakras** — mental rotation through specific psychic centres.
- **Awareness synchronization** — linking breath, mantra, and movement into a single loop of attention.

Its **aim** is not escape or trance but a precise inner engineering of energy and awareness.Through systematic circulation of prana, the nervous system is gradually re-patterned; the brain's dormant pathways are activated; the ida, pingala, and sushumna nadis become harmonized; and the **latent kundalini energy** begins to rise naturally.

The texts describe this as the **union of prana and consciousness**, the marriage of movement and stillness.In psychological terms, Kriya Yoga integrates the instinctive, emotional, and intellectual layers into one coherent rhythm. You begin to feel "one system" inside you instead of a collection of conflicting impulses.

3. The Principle: Circulation, Not Suppression

When people first learn meditation, they often attempt to stop thoughts by force. Kriya takes a different approach.Rather than fighting mental energy, it gives it a **route to move**.Imagine a river blocked by stones: the water

stagnates and breeds confusion. Move the stones, and the current purifies itself.In the same way, Kriya works by movement—through **circular awareness** and **cyclic breathing** —so that energy does not accumulate as tension.
It flows upward through the spinal channel (*sushumna nadi*), washing the mind clean as it moves.The practices use the **breath as the vehicle**, the **spine as the highway**, and **conscious awareness as the driver**.

At first the circulation is imagined; later it becomes perceptible—a subtle current of tingling, warmth, or pulsation.

That current is the language of prana, and learning to feel it marks the transition from mental practice to energetic yoga.

4. The Structure of Classical Kriya Yoga

In *Kundalini Tantra*, Swami Satyananda outlined a sequence of **twenty Kriyas**, divided into progressive stages.

Each combines breath, awareness, and internal focus. While the full training must be learned systematically under guidance, the principles can be understood and practiced safely through the foundational forms described below.

Returning to Yourself

A Closing Meditation

Every journey of the mind eventually circles back to the same question: Who is the one that is experiencing all this? Not the body—you have watched it change. Not the emotions—they rise and fall like weather. Not the thoughts—they come and go like passing birds.Not even the personality, which is only a pattern stitched from memory, culture, fear, longing.Everything you can observe is not you. Everything you can describe is not you. Everything that changes cannot be the one who witnesses change. Throughout this book, we have journeyed through the layers of the human system—the body, the breath, the emotions, the mind, the heart, the energy field, the discriminating intelligence, and finally the silent witness. Each chapter has been a window, and every practice a subtle turning of attention toward what is already present.If you look carefully, you will see the thread connecting all the teachings:Presence is the root of transformation.

Breath, energy, attention, memory, art, freedom, intelligence—all are branches of the same inner tree.The goal was never to sculpt a perfect mind, nor to escape the world, nor to accumulate spiritual experiences. Experiences come; experiences fade. What remains is the one who is aware.

You began with curiosity. You moved through perception, peeling, practice, digestion, expression.You learned how attention shapes reality, how the mind constructs worlds, how breath governs emotion, how energy follows awareness, how presence dissolves the hypnosis of time.You encountered the koshas, the chakras, the associative mind, the dream-mind, the shadow of conditioning, the illusion of freedom, the architecture of intelligence, the grammar of perspective.Every idea, whether scientific or mystical, pointed toward a single thing: knowing yourself without distortion.Inner work does not make you extraordinary.It makes you natural.It removes noise until the original clarity returns.This clarity is not dramatic. It is simple, like cold water on the face.It is as ordinary as walking, eating, breating, listening.It is the state in which life becomes transparent, and the mind stops interfering between you and reality.In earlier chapters, you encountered time as illusion, intelligence as alignment, freedom as essence, and art as the language of the soul.You saw how the mind generates perspectives, how thoughts are shadows, how conditioning shapes personality, how silence opens the door to the timeless.All these insights lead to one recognition:You are not the content of consciousness.

You are consciousness itself. This is not a belief. It is a direct experience available in the gap between two thoughts, in the pause after an exhale, in the moment of effortless awareness during Ajapa Japa, in the softening thathappens when you truly listen. The ancient mystics, neuroscientists, yogis, philosophers, and poets have all pointed—sometimes awkwardly, sometimes beautifully—to this same discovery. You are the sky in which every moment arises and dissolves. You are the open field in which time appears and disappears. You are the witness that has never aged.You are the silence behind all music, the canvas behind all art, the stillness beneath all breath.The real work of Yoga Psychology is not performed in meditation alone.It continues in conversation, in conflict, in creativity, in your relationships, in the tiny decisions that form the architecture of your days.Every moment asks you a simple question:Are you reacting from habit, or responding from awareness?If you can pause—just for a breath—your entire life begins to shift.A single conscious moment carries more intelligence than a thousand unconscious choices.This is the spiral of integration:Observe → Regulate → Reflect → Release → Realize → Live → Observe again. There is no final mastery.There is only deepening. Yoga is not a set of techniques. Yoga is the way you inhabit your own being. When you walk, walk fully. When you eat, eat with presence.When you speak, let awareness shape your words.When you feel, feel honestly.When you breathe, breathe as if life itself were flowing through you—because it is. There is no separation between the sacred and the mundane.Your ordinary life is the ashram. Your relationships are the teachers. Your breath is the mantra.Your awareness is the guru.And your mind—once a restless companion—becomes transparent, pliable, a tool instead of a tyrant.If this book has done its work, you will not remember every concept.But you will remember a feeling—a subtle shift,a clearer seeing,a deeper listening,a quiet confidence that your consciousness is infinitely larger than the stories you tell yourself. Take this with you. Practice gently. Study honestly.Rest deeply.Feel fully.Live simply. And return to yourself again and again.In that returning lies the whole path.

This is the end of the book.But it is the beginning of your real work.

Stage One – Establishing the Circuit

The goal here is to make the spinal pathway clear to perception.

1. Spinal Awareness (Meru Dhyana)

Sit upright. As you inhale, feel the breath travel from the base of the spine up to the crown. As you exhale, feel it descend back to the base.

Do not visualize light or colour; simply track sensation.

After a few minutes, you may sense a subtle "wire" of awareness running through the centre of the body.

This is the beginning of *sushumna dhyana*, the meditation on the central current.

2. Energy Lock (Moola Bandha + Jalandhara Bandha)

During exhalation, gently contract the pelvic floor (moola bandha) and the throat (jalandhara bandha).

This channels prana upward.

With practice, you will feel a light upward movement along the spine and a stillness behind the eyes.

Release the locks with the inhale.

> *Purpose:* Direct the vital energy upward and prepare the nervous system for steady flow.

Stage Two – Linking Breath and Awareness

Here we coordinate the **movement of attention** with **movement of breath**.

3. Spinal Breathing (Kriya Pranayama)

Inhale up the spine from base to crown while mentally chanting *So*.

Exhale down the spine while mentally chanting *Ham*.

Repeat for 10–20 cycles.

The mantra *So-Ham*—"I am That"—serves as a rhythmic pulse, keeping the mind anchored.

As you become sensitive, you'll notice each chakra responds differently: a heaviness near the root, a warmth at the navel, a vibration near the throat. These are normal; observe without chasing them.

4. Chakra Awareness (Shat-Chakra Kriya)
Once spinal awareness stabilizes, the focus can move through the chakras sequentially, synchronized with breath:

- Inhale: travel awareness from mooladhara to ajna, touching each centre.

- Exhale: descend back to the base.
  This "rotation" integrates the whole system—each breath becomes a miniature journey through your inner architecture.

Stage Three – Refinement and Stillness

When the current becomes steady, movement gives way to stillness.

5. Inner Silence (Khechari Mudra + Ajna Focus)
Roll the tongue back gently (or simply rest it on the palate) and bring attention to the space between the eyebrows.
Allow the breath to slow naturally.
Do not try to stop thought; let the energy circulate by itself.
Eventually, the body may feel magnetized upright, the breath pause spontaneously, and a sense of light or spaciousness may appear.
This is *Kriya in stillness*—the energy moving without effort.

> **Note:** The purpose of Kriya Yoga is not to awaken kundalini dramatically but to make the system so refined that awakening happens quietly and sustainably.

5. The Psychology of Kriya Yoga

Every Kriya movement has a corresponding **psychological transformation**:

Physical Axis	Energetic Effect	Psychological Result
Spinal ascent	Prana moves upward	Expansion of awareness
Spinal descent	Energy integrates	Emotional grounding
Retention (Kumbhaka)	Energy stabilized	Mental clarity
Circulation	Flow through nadis	Release of tension and past impressions (samskaras)

Practically, this means you will experience alternating phases of **activity and stillness**.
Sometimes the body feels charged, other times empty. Both are parts of the same cycle.
Do not cling to either.
The nervous system learns to tolerate higher voltage—what ancient texts called *tapas*, the inner heat of transformation.

If emotions surface—grief, anger, exhilaration—observe them as energy releasing from the unconscious.
Kriya does not erase emotion; it **digests** it.
As prana circulates through each chakra, the corresponding psychological contents rise and resolve: fear at the root, desire at the sacral, control at the navel, attachment at the heart, self-image at the throat, and so on.
This is why consistent, moderate practice is more effective than intense, sporadic sessions.

---

6. Preparation and Safety

Kriya Yoga is powerful because it acts directly on the nervous

system and brain.
Without adequate preparation, it can magnify imbalance.
The Bihar tradition emphasizes three safeguards:

1. **Purification (Shatkarmas):** Neti, dhauti, kapalbhati, and other cleansing techniques keep the physical body ready.

2. **Lifestyle:** Moderate diet, consistent sleep, honest work, and emotional transparency. Prana flows best through simplicity.

3. **Guided Progression:** Never rush from one stage to the next; let stability, not curiosity, decide advancement.

If agitation, insomnia, or headaches occur, pause energetic practices and return to grounding methods—walking, slow breathing, or relaxation.

Remember that the **goal is balance, not stimulation.**
A quiet nervous system is more spiritual than an excited one.

---

7. The Integration of Breath, Mind, and Awareness

As Kriya matures, three elements—**breath, mantra, and awareness**—merge into a single flow.
You are breathing, thinking, and observing all at once, without contradiction.
This is called *Ajapa Japa*, the natural mantra that continues by itself.

When breath and awareness merge completely, even the mantra dissolves, leaving only vibration.
The *Kundalini Tantra* describes this as **energy moving through the sushumna without effort**—the culmination of Kriya Yoga.
In ordinary life, this translates to an effortless mindfulness: actions flow cleanly, emotions are brief, thought becomes a

tool rather than a storm.

8. A Daily Framework for Practice

For a modern practitioner, the essence of Kriya Yoga can be experienced safely through this simple structure:

Phase	Duration	Key Practice	Purpose
Morning	15–25 min	Spinal Breathing + Chakra Awareness	Energize, clarify mind
Midday	5 min	Coherent Breathing or short relaxation	Balance during work
Evening	20–30 min	Spinal Circulation + Inner Silence	Integrate and rest
Before Sleep	2 min	Witnessing breath in heart centre	Complete the cycle

This framework ensures both activation and recovery.
Never skip rest after practice; the integration phase is when transformation consolidates.

---

9. The Real Awakening

In literature, kundalini is often dramatized, but in reality, true awakening is subtle.

You begin to feel alive in a new way—thoughts clearer, senses brighter, actions aligned.
The feeling of separation between inner and outer begins to blur.
That is Kriya Yoga working silently.

As *Swami Satyananda* emphasized:

> "Kriya Yoga does not belong to religion or belief; it is a science of experience."

When practiced steadily, it leads to a **state of natural meditation**—awareness continuously self-regulating through the body.
This is the *kriya currents*—life energy in conscious motion.

Kriya Yoga is not for escape but for **participation with precision**. You learn to live as a conductor of energy rather than a consumer of experience. Each breath becomes a subtle act of evolution.With time, the techniques fade, but the principle remains: breath, energy, and awareness move together as one current of intelligence.That current—the silent river through the spine—is the *Kriya Current*.It does not belong to yoga halls or traditions. It is the inherent movement of consciousness returning to itself, one breath at a time.

Appendix A – Classical Kriya Yoga Cross-Reference

Background

The *Kundalini Tantra* sequence consists of **twenty Kriyas** arranged in six progressive groups.
Each adds one new variable—breath pattern, awareness route, mantra, or bandha—so that prana and consciousness are circulated, balanced, and finally stilled in *sushumna nadi*.
Below, every practice from your chapter is traced to its classical equivalent.

Your Section / Practice	Classical Name (KT chapters 12–13)	Main Components	Purpose / Energetic Logic	Practical Notes
Spinal Awareness (Meru Dhyana)	**Kriya 1 – Vipareeta Karani Mudra (mental form)** and **Kriya 2 – Chakra Sanchalana (awareness movement)**	Awareness of breath moving along spine; gentle inversion or upright awareness of base-to-crown flow	Establishes perception of *sushumna nadi*; awakens sensory map of spinal axis	Keep physical body still; subtle sensing only, no visualization excess
Energy Lock (Moola Bandha + Jalandhara)	**Kriya 3 – Moola Bandha & Kriya 4 – Uddiyana + Jalandhara Combination**	Root and throat locks with breath suspension	Seals prana, prevents downward dissipation, drives current upward	Begin after mastering normal breath; never hold beyond comfort
Spinal Breathing (So-Ham Kriya)	**Kriya 5 – Spinal Breathing with So-Ham Mantra (Sthula Pranayama)**	Inhale "So" up sushumna, exhale "Ham" down	Coordinates breath, mantra, and awareness; harmonizes *ida-pingala*; initiates current	Daily 10–20 cycles max; pause if heat or restlessness increase
Chakra Awareness (Shat-Chakra Kriya)	**Kriyas 6–10 – Chakra Rotation (Shat Chakra Bhedan Sequence)**	Awareness moves through 6 psychic centres with each breath	Sequential activation and balancing of psychic-emotional layers	Keep mapping consistent (base → ajna → base); dwell briefly, avoid forcing visions
Inner Silence (Khechari Mudra + Ajna Focus)	**Kriya 11 – Khechari + Ujjayi Integration → Kriya 12 – Nada Sanchalana**	Tongue-lock, throat awareness, spontaneous inner sound	Allows spontaneous *kumbhaka* and perception of subtle vibration	Mild tongue placement on palate is sufficient; advanced form optional
Breath of Transformation (gentle Kapalabhati)	**Preparatory Shatkarma & Kriya 13 – Bhastrika Pranayama**	Rapid exhalations, passive inhalations	Increases pranic pressure to clear *manipura chakra*	Practice only when calm; end with grounding breath
Coherent Breathing (Heart Centre)	**Kriya 14 – Hridaya Dhyana + Kriya 15 – Prana Sanchalana in Anahata**	Equal 5-5 rhythm; heart focus	Balances sympathetic-parasympathetic tone; emotional integration	Excellent midday stabilizer; keep breath silent and unforced
Steady Gaze (Trataka)	**Kriya 16 – Trataka on Bindu / Ajna**	Candle or bindu gazing	Concentrates *ajna chakra*, strengthens mental steadiness	Tear-free eyes indicate correct duration; stop at strain
Witness Meditation / Inner Silence	**Kriya 17 – Ajapa Japa (So-Ham Spontaneous Flow)**	Breath-linked mantra continues automatically	Converts effort into effortless awareness; merges prana and chitta	Let mantra fade naturally; don't count repetitions
Full Body Awareness Scan	**Kriya 18 – Prana Sanchalana (Whole-Body Circulation)**	Awareness sweep through all nadis	Distributes energy evenly; grounds awakening	Finish each session with this to prevent localized tension
Integration / Natural Flow	**Kriyas 19–20 – Nada Anusandhana & Sushumna Sanchalana (Spontaneous Kriya)**	Listening to inner sound, perception of central current	Final stage—prana moves independently; spontaneous meditation	Do not seek phenomena; stability, rest, service are the marks of maturity

Energetic Progression Summary

1. **Purification (1–4):** prepare the channels, awaken awareness of the spine.
2. **Activation (5–10):** coordinate breath, mantra, and chakra rotation.
3. **Stabilization (11–15):** refine current through mudra, bandha, and heart rhythm.
4. **Integration (16–20):** establish inner sound, spontaneous circulation, and continuous awareness.

Each stage parallels the natural evolution of practice in your book—from bodily grounding to living meditation.

Guidelines for Modern Practitioners

- **Frequency:** Once daily is enough; over-practice agitates prana.
- **Sequence:** Always begin with grounding (Moola Bandha Awareness) and end with relaxation.
- **Health contra-indications:** Avoid strong kumbhaka or bandha work during high blood pressure, pregnancy, or acute illness.
- **Psychological integration:** Journal emotional shifts rather than analysing them; energy work must translate into behavioural clarity.

Comparative Perspective

Textual Source	Parallel Concept
Patanjali Yoga Sutra 2.1 — Tapaḥ Svādhyāya Īśvarapraṇidhāna	Kriya Yoga as disciplined self-transformation, not a posture set
Hatha Yoga Pradipika 2.1–10	Purification through pranayama before awakening
Shiva Samhita 5.78–90	Description of energy rising through six lotuses identical to Kriya rotation
Kundalini Tantra ch. 12–13	Practical codification into 20 Kriyas, modern Bihar School lineage

Appendix A: The Classical Lineage of the Kriya Currents

(Adapted from *Swami Satyananda Saraswati, Kundalini Tantra*, Bihar School of Yoga)

Appendix B – Practical Sequencing for Teachers

(Eight-Week Progressive Curriculum Based on the Bihar School / Kundalini Tantra Kriyas)

Purpose: give students a clear, methodical structure that develops sensitivity before intensity — balancing purification, activation, and integration.
Format: each week adds one new element while keeping earlier layers short and stable.
Session length: 25–40 minutes unless otherwise noted.
Environment: quiet, ventilated, empty stomach, consistent time of day.
Prerequisite: comfortable in basic asana and relaxation (shavasana).

Week 1 – Foundation & Grounding

Theme: body awareness and spinal orientation.
Practices (approx 25 min):

1. **Centering breath** (5 min) – observe natural breathing.

2. **Meru Dhyana / Spinal Awareness** (10 min) – feel inhale up, exhale down the spine.

3. **Moola Bandha Awareness** (3 min) – gentle pelvic-floor contraction on exhale.

4. **Witness Meditation** (5 min).

5. **Rest / Journal Reflection** (2 min).
   Checkpoint: steadier posture, calmer breath, easier concentration on spine.

Week 2 – Balancing Currents

Theme: harmonizing Ida and Pingala.
Add: *Nadi Shodhana Pranayama* (10 cycles).
Continue Week 1 sequence → add **So-Ham Spinal Breathing** (10 rounds).
Checkpoint: sense of symmetry between left/right nostrils, even mood.

Week 3 – Energetic Containment

Theme: introduce gentle bandhas.
Add: Moola + Jalandhara bandha with exhalation; hold 2–3 seconds.
Maintain earlier work but shorten to keep session ≈ 30 min.
Checkpoint: feel upward flow or inner stillness after release — no strain.

Week 4 – Chakra Rotation Basics

Theme: awareness through six centres.
Practice: inhale from mooladhara to ajna, exhale back down (6–8 rounds).
Keep So-Ham mantra optional.
Checkpoint: mild warmth, clarity, or distinct sensation per centre.

Week 5 – Heart Integration

Theme: coherence of breath and emotion.
Add: 5-5 coherent breathing at heart centre (5 min).
End with short Kriya pranayama rounds.
Checkpoint: easier emotional regulation, softer tone in speech.

Week 6 – Fire & Focus

Theme: ignite Manipura without agitation.
Add: Gentle Kapalabhati (3 × 20 pulses) → normal breathing → Heart coherence.
Introduce **Trataka** (1 min gaze + 1 min eyes closed × 3).
Checkpoint: bright mental state, no fatigue or headaches.

Week 7 – Inner Silence and Sound

Theme: transition from movement to stillness.
Add: simple Khechari (tongue to palate) and Ajna focus in silence (10 min).
Let So-Ham mantra arise spontaneously (Ajapa Japa).
Checkpoint: spontaneous pause in breath, effortless attention.

Week 8 – Integration & Sushumna Flow

Theme: whole-body circulation and stabilization.
Sequence (≈ 35–40 min):

1. Centering & Bandha Warm-up (5 min)

2. Spinal Breathing with Chakra rotation (10 min)

3. Heart Coherence (5 min)

4. Ajna Silence (10 min)

5. **Full-Body Awareness Scan** (8 min) → Rest.
   Checkpoint: balanced energy, clear perception, no

craving for experience.

Post-Course Maintenance

- **Daily Short Form (20 min):** Spinal Breathing → Heart Coherence → Silence.
- **Weekly Long Session (40 min):** add Chakra rotation + Full-Body Scan.
- **Integration:** encourage journaling of bodily, emotional, and behavioural changes rather than visionary events.

Safety and Teaching Cues

- End every session with **grounding** (feet awareness or a few normal breaths).
- Encourage **progress by comfort**, not by calendar; remain in any week's sequence for 2–3 weeks if stability isn't clear.
- Emphasize **functional benefits** – better sleep, mood, focus – as indicators of correct energy flow.
- Avoid teaching advanced bandhas or long kumbhaka outside supervised settings.

Integration Principle

> "Expansion of energy must equal expansion of awareness." — Swami Satyananda Saraswati

If practice expands sensation faster than understanding, pause and reflect.

The mark of success is calmness in action, not stimulation in meditation.

Appendix C – The Integrated Approach

Bridging Mind, Energy, and Consciousness

---

1. The Purpose of an Integrated Path

Every major stream of Yoga—Raja, Hatha, Kriya, Bhakti, and Jnana—addresses one layer of the human system:

Aspect	Classical Focus	Modern Expression
Body / Behavior	Hatha Yoga	Somatic awareness, lifestyle hygiene
Breath / Energy	Pranayama & Kriya	Nervous-system regulation
Mind / Emotion	Raja Yoga	Cognitive-emotional literacy
Heart / Relationship	Bhakti Yoga	Compassion, service, connection
Insight / Awareness	Jnana Yoga	Reflective understanding

An *integrated approach* weaves these into one functional psychology: the **energy of the body, the clarity of the mind, and the stability of awareness move as a single current**.
All methods in this book—breath, posture, attention, journaling, or Kriya circulation—serve that one purpose: **integration before transcendence.**

---

2. Three Stages of Development

Each student passes through recurring phases rather than linear steps.
Teachers can diagnose them by observing language, breath rhythm, and emotional tone.

Stage	Core Process	Observable Signs	Primary Practices
A. Grounding / Stabilization	Safety, embodiment, rhythm	Erratic breath → steadier; reduced anxiety	Earth & root practices, coherent breathing, journaling
B. Activation / Flow	Mobilizing energy, emotional release	More vitality, creativity; occasional mood swings	Spinal breathing, chakra rotation, gentle bandhas
C. Integration / Insight	Harmonizing currents, witness consciousness	Calm alertness, natural compassion, simplicity	Ajapa Japa, inner silence, service, reflection

Students may oscillate between them. The teacher's job is to **balance—not accelerate—the process.**

---

3. The Five-Layer Diagnostic Model (Pancha Koshas + Psychology)

Layer	Yogic Term	Psychological Lens	Corrective Focus
1. **Annamaya Kosha** (Physical)	Body habits, diet, fatigue	Grounding, asana, rest	
2. **Pranamaya Kosha** (Energetic)	Breath pattern, vitality	Pranayama, bandha, rhythm	
3. **Manomaya Kosha** (Mental-Emotional)	Thought loops, reactivity	Witnessing, journaling, emotion labeling	
4. **Vijnanamaya Kosha** (Discriminative Mind)	Insight, values alignment	Self-inquiry, contemplative reading	
5. **Anandamaya Kosha** (Bliss / Integration)	Ease, compassion, silence	Seva, gratitude, meditation without object	

Assessment tip: imbalance in a lower layer distorts higher ones; always begin correction from the base upward.

---

4. Integrating Teachings from the Whole Text

Source Chapter	Core Insight	Practical Translation
Everything's Alive(Previous book by Author)	Consciousness precedes thought	Cultivate direct awareness of sensation before analysis
Touching the Mind (earlier chapters)	Observation transforms	Use witnessing instead of suppression
Awakening the Centres	Awareness has structure	Map emotion to chakra field; work bottom-up

The Kriya Currents	Energy follows awareness	Circulate breath through spine daily
Practical Yoga Psychology overall	Mind is educable	Journal reactions, refine intention, act ethically

Together they form a **closed circuit**: awareness → breath → energy → insight → action → awareness again.

---

5. Teacher's Toolkit by Domain

Domain	Tools	Key Cautions
Body	Asana, grounding walks, diet simplicity	Avoid aesthetic obsession; favor comfort over display
Breath	Nadi Shodhana, Kriya Pranayama, Coherent Breathing	Do not extend retention until spontaneous
Energy	Bandhas, mudras, chakra focus	Always end with grounding; never teach locks in fatigue
Mind	Witness meditation, emotion journaling	Don't analyse during session; integrate after
Heart	Gratitude, compassion reflection, service	Balance empathy with boundaries
Insight	Self-inquiry ("Who observes?"), philosophical study	Prevent dryness—alternate study with felt experience

---

6. Psychological Markers of Progress

Marker	Early Indication	Mature Expression
Breath awareness	Can notice pauses	Breath self-regulates under stress
Emotional literacy	Names feelings post-event	Recognizes and releases in real time
Energy perception	Heat, tingling, vibration	Stable, even current without restlessness

Attention span	2–3 min steady	15 min single-pointed or effortless open awareness
Ethical alignment	Fewer contradictions	Spontaneous integrity; no inner conflict
Service orientation	Occasional generosity	Natural responsibility without pride

Teachers assess through dialogue, not display: how the student lives, not what they feel in meditation.

---

7. Designing Integrated Sessions

A 60-minute template blending body, breath, mind, and inquiry:

Phase	Duration	Focus	Corresponding Chapter
Grounding & Asana	10 min	Rooting, release tension	*Awakening the Centres* (Muladhara–Manipura)
Breath Regulation	10 min	Nadi Shodhana → Coherent Breath	*Kriya Currents*
Kriya Flow	15 min	Spinal breathing + chakra rotation	*Kriya Currents*
Meditation	15 min	Witness / Ajapa Japa	*Touching the Mind*
Reflection & Integration	10 min	Journaling / discussion	*Practical Yoga Psychology* principles

Rotate emphasis weekly—body, breath, emotion, insight—to keep adaptation balanced.

---

8. Ethics and Psychological Ground Rules

1. **Transparency:** explain physiological bases; remove mystique that breeds fear or superiority.

2. **Consent & Autonomy:** students may decline touch, mantra, or visualization.

3. **Mental-Health Awareness:** agitation, insomnia, or dissociation are red flags; shift to grounding, not

deeper practice.

4. **Integration into Life:** measure progress by relationships, work stability, and emotional honesty —not by sensations.

---

9. The Spiral of Integration

Real development cycles through the same themes at subtler levels:

1. **Observation** – recognize pattern.
2. **Regulation** – apply breath or posture.
3. **Reflection** – understand cause.
4. **Release** – drop identification.
5. **Realization** – live newly.

This spiral repeats, each turn quieter and wider.
Teachers remind students that "setbacks" are revisits at higher resolution.

---

10. The Role of the Teacher

- **Mirror, not model:** show awareness rather than perfection.
- **Diagnose by energy:** Is the student scattered (add structure) or compressed (add softness)?
- **End every session with integration:** a few normal breaths, grounding, or short dialogue ensures awareness

returns to ordinary consciousness.

---

11. Integration with Psychology and Science

Modern research on breath, vagal tone, and neuroplasticity validates ancient principles:

Yogic Concept	Physiological Parallel
Ida–Pingala balance	Left–right autonomic regulation
Sushumna activation	Prefrontal–limbic coherence
Kumbhaka (pause)	Baroreceptor reset, parasympathetic rebound
Ajapa Japa	Default-mode network quieting
Seva (service)	Oxytocin-mediated prosocial circuits

Use this knowledge not for reductionism but to **translate Yoga into universal human science**—accessible to students of any background.

---

12. Final Integration Principle

> "When breath becomes steady, the mind becomes transparent;
> when the mind becomes transparent, awareness becomes continuous;
> when awareness becomes continuous, life itself becomes Yoga."

At the mature stage, the distinctions between asana,

pranayama, meditation, and action fade. Work, conversation, creativity, and rest all express the same current—the *Kriya Current* alive in daily living.

The practitioner becomes an ordinary, clear, compassionate human being: efficient, calm, awake.

SOURCE

Conscious Awareness

("Witness / Pure Observation")

▼

LEVEL 5 – INSIGHT

(Vijnanamaya /

Anandamaya Kosha)

• Ajapa Japa

• Self-Inquiry

• Service & Ethics

Awareness guides action

▼

┌──────────────────────────

┐

| LEVEL 4 – MIND & |
| EMOTION INTEGRATION |
| (Manomaya Kosha) |
| • Witness Medit. |
| • Journaling |
| • Heart Coherence |

└─────────────┬────────────

┘

| Breath regulates mind

▼

┌──────────────────────────

┐

| LEVEL 3 – ENERGY / |
| PRANIC FIELD |
| (Pranamaya Kosha) |
| • Nadi Shodhana |
| • Kriya Pranayama |
| • Bandha / Mudra |

└─────────────┬────────────

┘

| Energy animates body

▼

┌──────────────────────────

┐

| LEVEL 2 – BODY / |

| BEHAVIOR |
| (Annamaya Kosha) |
| • Asana |
| • Grounding |
| • Diet / Rest |
└───────────┬───────────
┘

| Body expresses awareness
▼

┌──────────────────────
┐

| LEVEL 1 – ACTION / |
| DAILY LIFE |
| • Speech & Work |
| • Relationship |
| • Creativity |
└───────────┬───────────
┘

| Experience reflects growth
▼

┌──────────────────────
──────────────────────┐

| FEEDBACK LOOP OF INTEGRATION |
| Observation → Regulation → Reflection → |
| Release → Realization → (back to life) |
└──────────────────────
──────────────────────┘

References

Primary Classical Yogic Texts

Patañjali. Yoga Sūtras. Various translations by Swami Vivekananda, Swami Satchidananda, and I. K. Taimni.

Svatmarama. Hatha Yoga Pradipika. Commentary by Swami Muktibodhananda. Yoga Publications Trust.

Gheranda Samhita. Translated by James Mallinson. Yoga Vidya.

Shiva Samhita. Translated by Rai Bahadur Srisa Chandra Vasu.

The Upanishads. Especially Katha, Mandukya, Taittiriya, and Prashna Upanishad. Various translators.

Secondary Yogic & Tantric Sources

Swami Rama. Path of Fire and Light. Himalayan Institute Press.

Swami Rama, Rudolph Ballentine, & Swami Ajaya. Yoga and Psychotherapy: The Evolution of Consciousness. Himalayan Institute Press.

Swami Satyananda Saraswati. Asana Pranayama Mudra Bandha. Yoga Publications Trust.

Swami Satyananda Saraswati. Kundalini Tantra. Yoga Publications Trust.

T. K. V. Desikachar. The Heart of Yoga: Developing a Personal Practice. Inner Traditions.

B. K. S. Iyengar. Light on Pranayama. HarperCollins.

Georg Feuerstein. The Yoga Tradition. Hohm Press.

Sufi Texts & Islamic Mystical Literature

Rumi, Jalaluddin. Masnavi (Mathnawi). Translations by R. A. Nicholson and Coleman Barks.

Rumi, Jalaluddin. Fihi Ma Fihi (Discourses of Rumi).

Shams-i-Tabrizi. Maqalat-e-Shams (Discourses of Shams of Tabriz).

Al-Ghazali, Abu Hamid. Ihya Ulum al-Din (The Revival of the Religious Sciences).

Al-Ghazali, Abu Hamid. The Alchemy of Happiness.

Ibn Arabi, Muhyiddin. Futuhat al-Makkiyya (The Meccan Revelations).

Ibn Arabi, Muhyiddin. Fusus al-Hikam (The Bezels of Wisdom).

Attar, Farid ud-Din. The Conference of the Birds.

Esoteric, Tantric & Alchemical Sources

Kashkul (The Beggar's Bowl). A Persian compendium of Sufi, esoteric, and alchemical teachings; circulated across Qadiri and Nurbakhshi lineages.

Abhinavagupta. Tantraloka. Kaśmiri Shaivism's foundational esoteric text.

The Six Yogas of Naropa. Teachings on inner heat (tummo) and subtle-body transformation.

Mahasiddha Teachings (Tilopa, Naropa, Saraha, Luipa). Oral yogic-tantric literature from Indian Buddhist adepts.

Modern Mindfulness, Psychology & Consciousness Studies

Kabat-Zinn, Jon. Wherever You Go, There You Are: Mindfulness Meditation in Everyday Life.

Goleman, Daniel. The Varieties of the Meditative Experience.

Jung, Carl Gustav. Collected Works. Princeton University Press.

Eliade, Mircea. Yoga: Immortality and Freedom.

Mallinson, James & Singleton, Mark. Roots of Yoga. Penguin Classics.

Feuerstein, Georg. The Psychology of Yoga.

www.ingramcontent.com/pod-product-compliance
Ingram Content Group UK Ltd.
Pitfield, Milton Keynes, MK11 3LW, UK
UKHW041350190726
13845UKWH00026B/528

9 789334 307214